AN ENEMY OF

AN ENEMY OF THE CROWN
The British Secret Service Campaign against Charles Haughey

DAVID BURKE

MERCIER PRESS

Dedication

This book is dedicated to Fred Holroyd and Colin Wallace, two British intelligence whistle blowers who paid a heavy price for resisting the pressure to engage in criminal activity in Ireland. The revelations they made in the 1980s about assassination operations, collusion with loyalist paramilitary gangs and the exploitation of child abuse networks led to a decision by the British government to place MI5 on a legislative footing with a modicum of oversight, something one hopes has curtailed the worst impulses of the people who work for it.
Long may Holroyd and Wallace continue to shine a light on the nefarious activities of British intelligence.

MERCIER PRESS
Cork
www.mercierpress.ie

Cover design: Sarah O'Flaherty

© David Burke, 2022
ISBN: 978-1-78117-821-8
eBook: 978-1-78117-822-5

A CIP record for this title is available from the British Library.

Printed and bound in the EU.

CONTENTS

DRAMATIS PERSONAE

AINSWORTH, Joseph: Garda intelligence chief.

ASTOR, David: co-chair of the British-Irish Association, former officer of the Special Operations Executive (SOE) and owner of *The Sunday Observer*.

BARKER, Thomas Christopher: head of the IRD, November 1971 to October 1975.

BERRY, Peter: secretary to the Department of Justice.

BLANEY, Neil: Fianna Fáil politician. Charged along with Charles Haughey in 1970 for attempting to import arms illegally. The charges against him were dropped at an early stage.

CARRINGTON, Peter: Britain's Secretary of State for Defence, 1970–1974.

CAVENDISH, Anthony: former MI5 and MI6 officer who was a close friend of Sir Maurice Oldfield. Author of *Inside Intelligence*.

CHICHESTER-CLARK, James: prime minister of Northern Ireland, 1969–1971.

COLLEY, George: Fianna Fáil politician.

COLLINS, Gerry: Fianna Fáil politician.

COSGRAVE, Liam: leader of Fine Gael, 1966–1977; taoiseach 1973–77.

CROZIER, Brian: a propagandist who worked for MI6, the IRD and the CIA. He was a friend of Maurice Oldfield.

DALY, Michael: head of Chancery at the British embassy in Dublin with responsibility for 'information', 1973–76.

DEACON, Richard: a friend and biographer of Maurice Oldfield.

EVANS, Peter: MI6 officer stationed at the Dublin embassy, 1970–72.

EWART-BIGGS, Christopher: British ambassador to Dublin,

1976. An official of the FCO who had extensive dealings with MI6. The Provisional IRA assassinated him in 1976.

FAULKNER, Brian: prime minister of Northern Ireland, 1971–1972.

FITZGERALD, Garret: leader of Fine Gael, 1977–1987, taoiseach 1981–1982; 1982–87

FULLER, Bill: owner of the Old Shieling Hotel.

GALSWORTHY, Arthur: British ambassador to Dublin, 1973–76.

GARVEY, Ned: Garda commissioner, 1975–78.

GIBBONS, James: Fianna Fáil politician, Minister for Defence, 1969–70.

GILCHRIST, Andrew: British ambassador to Dublin, 1966–70.

HAUGHEY, Charles: leader of Fianna Fáil, 1979–92; taoiseach 1979–81; 1982; 1987–92.

HAUGHEY, Jock: brother of Charles.

HAYDON, Robin: British ambassador to Dublin, 1976–80.

HEATH, Edward: Conservative Party prime minister of the UK, 1970–74.

HEFFERON, Michael: director of Irish Military Intelligence.

HILL, Cliff: IRD officer assigned to Stormont Castle in 1971.

HUME, John: SDLP politician.

KELLY, Captain James: an officer of Irish military intelligence (G2).

KELLY, John: a veteran of the IRA's Border Campaign. He stood trial with Charles Haughey in 1970 for the alleged illegal importation of arms and was acquitted.

KENNEDY, Edward: US senator and brother of President John F. Kennedy. Edward Kennedy was a target of the IRD and Brian Crozier of the ISC. His character was called into question alongside that of Charles Haughey in *Private Eye* magazine.

LAWLESS, Gerry: former member of IRA. Journalist with the *Sunday World*.

LEAHY, John: a FCO diplomat who served as head of the News Department at FCO in 1971, and under-secretary at the NIO, 1975–77.

LITTLEJOHN, Keith: criminal and MI6 agent [brother of Kenneth].

LITTLEJOHN, Kenneth: criminal and MI6 agent [brother of Keith].

LUYKX, Albert: defendant at the Arms Trial alongside Charles Haughey, Capt. James Kelly and John Kelly.

LYNCH, Jack: leader of Fianna Fáil, 1966–79; taoiseach 1966–73; 1977–79.

McDOWELL, Maj. Thomas: Ex-MI5 officer and managing director of *The Irish Times*.

MAINS, Joseph: Warden of Kincora Boys' Home in Belfast. He helped run a paedophile network with links to MI5 and MI6.

MALONE, Patrick: head of C3, the intelligence directorate of An Garda Síochána, in the late 1960s until 1971; garda commissioner, 1973–75.

MIFSUD, 'Big' Frank: a London pimp who ran the 'Syndicate' in West London with his partner Bernie Silver. Mifsud lived beside the Old Shieling hotel, Raheny, Dublin in the early 1970s.

MARKHAM-RANDALL, Capt. Peter: *nom de guerre* of a British intelligence agent who visited Dublin in November 1969.

MOONEY, Hugh: Foreign Office official who worked for the Information Research Department (IRD).

MOORE, John D: US ambassador to Ireland, 1969–75.

O'DONOGHUE, Professor Martin: Fianna Fáil politician.

O'MALLEY, Desmond: Fianna Fáil politician, Minister for Justice, 1970–73.

Ó MORÁIN, Mícheál: Fianna Fáil politician, Minister for Justice, 1968–70.

OLDFIELD, Maurice: deputy chief of MI6, 1964–1973 and chief of MI6, 1973–78. Northern Ireland Security Co-ordinator 1979–80.

OWEN, David: British Foreign Secretary, 1977–79.

PARK, Daphne: senior MI6 officer and associate of Maurice Oldfield.

PAYNE, Denis: director and controller of intelligence (DCI), 1973–75.

PECK, Edward: MI6 officer, chairman of the Joint Intelligence Committee, 1968–70.

PECK, John: head of the IRD, 1951–53; director-general of the BIS in New York, 1956–59; British ambassador to Dublin, 1970–73.

PINCHER, Chapman: British journalist with multiple ties to MI5 and MI6.

PIPER, Reuben W.: counsellor at the British embassy in Dublin, 1968–1971.

RANDOLPH, Virgil: political officer at the US Embassy in 1971.

RENNIE, Sir John Ogilvy: chief of MI6, 1968–73. Director of the IRD, 1953–58.

ROWLEY, Allan: director and controller of intelligence (DCI), 1972–73.

SILVER, Bernie: London pimp who helped MI6 set up brothels in Belfast in 1970. He was a partner of 'Big' Frank Mifsud. The pair ran the Mifsud-Silver criminal 'Syndicate' in West London.

SMELLIE, Craig: MI6 head of station Belfast in the mid-1970s.

SMITH, Howard: Foreign Office official appointed by Edward Heath as the UK Representative (UKREP) to the Stormont government of Northern Ireland. He later became the director-general of MI5, 1978–1981.

STEELE, Frank: MI6 officer stationed in Northern Ireland in the early 1970s.

TUGWELL, Col Maurice: the officer in charge of the IPU in Northern Ireland in early 1970s.

UTLEY, T.E.: journalist with ties to Chatham House and the IRD.

WALSH, Dick: *Irish Times* journalist and adviser to Cathal Goulding, chief-of-staff of the Official IRA. Negotiated on behalf of the Official IRA during its feud with the Provisional IRA.

WARD, Andrew: secretary of the Department of Justice, 1971–86.

WAUGH, Auberon: *Private Eye* journalist with ties to MI5 and MI6.

WREN, Larry: head of C3, the intelligence directorate of An Garda Síochána 1971–79; garda commissioner 1983–87.

WALLACE, Colin: psychological operations officer with the IPU at HQNI in the early and mid–1970s.

WYMAN, John: MI6 officer. Served a term of imprisonment in Ireland, 1972–73.

Key to terms used

Ard Fheis: political conference.

BIS: British Information Service. It disseminated IRD propaganda in the USA.

B-Specials: members of the Ulster Special Constabulary, a part-time force disbanded in 1970.

C3: The department that co-ordinated garda intelligence.

CDCs: Citizen Defence Committees.

Dáil Éireann: the lower house of the Irish parliament located in Dublin.

DFA: Department of Foreign Affairs, Dublin, Ireland.

DoJ: Department of Justice, Dublin, Ireland.

FCO: Foreign and Commonwealth Office, King Charles Street, London, England.

Fianna Fáil: Irish political party led by Éamon de Valera, Seán Lemass, Jack Lynch and Charles Haughey.

Fine Gael: Irish political party led by Liam Cosgrave who was succeeded by Garret FitzGerald.

Forum World Features (FWF): conduit for MI6, IRD and CIA propaganda.

G2: Irish Military Intelligence.

Garda Síochána: the police force of the Republic of Ireland [also referred to as garda/gardaí].

GIB: Government Information Bureau (Dublin).

HMG: Her Majesty's Government.

HQNI: Headquarters NI, British army HQ located at Thiepval Barracks in Lisburn.

IPU: Information Policy Unit, the Psy Ops wing of the British Army in Northern Ireland.

IRD: Information Research Department. A propaganda and forgery department attached to the FCO.

ISC: Institute for the Study of Conflict, an outlet for CIA and MI6 propaganda, publisher of the book, *The Ulster Debate*.

JIC: Joint intelligence committee. The body that analyses the work of MI5, MI6, GCHQ and British military intelligence for the British government.

MI5: Britain's internal security service, active inside the United Kingdom and her overseas colonies. It is attached to the Home Office.

MI6: Britain's overseas intelligence service. It is attached to the Foreign Office. Also known as SIS, Secret Intelligence Service.

MoD: Ministry of Defence.

MRF: Military Reaction Force, an undercover unit of the British army.

NICRA: Northern Ireland Civil Rights Association.

NIO: Northern Ireland Office.

North Atlantic News Agency: conduit for MI6, IRD and CIA propaganda.

Official IRA: the Marxist wing of the Republican Movement which emerged after the split in the IRA in December 1969. Its chief-of-staff in the 1970s was Cathal Goulding.

***Preuves Internationales*:** conduit for MI6, IRD and CIA propaganda.

Provisional IRA: the wing of the IRA which emerged after the IRA split in December 1969 with the intention of ending British rule in Northern Ireland.

PSY OPs: Psychological Operations.

RHC: Red Hand Commando. A loyalist paramilitary organisation led by John McKeague.

RUC: Royal Ulster Constabulary, the police force of Northern Ireland.

RUCSB: RUC special branch.

Saor Éire: republican socialist paramilitary organisation responsible for an attack on Fianna Fáil's HQ in 1967 and the death of Garda Richard Fallon in April 1970.

SDLP: Social Democratic and Labour Party – a nationalist political party active in Northern Ireland.

Sibs: a word derived from *sibillare*, the Latin for whispering. Sibs are hostile or negative comments spread by way of rumour to undermine an opponent

SLO – Senior Liaison Officer: a MI5 officer assigned to assist a police force such as the RUC during an 'emergency', typically an anti-colonial insurgency.

SMIU: Special Military Intelligence Unit. SMIU soldiers in Northern Ireland were permitted to perform fieldwork for MI6.

SOE: Special Operations Executive, a British intelligence organisation which was created by Winston Churchill during the Second World War to aid anti-Axis resistance forces.

Stormont: seat of the Northern Ireland parliament.

Tánaiste: Ireland's deputy prime minister.

Taoiseach: Ireland's prime minister.

Trans World News: a conduit for MI6, IRD and CIA propaganda.

UCD: University College Dublin.

UDA: Ulster Defence Association.

Ultras: a group of right wing MI5 and MI6 officers who were involved in plots against British politicians such as Harold Wilson.

UVF: Ulster Volunteer Force.

Author's Note

The events of 1969–70, known as the Arms Crisis, were the subject of a book I published in 2020, *Deception & Lies*. It concerned allegations that two Fianna Fáil government ministers had engaged in an illegal attempt to import arms with the assistance of Irish military intelligence. One chapter of that work focused on the role played by the British Secret Service, MI6, in the affair. Other chapters touched upon other features of their involvement. Some of the information in that book is revisited here. The overlap includes the Markham-Randall affair, the provision of information about Irish military intelligence by an Irish TD, and the attempt to suppress a book about the crisis by Capt. James Kelly. The overlap was unavoidable if a full picture of the MI6 campaign against Charles Haughey is to be understood. While there is an overlap, a lot of new information is supplied in this book about those events.

INTRODUCTION

In the early 1970s, Sir Maurice Oldfield of the British Secret Service, MI6, embarked upon a decade–long campaign to derail the political career of Charles Haughey of Fianna Fáil.[1] Dirty tricks were employed by the Englishman to thwart Haughey's efforts to revive his career in the wake of his dismissal from cabinet in 1970 after he was alleged to have attempted to import arms illegally. The dismissal was followed by MI6 intrigues to impede his bid to secure a position on Fianna Fáil's front bench and a return to respectability while his party was in opposition, 1973–77. After Fianna Fáil returned to power in triumph in 1977, with a large majority, there was no let-up in the drive against Haughey by Oldfield. At this juncture, Haughey was seeking a place in Jack Lynch's new cabinet. Oldfield also played a part in trying to prevent Haughey succeed Lynch as taoiseach in 1979.

While Haughey was suspicious of MI6 interference, he had no inkling of the full extent of Oldfield's clandestine efforts to destroy him.

The English spy did not understand the intricacies of Irish politics and believed Haughey was close to the Provisional IRA and therefore, in his eyes, a threat to Britain. Oldfield's obsession with the Irishman can be aptly compared to that of Ahab's fixation with the whale in *Moby Dick*.

During the period under review, 1968–1980, Oldfield and his ilk unleashed assassins, bombers, bank robbers, blackmailers, brothel keepers and child traffickers to further London's interests in Ireland. This book, however, will focus primarily on the manoeuvrings against politicians, especially Haughey.[2] The task involved the assembly of massive amounts of information from disparate sources about Haughey and his associates, and tracking the incessant circulation of smears that impugned Haughey's character on a multiplicity of fronts.

The English spymaster was assisted in his machinations by a shadowy group of conspirators inside Dublin's security apparatus who shared Oldfield's distrust of Haughey. They have escaped scrutiny for their actions until now. As this history unfolds, more than a dozen instances of their activities will be described; many of which employed dirty tricks. Crucially, some of these operations involved a high-level official from the Department of Justice (DoJ). In addition, a number of gardaí lent a helping hand.

Oldfield was ideal for the secret world of espionage and dirty tricks. He was conspiratorial by nature and lacked a moral compass. It is no exaggeration to say that he was one of the most noteworthy figures of the early years of the Troubles. He was assisted by an array of spies, ambassadors, diplomat–spies and black propaganda operatives in his campaign to thwart Haughey. The most important of these are outlined below:

Peter Evans who presented himself to the Irish public as the innocuous sounding 'information' officer at the British embassy in Dublin, 1970–72. He was in fact one of Oldfield's most valuable operatives. Insofar as it is possible to disinter the bones of MI6's activities in Ireland in the early 1970s, he emerges as one, if not the most significant, of the dirty tricks operatives to serve in Dublin.

Hugh Mooney who worked for the Information Research Department (IRD), Britain's black propaganda and forgery directorate. The IRD worked closely with MI6. Mooney was a key figure in the smear campaigns directed against Haughey and other Irish politicians including John Hume of the SDLP. He was an ideal choice for the task as he had studied at Trinity College Dublin before working as a sub-editor at *The Irish Times*.

Sir Andrew Gilchrist who served as Britain's ambassador to Dublin, 1966–70. He was what can be fairly described as a 'diplomat-spy', as he had a special forces and intelligence background. His actions in trying to unravel Fianna Fáil ministers' activities during the Arms Crisis will be examined in the first part of this book.

Sir John Peck who succeeded Gilchrist as ambassador, 1970–73. He had served as director of the IRD in the 1950s. He was a master of dirty tricks. While at the IRD, he was central to multiple regime change plots including the one that succeeded in ousting the prime minister of Iran in 1953.

There was as much intrigue in Dublin in the 1970s as there was in Berlin, Moscow or Havana. The full extent of it has been buried so deeply that it may never see the light of day. This book is an attempt to shed light on at least some of the conspiracies that took place on this island during the 1960s to the early 1980s. An even fuller picture may eventually emerge if MI6's files become available one day.

Haughey's Republican Pedigree

Seán Haughey was one of the most capable and trusted officers who served under Michael Collins during the War of Independence. He was a man to whom Collins entrusted a vital role in a secret mission, one that could have changed Irish history had Collins not perished at Béal na mBláth in August 1922. Seán and his wife Sarah (née McWilliams) were born and reared almost next door to each other on small farms in the adjacent townlands of Knockaneil and Stranagone, near 'Fenian' Swatragh, a few miles from Maghera town, Co. Derry. It was deep inside unionist territory. Seán Haughey, who was born in 1897, served as the second in command and later officer in command of the South Derry Battalion of the Irish Volunteers during the War of Independence. Sarah, who was born in 1901, also played an active part during the campaign. A price was placed on Haughey's head and he was hunted relentlessly by the Black and Tans. One of his hiding places was an underground bunker, where he and his colleagues had to live in cold, damp and wet conditions.

The Anglo-Irish Treaty was signed on 21 December 1921 and ratified the following January. Yet, hostilities persisted in the north.[1] On 19 March 1922, 200 men surrounded the town of Maghera. They cut the telephone wires before attacking the Royal Irish Constabulary barracks from which they removed 17 rifles, 5,000 rounds of ammunition and a sergeant as a hostage. The next day the IRA in Derry attacked a series of mills, sawmills, stables and outhouses. Burntollet Bridge (which would become infamous in 1968) was blown up.

On 30 March 1922, Michael Collins and Sir James Craig attempted to bring about an end to this cycle of violence. In return for a halt to IRA operations, it was agreed that it would be open to Catholics to join the Special Constabulary (B-Specials) and to assume responsibility for policing nationalist areas. In mixed nationalist/loyalists areas, an equal force of Catholic and Protestant officers would be deployed. Meanwhile, mixed units would conduct all searches, with British soldiers in attendance. The B-Specials were to wear uniforms with identification numbers and surrender their arms once they had finished their duties.

On 31 March 1922, royal assent was given to the Free State Bill that would evolve after further deliberations into the new constitution of the Free State. The ceasefire which Collins and Craig negotiated proved a failure. On 2 April 1922, 500 B-Specials swooped across Derry and Tyrone detaining up 300 men for questioning. Only four were found to be in the IRA. The remainder of the IRA membership escaped to Co. Donegal.

By now the IRA was on the verge of a split into pro- and anti-Treaty factions. The volunteers who lived in the new jurisdiction in Northern Ireland were virtually all anti-Treaty. Collins did not intend to abandon them. He arranged to supply them with arms, something that offered him a possible way to prevent a split in the IRA. It also provided an opportunity to covertly undermine the new unionist regime across the new border.

Seán Haughey became involved in the clandestine

operation overseen by Collins to smuggle weapons across the new border to nationalists so they could defend themselves.[2] Most, if not all, of the arms were supplied by the IRA in Cork. Commandant-General Joseph Sweeney, of the First Northern Division of the IRA in Donegal, revealed that Collins sent an emissary to him 'to say that he was sending arms to Donegal, and that they were to be handed over to certain persons – he didn't say who they were – who would come with credentials to my headquarters. Once we got them we had fellows working for two days with hammers and chisels doing away with the serials on the rifles ... About 400 rifles and all were taken to the Northern volunteers by Dan McKenna and Johnny [aka Seán] Haughey.'[3]

Some of the guns were stored in rural Donegal at the home of George Diver of Killygordon, albeit against his wishes. They were hidden by his daughter Kathleen, under the mattress where she slept. George feared that the family's house would be burned down if word reached unionists about the guns. Killygordon, a remote rural village, was close to the Tyrone border.[4]

Another IRA man, Thomas Kelly, collected a consignment of 200 Lee-Enfield rifles and ammunition from Eoin O'Duffy, the leader of the Monaghan Brigade of the IRA. Many years later, Kelly revealed that the 'rifles and ammo were brought by Army transport to Donegal and later moved into County Tyrone in the compartment of an oil tanker. Only one member of the IRA escorted the consignment through the Special Constabulary Barricade at the Strabane/Lifford Bridge. He was Seán Haughey, father of Charles Haughey.'[5]

The death of Collins in August 1922 brought about an end to the arms smuggling operation.[6] Seán Haughey subsequently joined the Irish Army and rose to become a commandant. He was stationed in Castlebar in September 1925, when his third child Charles was born at the barracks in the town. After he retired in March 1928, the family went to live in Sutton, Co. Dublin, before moving on again in 1930 to Dunshauglin, Co. Meath, where they took up farming on a 100-acre holding. All told, the couple had seven children: Maureen, Seán, Charles, Eithne, Bridie, Pádraig, and Eoghan.

Seán Haughey developed multiple sclerosis, became severely incapacitated and was forced to sell his farm. His family blamed the atrocious conditions at the bunker in which he had camped during the War of Independence for the destruction of his health. In 1933, he moved his family to a small two-storey house, 12 Belton Park Road, Donnycarney, in Dublin. After this, the children were reared in modest circumstances. While they were growing up, they received regular visits from their northern relatives and friends with news and stories about what was going on across the border. In the other direction, Charles and his brother Seán spent extended summer holidays in Swatragh, Co. Derry. Charles stayed with his mother's parents at Stranagone, about half a mile up the mountain road leading from Swatragh. During these holidays, Charles Haughey and his cousins were sometimes stopped at night by B-Special patrols, something he found unpleasant, sinister and often quite intimidating. These patrols usually intercepted them as they were returning to Stranagone and were made up of men from the neighbouring areas who were known to them, but were never friendly; all were drawn from the loyalist community. They were quick to display their authority. Charles Haughey felt there was an element of 'croppies lie down' in their behaviour.[7]

The threat of violence in Northern Ireland was ever present. In 1935, sectarian rioting cost eleven deaths and 574 injuries in Belfast. In 1938, after a visit to the cinema at Maghera, Charles Haughey, his brother Seán and uncle Owen emerged from the building to witness a riot, during which loyalists fired rifles at unarmed nationalists. The event forged a lasting impression on Haughey. It was, he felt, a visceral experience of what life was like for some nationalists in Northern Ireland; an insight that was shared by very few, if any, of his contemporaries in Dublin, especially the middle-class children he would soon encounter at University College Dublin (UCD).[8] Many of them looked down on him as a 'scholarship boy'.

***

Despite the difficulties his family faced, Charles flourished.[9] Having come first in the Dublin Corporation scholarship examination, he went on to study commerce at UCD, and won a bursary. In 1941, at the age of fifteen, Haughey joined the Local Defence Force, the then reserve force of the Irish Army. He rose to become a lieutenant and enjoyed it so much at one time that he considered a career in the army.[10]

On 7 May 1945, the British government announced that Nazi Germany had surrendered to the Allies. This triggered jubilant celebrations by Trinity College students who raised a string of flags, including a Union Jack, over College Green. Word soon spread to UCD, then located a few minutes' walk away from Trinity College at Earlsfort Terrace, where Haughey was a student. 'This generated a wave of anger. The reason we were so furious was because the [Trinity] students were goading and insulting the rest of us', said Seamus Sorohan, a friend of Haughey's who later had a distinguished career as a barrister.[11] Some of the students on the roof of Trinity were singing 'God Save the King' and 'Rule Britannia' while the Irish Tricolour fluttered beneath those of Allied flags, something which provoked criticism from the passing public. In response to the complaints, some of the Trinity students hauled the Tricolour down and set it ablaze, before throwing it onto the ground beneath them. This 'inflamed the fury' of Sorohan, Haughey and others from UCD. That night they tore down a Union Jack flag which they found hanging on a lamppost at the bottom of Grafton Street and set it alight. They then congregated on Middle Abbey Street and marched over O'Connell Bridge towards Trinity College, breaking windows in the offices of *The Irish Times* on Fleet Street en route. They perceived the paper to be pro-British. It was reported the next day that the march was led by a 'young man [i.e. Haughey] waving a large tricolour hoisted on the shoulder of his comrades'. When they found the gates of Trinity were closed, a group of them tried to scale the railings, but were repelled by the police who baton charged them.

One of the eyewitnesses to the event was a future taoiseach, Garret FitzGerald, also at UCD at the time, who recalled watching Haughey leap over bicycles before bolting up Trinity Street. 'My views and his views would have been different. I was strongly pro-Allied', he said years later, thereby implying Haughey was pro-Nazi rather than merely infuriated by the burning of the Tricolour.[12] The provost of Trinity later apologised for the burning of the Tricolour.

Haughey would dine out on this escapade for decades.

A few years later Sorohan approached Haughey. 'I was in the IRA. I told him so, and asked him to join,' Sorohan revealed.[13] But he had misjudged Haughey, who declined the offer, albeit having considered – or more likely having pretended to consider – the offer seriously. An indication of his reasoning may be gleaned from a speech he made on 25 March 1958 in the Dáil, extolling the merits of the FCA.[14] Haughey felt it gave young men 'from the ages of 17 to 20 ... an opportunity of being inculcated with patriotism, proper national ideals, a sense of discipline and all the other advantages that go with military training at that early age'. Moreover, he argued the patriotism the FCA inspired in young men offered an alternative to the IRA: 'A lot of young men who find themselves caught up in movements without realising fully what is involved in the ultimate, would never get into these difficulties if the career of a member of the FCA were made more attractive and interesting.'

According to Sorohan, Haughey 'discussed the invitation with Seán Lemass', who was the father of his girlfriend and future wife, Maureen. Not surprisingly, Lemass, a senior Fianna Fáil politician and future taoiseach,[15] 'told him not to join'.[16]

When Seán Haughey died prematurely on 3 January 1947, his old comrades provided a guard of honour at his funeral. He had remained an ardent supporter of Michael

Collins throughout his life, while maintaining an aversion to De Valera and Fianna Fáil. Whether a coincidence or not, Charles Haughey did not become active in Fianna Fáil until after his father's death.

News of Sorohan's invitation to Haughey reached the ears of garda special branch officers by the 1960s. The garda version was that Haughey had failed to 'say no outright'. This is at odds with Sorohan's recollection. His account of what Haughey said is more likely to be accurate, as he was directly involved in the discussions. Perhaps Haughey was being diplomatic when he said he would consider the offer, knowing all along that he would reject it. 'That is quite possible', was how Sorohan replied to this scenario, when I put it to him.[17]

After UCD, Haughey pursued a career in accountancy, while making a few attempts at securing a seat for Fianna Fáil in the Dáil.[18] On 18 September 1951, he married Maureen Lemass, who had also studied commerce at UCD. Together they would have four children: Eimear, Conor, Ciaran, and Seán.

Haughey, the RUC and MI5

In 1920, the 'Twelve Apostles', an IRA unit that reported to Michael Collins, killed twelve of a group of eighteen to twenty members of the 'Cairo Gang', a British unit, which had been sent to Dublin to gather intelligence and assassinate Collins and his senior commanders. That operation sparked the Bloody Sunday massacre at Croke Park in Dublin in reprisal. British soldiers, the RIC and auxiliaries killed fourteen people. Remarkably, despite the spillage of all this blood, the secret services of Britain and Ireland would begin to co-operate with each other within a few decades.

MI5 helped the Irish state set up the first modern spy agency in Ireland, G2. It came into existence after a secret consultation between Guy Liddell of MI5, and J.W. Dulanty, the Irish high commissioner, in London on 31 August 1938. Joseph Walshe, the Secretary of the Department of External Affairs, also attended. At the meeting, Walshe explained that the taoiseach, Éamon de Valera, was concerned about Nazi links to the IRA, a partnership that had been forged in 1935. He wanted to set up Ireland's equivalent to MI5 to counteract such mischief. This was music to British ears. MI5 offered to assist them in 'every possible way'.[1] It was also agreed that an 'exchange of information would be made between [MI5] and the Eire counter-espionage department on the activities of Germans in Eire'.

The new organisation, G2, was set up under the auspices

of the Department of Defence. It was soon busy disrupting the relationship between the Nazis and the IRA. In addition, Britain's signals intelligence succeeded in intercepting communications from the German legation in Dublin to Berlin. On 3 May 1943, Clement Attlee, the British deputy prime minister (and future premier) wrote to Winston Churchill describing how G2 was working 'with our Security authorities'.[2]

Britain did not have an embassy in Dublin during the Second World War, rather a Representative Office run by Sir John Maffey. John Betjeman took up the post of press attaché in that office in January 1941. This was cover for his real assignment, which was as a propagandist on behalf of the Ministry of Information. His work was performed in co-ordination with the Special Operations Executive (SOE), MI6 and MI5. One of Betjeman's tasks was to undermine support for Hitler and his Axis partners by nurturing favourable press coverage of Britain's military successes. Betjeman also recruited 'agents of influence' to advance Britain's cause. One of them was George Furlong, the director of the National Gallery of Ireland, who had strong social links with the Italian legation.[3]

Betjeman acted for the Political Warfare Executive (PWE) too. It assigned him the task of circulating so-called 'sibs', a word derived from *sibillare*, the Latin for whispering. Betjeman spread 'sibs' to damage the image of the Axis forces. Within six months of his arrival, he became 'a well-known and popular figure, frequently encountered in the pub, and at house parties and literary functions'.[4] 'They used to paint on walls that I was a spy but nobody really believed it',

Betjeman said decades later.[5] An IRA plot was hatched to assassinate him. In what is one of the few charming episodes in the entire history of the IRA's confrontation with British intelligence, the operation was called off because of admiration on the part of a senior IRA figure for Betjeman's skill as a poet. Betjeman went on to become poet laureate of the UK, 1972–84.[6]

Cooperation continued between MI5 and G2 after the defeat of Hitler. In the late 1940s, MI5 and the gardaí placed Robert Briscoe, a Jewish IRA veteran, under surveillance because of his links with militant Zionists in Palestine.[7]

In April 1955, Haughey's old friend from UCD, Seamus Sorohan, addressed an Easter rally in Galway, at which he called on young men to volunteer for the IRA 'and be trained in the use of arms to achieve the complete freedom of the Nation'. He was followed by Joe Christle, another IRA volunteer, who told the crowd that the Republican Movement would soon be making 'the Six Counties so hot that England won't be able to hold them'. These declarations heralded the IRA's Operation Harvest (better known as the border campaign), which, as the name suggests, was directed against the security forces of Northern Ireland posted along the border. It began in 1956 and ended in early 1962. At the outset, the British ambassador to Dublin, Sir Alexander Clutterbuck, tried to construct a framework for intelligence co-operation between the UK and Ireland. However, having made his pitch in Dublin, he was politely rebuffed by Frederick Boland, the secretary at the Department of External Affairs, who told him that the liaison between the police forces of both countries 'would continue to be of the personal and informal character that he thought at present existed between individuals in the two police forces and that the more informal it was and the less that was known about it the better'.[8] Despite Boland's instinctive preference for informality, a limited degree of co-operation was achieved at the highest levels of power, when the two governments exchanged aide memoires on the IRA in January and February 1956.

In Northern Ireland, the RUC special branch led the campaign against the IRA during the border campaign with assistance from a MI5 Security Liaison Officer (SLO) who was dispatched to Belfast for the duration of the offensive. The secretary of the Department of Justice (DoJ) in Dublin maintained a direct line of communication to his counterpart in the Home Office in London. According to Joe Ainsworth, a future deputy garda commissioner and intelligence supremo, who worked alongside Garda Commissioner Daniel Costigan, 'It was as simple as picking up a phone'.[9]

John A. Costello's Fine Gael-led government was in power when the campaign began. Insofar as security policy was concerned, the election turned into a wrestling match over who could best crush the IRA. Fianna Fáil criticised Fine Gael for allegedly not taking a sufficiently hard line against the IRA, purportedly because of Seán MacBride's presence in cabinet. MacBride was leader of Clann na Poblachta, a smaller party which was sharing power with Fine Gael. MacBride was also a former IRA chief-of-staff. During the 1957 general election, Fianna Fáil asserted that it was the only political party with 'the unity, capacity and will to curb the IRA'. As the campaign intensified, Fianna Fáil pursued the issue with vigour. Gerald Boland of Fianna Fáil accused the government of providing 'illegal organisations' with a 'carte blanche' to 'arm, drill, openly recruit, hold public collections ... and publish a newspaper'.

Fianna Fáil won the election. De Valera assumed the role of taoiseach again. He moved quickly to suppress the IRA. Sitting in his prison cell in England, an IRA prisoner, Seán MacStíofáin,[10] a man who would generate a lot of trouble for Haughey in the future, was convinced that the new Fianna Fáil administration would come down hard on the IRA: 'We knew, even from the Scrubs hundreds of miles away, what De Valera's return meant for our comrades in Ireland. The persecution of republicans would now begin in earnest and collaboration with the British forces would be stepped up.'[11]

Garda-RUC liaison was indeed intensified, while extra police and soldiers were deployed to border areas. Sir John Hermon, who later became RUC chief constable, was a witness to the discreet exchange of information that flowed between the RUC and Dublin Castle during the border campaign. In his memoirs, he described how the sharing of 'sound intelligence and practical co-operation between the Garda Síochána and the RUC was given tacit approval by the Irish and British governments, much to the mutual benefit of both forces. This relationship, which strengthened over the years, was quickly and warmly extended beyond policing into other areas, including recreational and social activities.'[12]

De Valera reintroduced internment – arrest and detention

without trial – after a cabinet decision in July 1957. The policy encountered a robust legal challenge from an internee called Gerald Lawless, which eventually wound its way to the European Court of Human Rights. The Curragh internment camp was closed in March 1959, long before the Lawless case was determined. Lawless would become a journalist in later life and produce some intriguing reports about British intelligence interference with Haughey's career.

Seán Lemass succeeded De Valera as taoiseach on 23 June 1959. He resolved to end the IRA's border campaign 'by making its futility obvious rather than making martyrs of those who practised it'.

Haughey, who had been elected as a TD in the 1957 general election, was beginning to make a name for himself in the Dáil as a moderniser. He became parliamentary secretary (i.e., junior minister) at the DoJ in March 1960. He was promoted to cabinet as the department's full minister in October 1961. After the European Court of Human Rights condemned aspects of Ireland's laws on internment, Haughey let it be known that the cabinet felt that the 'powers of detention should not again be exercised except as a last resort and only where any other effective means of a less repugnant kind were not available'.[13]

Now, in his late thirties, Haughey was faced with the task of defeating the IRA as it attempted to resuscitate its campaign, without the tool of internment at his disposal. He examined the available options with his officials, particularly Peter Berry, the secretary of the DoJ. Born in 1910, Berry served under every minister for justice from the foundation of the state until his retirement at the end of 1970.[14] The IRA in Dublin assassinated the first of these ministers, Kevin O'Higgins. The killing took place in July 1927, six months after Berry's arrival at the DoJ. Within a decade, Berry became a key figure in the on-going struggle against the IRA. He compiled books on the organisation as well as other groups perceived as a threat to the state. They were circulated within the DoJ and to Berry's ministers. He maintained the direct line of communication to his counterparts in the British Home Office, the department responsible for MI5.

During the Second World War, Gerry Boland, the Fianna Fáil Minister for Justice, had given Berry the task of co-ordinating and supervising the nation's security apparatus. Berry liked the cloak and dagger brief and retained responsibility for it after his promotion to permanent secretary, the position that put him in overall charge of the DoJ. The Irish police force was set up by legislation as an independent organisation and was not controlled by the DoJ. Yet, Berry, through sheer force of personality, managed to exert an enormous influence over it, almost as if it was a subordinate section of his department. Garda commissioners, C3 intelligence chiefs and heads of the special branch liaised with him.[15] Berry became particularly close to John Fleming, the head of Special Branch in the late 1960s and early 1970s and they played handball at Garda HQ on Sunday mornings.

The plan Haughey and Berry formulated in 1961 involved the reactivation of the Special Criminal Court. He also launched a publicity drive designed to highlight the futility of the IRA's campaign. The Special Criminal Court sat with military officers and enjoyed special powers. There was no jury. It was empowered to hand down longer custodial sentences than the ordinary courts. Overall, the public accepted its existence, despite attempts by Sinn Féin to incite outcry against it. In its first month, twenty-five republicans were sentenced to a combined total of forty-three years imprisonment. The shortage of manpower was devastating for the IRA. Seán Garland, one of the movement's leaders, felt that the severe sentences that had been handed down by the court were a decisive factor in the ending of the border campaign.[16] In February 1962, the IRA threw in the towel.[17]

After the IRA announced the end of its campaign, Haughey made a statement during which he recognised the desire in the country to end partition, but condemned what he described as the IRA's 'foolish resort to violence' in furtherance of that aim. Berry deemed the IRA's collapse as 'a great personal triumph' for the young minister. To his intense satisfaction, Haughey had managed to defeat the IRA without turning the volunteers into martyrs, in line with the policy advocated by Lemass.

A Hate Figure among Republicans

By the end of the border campaign in 1962, Haughey had become deeply unpopular in republican circles. Later in 1962, his stock among those camps declined even further with the passing of the Street and House to House Collection Act, 1962, which required individuals and organisations engaged in street collections to apply to the state for permits. Republicans refused to request such authorisations, since they did not recognise the legitimacy of the state. This allowed the gardaí to confiscate monies amassed by republicans from such endeavours as the sale of lilies to celebrate the Easter Rising. It also led to the imposition of fines, which objectors refused to pay. One of the collectors, Richard Behal, was incarcerated for a month. He embarked on a hunger strike when he was not recognised as a political prisoner. He survived, but was in a pitiable state when he left prison.

In 1961, Austin Currie became president of the New Ireland Society, a student debating forum at Queens University.[1] In his autobiography, Currie recalled that among those who spoke to its members were 'two future Taoisigh, Charles Haughey TD and Liam Cosgrave TD.'[2] Haughey spoke at a debate in November 1962, which concerned the future of the 'Protestant Minority in a United Ireland'. The young minister expressed the view that it would be 'difficult to conceive of a structure in which individual liberty and religious freedom would be more adequately safeguarded' than in a united Ireland. Southern Protestants, he stressed, had not suffered discrimination. 'What is really important,' he argued, 'is not that there is no unfair treatment of minorities – but the fact that there couldn't be. There is no longer any argument about it.'

In 1962, Seán Lemass dispatched Haughey and Jack Lynch to Belfast to explore the possibility of free trade with Northern Ireland. The choice of Lynch, who was then Minister for Industry and Commerce, was obvious; Haughey less so as he was Minister for Justice, a department not involved in trade. However, his credentials as a moderniser and foe of the IRA made him an ideal emissary. Added to this was the fact that Haughey had become an enthusiastic horseman and was acquainted with Brian Faulkner, the Stormont minister (and future prime minister) through the sport.

Around this time, there were further points of friction between Haughey and the Republican Movement. In 1963, he announced 'that the death penalty for murder generally will be abolished but it will be retained for certain specific types of murder.' The following year the Criminal Justice Act, 1964, abolished the death penalty for piracy, certain military crimes and most murders, but maintained it for the type of activity in which the IRA could become entangled, if they were ever to return to a war footing.

After the border campaign Haughey remained vigilant against a possible resurgence of the IRA. He permitted the relay of information about the organisation from Garda

HQ to New Scotland Yard and the RUC special branch, and sanctioned meetings between the heads of the RUC and garda intelligence.[3]

Peter Berry was directed by Haughey to meet William Stout, the secretary of the Ministry of Home Affairs, in secret at Stormont on 4 October 1963. Stout's minister was William Craig. The latter had claimed publicly that a 'sizeable splinter-group' of the IRA was active in the Republic before proceeding to criticise the failure of the 'Dublin Authorities' to curtail them.[4] According to Berry: 'I said that within the previous 48 hours I had seen Chief Superintendent Moore and Superintendent [Philip] McMahon [of the special branch] and I had had the most categoric assurances that the Gardaí were not aware of any activities in Border counties. I told them that the Gardaí hadn't a shred of evidence which would lead them to think that a Border campaign would be reopened this winter.'[5]

Berry suspected that the RUC was acting on false information from deceitful informers about the IRA, a problem that plagued both the RUC and the gardaí. Sources often invented stories to extract more money from their handlers. 'I suggested that somewhere along the line somebody was passing false information,' Berry wrote.[6]

Craig said he was greatly relieved to hear what Berry had conveyed to him and would give this matter serious consideration. Berry, however, felt Craig 'was not convinced that the IRA were not actively preparing for a fresh campaign but that he did accept the suggestion that newspaper publicity should be avoided. I formed the impression that the Minister (and the Secretary) knew very little about the IRA and the police machinery for dealing with the organisation.'

As he was about to embark on his return trip to Dublin, Stout 'came out in the rain, bareheaded, to see me to my car but, nevertheless, I could discern no warmth. I think that he was nervous of being seen alone with me.'[7] Nonetheless the pair had managed to arrange that if 'the occasion required it communication about IRA matters could be made direct between ourselves. (I had feared a request for communication at various levels within the police).'

Haughey's willingness to engage with his ministerial counterpart in Northern Ireland was matched by Jack Lynch. Their bridge-building exercises helped pave the way for the historic meeting between Seán Lemass and the prime minister of Northern Ireland, Captain Terence O'Neill, which took place on 14 January, 1965, at Stormont House. That development caught the public completely by surprise. Lemass had not even conveyed to his wife where he was going on the morning of his visit; his driver was told only after he had picked him up. Haughey later disclosed that Lemass had informed the cabinet about it, but they had not debated the matter; an indication of the support Lemass enjoyed for the initiative. The meeting was the first of two historic encounters between the premiers.

O'Neill had extended the invitation to Lemass. After Lemass emerged from his car, he was greeted by O'Neill, but maintained a silence. Later, however, Lemass appeared to thaw at a lunch with O'Neill and some of the Stormont cabinet including Brian Faulkner, who was now Minister for Commerce. Lemass had met Faulkner before. Haughey had briefed Lemass about Faulkner's interest in hunting. When Jonathan Bardon for BBC Radio Ulster interviewed Faulkner in 1976, he recalled that: 'the first thing Lemass said to me was "I hear you had a great day with the Westmeaths [i.e. the Westmeath hunt] a few weeks ago."

'"That's right indeed, I didn't realise you knew."

'"Ah," he said, "the boys told me."

'He said, "Have you had a day with Charlie [Haughey] lately?"'[8]

Faulkner then began to reminisce about a number of other hunt meetings he had attended with Haughey, which kept the conversation flowing. Faulkner was no stranger to the south. He had been educated at St Columba's College in Dublin, where he had befriended Catholic students, one of whom, Michael Yeats, went on to become a Fianna Fáil senator. After St Columba's, Faulkner spent a year in Trinity College Dublin, before returning home during the Second World War to help his father run his clothes factories, including one in Co. Donegal. He had also holidayed in the Republic, where he became acquainted with Liam Cosgrave, another equestrian enthusiast and future taoiseach. On top of all this, he was a regular visitor to the annual Horse Show at the RDS in Dublin, where he regularly met Haughey.

TAKING THE GUN OUT OF
REPUBLICAN POLITICS

While Seán Lemass, Jack Lynch and Charles Haughey were developing good relations with their counterparts in Northern Ireland, the IRA was becoming less militant. Overall, the prospects for peace and reconciliation on the island of Ireland looked promising.

The IRA killed no one during the *interregnum* between 1962 and 1969. The relative calm during that interlude was due primarily to the influence of people like Dr Roy Johnston, Anthony Coughlan and others who supported the policy of the new chief-of-staff of the IRA, Cathal Goulding, whose focus was directed towards the development of left-wing politics, rather than military action.

Reluctantly, Goulding had succeeded Ruairí Ó Brádaigh as the IRA's chief-of-staff in late 1962. He concluded that the decisive factor in the failure of the border campaign was the indifference toward it of the overwhelming majority of the population in the Republic. Beyond lip service, few self-professed nationalists had been prepared to make a real contribution to the campaign.

Goulding was a short, burly, charismatic man.[1] Born in 1922, he was the scion of a distinguished republican family. His grandfather had been a member of the Fenians and his father had participated in the 1916 Rising. Goulding had been involved with the IRA since the 1940s and had served a number of terms of imprisonment. He had also been interned at 'Tintown', the Curragh internment camp during the Second World War. In 1953, he participated in an arms raid on the Officers' Training Corps School at Felstead in Essex, England. He, Seán MacStíofáin and Manus Canning were arrested, convicted and sentenced to eight years imprisonment for the offence. Goulding was released in 1961.

The failure of the IRA's border campaign instigated a re-appraisal about where the Republican Movement should go. An internal report was produced which concluded that it had 'no solid political base among the people' and displayed 'no clear-cut ideology which could define for the people what the struggle was all about'. Goulding decided to open up both Sinn Féin and the IRA to left-wing influences. He was an admirer of Wolfe Tone, who had attempted to rid Ireland of the English crown by uniting 'Protestant, Catholic and Dissenter'. Now, in the tradition of Tone, Goulding promoted the principle of non-sectarianism. To Goulding, the real enemy was British imperialism.

Goulding set out to nudge the Republican Movement to the left through the establishment of Wolfe Tone societies. They were inaugurated during Tone's bicentenary in 1963. Notable members included Jack Bennett of the Communist Party of Northern Ireland, Dr Roy Johnston and Anthony Coughlan. The meetings of the Wolfe Tone societies created opportunities for the discussion and cross-fertilisation of left-wing concepts.

Dr Roy Johnston, who shared Goulding's vision of winding down the IRA, became embarrassed by its on-going existence, especially as it was his specific task to achieve its disappearance. He found it a slow process. He told me that the excuse he gave when challenged about its continued existence by those impatient to have him move faster was 'that they might be required in the event of a counter-revolution'.

On the other side of the republican fence sat Seán MacStíofáin. He was far from happy about the new direction the movement was taking: 'At the top level of the organisation, therefore, three of us were against the new proposals to defer the IRA into the never-never land of theoretical Marxism and parliamentary politics. Three others were in favour of them. The seventh member, the chairman of the Army Council, maintained an ambiguous position on this issue, and kept it up for the next three years.'[2]

The IRA would split into the Official and Provisional wings, but not until December 1969.

Although the *interregnum* period between the border campaign and the 'Troubles' was comparatively peaceful, the special branch still had a lot on their plate. Republicans began to agitate against multinational agribusiness and opposed privately owned fishing rights and ground rents. They burned German owned farm buildings and destroyed an oyster boat, the *Mary Catherine* arguing that the Germans were undermining the livelihoods of local farmers and fishermen. Buses ferrying strike-breakers were destroyed. Less dramatically, some agitated for the preservation of Georgian architecture in Dublin, while others joined trade unions. On 29 January 1967, the Northern Ireland Civil Rights Association was established in Belfast and featured some of Goulding's acolytes among its members.

By now Goulding had swung sufficiently to the left

that he had no qualms about personally visiting the Soviet embassy in London to look for support for the Republican Movement. An official who informed him that the Soviets supported revolutionary governments, not revolutionary movements, rebuffed him.

Joe Cahill, a Belfast IRA leader, was 'convinced that [Goulding] developed his Marxism in jail through his association with the [German-born Soviet] spy Klaus Fuchs'.[3]

Despite opposition, Goulding succeeded in bringing some left-wing ideas to bear on his movement. In tandem with this, the IRA's ability to wage war was scaled down: in 1968, the IRA sold some explosives they had stored in Birmingham to the Free Wales Army. The Welsh activists were arrested and the explosives confiscated. Goulding's motivation for emasculating the IRA flowed from his desire to avoid conflict with the working-class Protestants of Northern Ireland. Instead, he felt he could convince working class loyalists to join with the southern workers, in a common crusade to overthrow the ruling capitalist classes on both sides of the border. Before the outbreak of serious violence at the end of the 1960s, Goulding had sometimes visited Northern Ireland where he made contact with left-wing figures, while ignoring opportunities to meet the ever-dwindling number of Northern IRA men ostensibly under his command.

During all this time, the Joint Intelligence Committee (JIC) at Downing Street, the body which co-ordinates the activities of the various intelligence bureaucracies serving the British government, was keeping a weather eye on Goulding's IRA. In 1966 one of their fears was that there might be an outbreak of violence in the run-up to the fiftieth anniversary of the 1916 Rising.[4] The information at their disposal was supplied by MI5, then led by Sir Martin Furnival-Jones. On the anniversary, the IRA in Belfast only managed to fill a single minibus for the 1966 Wolfe Tone commemoration at Bodenstown. Billy McKee, who later emerged as a key Provisional IRA leader, felt the IRA 'was dead, completely dead. And it was except in the minds of myself and other old Republicans. We lived in hope.'[5]

If the RUC had any sources inside the IRA, they were little more than opportunists who were feeding them yarns for payment. These 'misinformers' upped the ante by claiming Goulding and his associates were preparing to carry out a series of assassinations. There was no hard evidence for this. No names, places or dates were supplied. In this void, the JIC reasoned that 'if the threat materialised, intelligence relating to specific targets for attack could only be obtained at short notice owing to the IRA practice of making last minute decisions'.[6]

No less a figure than the British cabinet secretary, Sir Burke Trend, was appointed to prepare for an outbreak of IRA violence. Intensive security precautions were put in place. The border was sealed off. The B-Specials were put on overtime. Then, nothing happened. After the 1916 anniversary passed without any IRA violence, a delighted intelligence community patted itself on the back. MI5 and the RUC were singled out for compliments by the JIC. London attributed the perceived success to the deterrent effect of the heightened level of security they had put in place in the run up to the Easter Rising celebrations.

In the south, the garda C3's intelligence division had predicted that Goulding had merely planned a number of commemorative parades.

The fact that there was such a variance between what the gardaí had predicted was going to happen on the anniversary, and what the RUC and MI5 believed was afoot, indicates that British intelligence had not penetrated garda intelligence, and that communication between the two groups was poor.

The combination of negligence, ineptitude and paranoia on the part of MI5, the JIC and the RUC special branch – aggravated by the lies of unknown informers – created the impression in 1966 that the IRA was determined to go on the offensive. The toxic atmosphere this created, triggered the rebirth of the Ulster Volunteer Force (UVF) which went on to carry out a series of killings later in the year.

With the 1916 anniversary safely behind him, Seán Lemass decided to step down as taoiseach. He announced his decision in late 1966. One of the issues in the contest revolved around the new policy of rapprochement against more traditional republicanism. Charles Haughey threw his hat into the ring to succeed Lemass. Haughey asked his colleague, Neil Blaney, Minister for Local Government, for his backing. According to another minister in the government, Kevin Boland, Blaney rebuffed Haughey saying: 'No Charlie, you haven't got the [republican] background'.[7] In any event, Blaney was interested in becoming taoiseach himself.

George Colley entered the fray too. James Gibbons acted as his campaign manager.

Haughey realised that he was not going to win and backed

down in favour of Jack Lynch, who had emerged as a reluctant compromise candidate. Blaney backed out too, while Colley forged ahead, only to be defeated 52 votes to 19 in the contest against Lynch who became taoiseach on 10 November 1966. Haughey then succeeded Lynch as Minister for Finance, a position that saw him enhance his reputation as an effective minister.

On the other side of the fence, Goulding pressed ahead with his political agenda. In June 1967, he told a gathering at Bodenstown, that 'revolution is a matter of organisation and demonstration' and ruled out the 'physical force tradition of Dan Breen'.[8]

Bishop and Mallie, authors of *The Provisional IRA,* record that by 1969 'all military activity had ceased. No drilling or arms training had taken place for years, and little attempt was made by the traditionalists to get into a more military posture as the year progressed and the likelihood of widespread violence increased'.[9]

At this time, the IRA was a mere shadow of its former self. As if in reflection of its decline, the organisation's ruling body, the Army Council, met in the ghostly shell of a dilapidated mansion in Co. Meath. Those attending it had to take a right turn off the road somewhere between Navan and Kells and follow a narrow lane to the ballroom of an old building, where an oak tree protruded through the roof. The leaders sat around an illuminated table: Cathal Goulding, Seán Garland, Seán MacStíofáin, Seamus Costello, Tomás McGiolla, Ruairí Ó Brádaigh and Paddy Murphy.[10]

THE MAN FROM 'GLOOM HALL'

'Gloom Hall' was the rather disparaging nickname some of the more cynical British Secret Service (MI6) officers ascribed to Century House, the drab high-rise building in London that served as their HQ during the swinging 1960s and beyond. The top floor office belonged to Sir Maurice Oldfield, the service's heavy-drinking chief, and reeked of the cheap cigarillos he chain-smoked and which had stained his fingers a mahogany brown. Oldfield and his colleagues would spend most of the 1970s trying to sabotage Charles Haughey's political career.

Oldfield became more famous than most of his contemporaries, in part because he courted publicity. He once dined with the actor Alec Guinness, to allow the thespian observe his appearance and absorb his mannerisms in preparation for his portrayal of George Smiley in the BBC's production of John Le Carre's *Tinker Tailor Soldier Spy*. Guinness drew on Oldfield's bespectacled appearance but, in a private letter to Le Carre, who had also attended the lunch, he explained that he was rejecting Oldfield's 'dreadful necktie [which] was beyond any wildest dreams'. He added that the 'ginger shoes, I felt, had been put on to shock quite deliberately. I see what you mean about his shirts. The cufflinks were surprisingly flashy ...'[1]

The glamour of the association with Smiley has served to eclipse the true nature of Oldfield's character for decades.

Oldfield was a tubby little man who waddled when he

walked, often dressed badly and was afflicted with psoriasis – or so he claimed as an excuse for not dating women. His sexual preference was for young men. He accumulated a library of pornographic photographs at his flat in London. In 2016, MI6 disclosed to the Hart Inquiry into child sex abuse committed in Northern Ireland, that it possessed a 'small collection of papers … which relate to the relationship [Oldfield] had with the Head of the Kincora Boys' Home (KBH) in Belfast'. The 'Head' of that monstrous establishment was the 'Warden of Kincora', Joseph Mains, who was convicted in 1981 for a series of rapes he had committed at the residence. The vice ring that revolved around Kincora exploited children as young as eight years of age and was protected by Oldfield for various nefarious intelligence related reasons. The relationship between the spymaster and the warden most likely related to intelligence gathering. Luckily for MI6, the mainstream media ignored the revelation made to the Hart inquiry about Oldfield and Kincora.

MI6 was – and is – part of the Foreign Office and is sometimes referred to as the Secret Intelligence Service (SIS). Oldfield's colleagues – and sometime adversaries – at MI5 were attached to the Home Office. MI5 is also known as the Security Service. In theory, MI5 protected the UK and Britain's colonies, i.e., anywhere the writ of the crown ran, whereas MI6 operated on foreign soil. The distinction is akin to that between the American FBI that operates within the borders of the USA, while the CIA acts abroad.

Oldfield was seen by many of his colleagues as a cunning and devious individual. Born in 1915 in Over Haddon,

Derbyshire, he could switch at will between his original rural accent and a more refined one, when it suited him. Deception was in the marrow of his bones. As a young man, he paid one of his friends from Over Haddon, Vic Smith, the sum of £1 to sit his car driving test for him on 27 May 1938 at Buxton, Derbyshire. Oldfield had failed an earlier test, during which, whilst driving his car, he narrowly avoided colliding with a bus and had rolled down a hill, whilst attempting a hill start. The ruse at the second test worked and Oldfield obtained a licence by fraud.

During the Second World War, Oldfield became a military intelligence officer and participated in deception campaigns. After the war, he fought attempts by Jewish groups to drive the British out of Palestine. In later years, he regaled his colleagues with tales about beating up Jews in Palestine and ducking their heads in buckets of water. He referred to them as 'snipcocks'

While Oldfield did not like being associated in the public mind with violence, his closest friend in the intelligence world, Anthony Cavendish, had no such qualms. The pair had worked together in the 1940s and 1950s and remained close right up until the day Oldfield died in hospital, alongside a picture of Cavendish's dog. One of Cavendish's earliest intelligence experiences had involved the beating and torture of a boy during the Second World War in Egypt, something he recounted in his memoirs, *Inside Intelligence*. The child had the misfortune to know the whereabouts of a truck that was carrying stolen grenades and ammunition. Cavendish was meant to be keeping the vehicle under surveillance, but had lost sight of it. His mistake cost the young Egyptian dearly. Cavendish and a colleague found the boy, whom they then abducted and drove to a police station, where he was 'bundled' into an interrogation room. There, 'the poor child was stripped of everything but his shoes and given a beating before even being asked any questions'. When he denied any knowledge of the arms, he was lifted on to a table where 'he was held down by three brawny Egyptian police'. One of them removed his shoes and began to 'whip the soles of his feet with a thin metal rod until, through the boy's screams and sobs, came the information' Cavendish wanted. It transpired that the elusive truck had made its way to a small village just outside Ismailia, where the arms had been hidden in a dry well. Cavendish and his team rushed off to it 'accompanied by a lorry load of armed police, while the poor boy who could no longer walk was dragged along as our guide'.[2]

There was nothing new about the toxic methods employed by Oldfield and Cavendish. Violence had been part of Britain's intelligence gathering *modus operandi* for decades, if not centuries. In the Middle East of the 1920s, terrifying amounts of brutality had been meted out to Arabs by former Black and Tans who had served in Ireland during the War of Independence.

Oldfield and Cavendish joined MI5 and later transferred to MI6. According to Cavendish, deceit was the starting point of an officer's career in MI6, because a recruit was destined to lie 'from his first day in the Service'. 'It is part of his cover. He says he is a member of the Foreign Service, or he works at the Ministry of Defence, or he is involved in the Post Office engineering, or whatever else his cover might be. As the years go by, the lies take over from the truth and morality accepts the other demands which are made on an officer to get the job done.'[3]

During a training exercise at the start of his career, Cavendish stole the plans of rival teams during a night-time raid. The following day when his stealth was uncovered, a man who had served with the Indian police, recoiled at what Cavendish had done and 'stood upright with anger and said that this was "not cricket", and that he no longer wished to be associated with such people. He resigned at no great loss to a service which has to be prepared to go to any lengths to achieve its objects.'[4]

Cavendish's portrayal of MI6 was not for the faint-hearted, something that would account for the steps the British government took to prevent the publication of his memoirs. He wrote about the use of blackmail to control MI6 agents and the use of 'threats to the family of valu-able informants. An operative member of MI6 cannot auto-matically rule out such methods of achieving the required result in an intelligence mission. Similarly, theft, deception, lies, mutilation and even murder are considered if and when necessary.'[5]

Oldfield served as deputy head of MI6's Singapore station, 1950–53, and as head, 1956–59. The Phoenix Park complex, where Oldfield was based, was 'a regional out-station of HMG with a coordinating role for promoting British interests in the whole of South-East Asia'.[6] One of his tasks was to monitor the flow of weapons and money to the communist guerrillas fighting the British in Malaya in 1949–53, with later American involvement.

Oldfield helped run MI6's guerrilla campaign against Albania in the 1950s during his stint as deputy chief of MI6's counter espionage directorate, R5. The Albanian campaign was a disaster. Most observers believe the MI6 traitor Kim Philby betrayed it from the inside.[7]

MI6 and the CIA were also behind attempted coups in Poland, Hungary, the former Czechoslovakia, Romania, Ukraine and the Baltic states at this time, all of which failed.

Viscount John Julius Norwich once provided a glimpse into the distorted world in which Oldfield was emerging as a star player. When he attended Oxford in the early 1950s, Norwich was approached by MI6 talent scouts, who persuaded him to attend a couple of interviews with the service. During the second one, he was asked if he thought he had the capacity to 'be very unscrupulous'. He did not, and turned down the opportunity to enrol, opting instead to become a regular diplomat.

One of the most unscrupulous operations run by MI6 in the 1950s was Operation Boot, which culminated in 1953 in the downfall of the Iranian prime minister, Muhammad Mosaddegh. Oldfield played a part in the planning of the coup, which involved bribery, the instigation of riots, black propaganda and murder.

British politicians and spies alike engaged in the practice of political assassination to further the interests of their realm. Many of them were hardened by their experiences during the Second World War. Prime Minister Anthony Eden was one such man and had no qualms about ordering the assassination of President Nasser of Egypt in 1956. Anthony Nutting, a British Foreign Office minister recalled decades later: 'I was horrified to get a telephone call over an open line ... in which Anthony Eden said, "What's all this poppycock you've sent me about isolating and quarantining Nasser? Can't you understand – and if you can't understand it, will you come to the Cabinet and explain why – that I want Nasser", and he actually used the word "murdered".'

Before his death, Oldfield described to his friends how MI6 had developed a plan to release a canister of nerve gas in Nasser's offices to kill the Egyptian leader. This would have taken the lives of anyone at the presidential palace, ranging from the most humble members of his domestic staff to his generals and political advisers. Oldfield's friend George Kennedy Young, a former deputy chief of MI6, was the driving force behind the plot. It was meant to have taken place during what became known as the Suez Crisis in 1956.

MI5 and MI6 had access to an assortment of poisonous substances for these types of operations. Peter Wright of MI5 (who frequently worked with MI6 and was an associate of Oldfield) described in his book *Spycatcher*, how he had once visited Porton Down for a demonstration of a cigarette packet, which had been fitted with a poison tipped dart by the staff of the Explosives Research and Development Establishment: 'We solemnly put on white coats and were taken out to one of the animal compounds behind Porton by Dr Ladell, the scientist there who handled all MI5 and MI6 work. A sheep on a lead was led into the centre of the ring. One flank had been shaved to reveal the coarse pink skin. Ladell's assistant pulled out the cigarette packet and stepped forward. The sheep started, and was restrained by the lead, and I thought perhaps the device had misfired. But then the sheep's knees began to buckle, and it started rolling its eyes and frothing at the mouth. Slowly the animal sank to the ground, life draining away, as the white-coated professionals discussed the advantages of the modern new toxin around the corpse.'[8]

In 1963, Dick White, chief of MI6, asked Oldfield and two other senior officers to submit nominations for the position of deputy chief, which was about to become vacant. Oldfield recommended himself with a three-page letter extolling his virtues. His two colleagues rowed in behind him and, in 1964, he became number two in the chain of command.

When White retired as chief of MI6 in 1968, Oldfield perceived himself as his rightful successor. Instead, Harold Wilson appointed Sir John Ogilvy Rennie, a FCO diplomat and Cold War propagandist.

During all this time, London behaved as if it could not make up its mind whether the south of Ireland was truly an independent entity or not. Until 1965, the British embassy in Dublin reported to the Commonwealth Office. This was the framework Britain employed in her dealings with her colonies, or very recently departed ones. Yet, Ireland had left the Commonwealth in 1949. This situation might have prevailed, but for the fact that the Foreign Office and the Commonwealth Office merged into one entity, the FCO in 1965. This development afforded MI6 primacy in espionage against the Republic, as MI6 was a department of the FCO and the latter was responsible for relations with Ireland.

A campaign of violence perpetrated by loyalists to suppress demands for civil rights in Northern Ireland ignited the Troubles in 1968. In response to the turmoil, MI5 sent a 'senior liaison officer' to Northern Ireland while MI6 concentrated on the Republic. Oldfield assumed control of Irish affairs and dominated them for the next decade. His man in Dublin was Peter Carter. Ostensibly a counsellor in the Dublin embassy, he was actually the head of the MI6 station, 1965–68. Carter left Dublin for Rhodesia (now Zimbabwe) from where he was expelled in 1969 'for spying activities' conducted from the post he held as part of the 'residual staff of the British High Commission'.[9]

The Joint Intelligence Committee (JIC) depended upon the Dublin embassy and Maurice Oldfield to keep them abreast of what was happening in the Republic of Ireland. In June 1969, the JIC carried out an assessment of the threat posed to the UK by the IRA and other nationalist movements, albeit in the context of helping the Soviet Forces of the Warsaw Pact.[10] On this occasion, they displayed a more accurate appreciation of what was afoot than during the run up to the anniversary of 1916. Their assessment was that: 'since 1966 the IRA, largely under Communist influence, have adopted a program of semi-constitutional activity designed to create a political situation favourable to a military takeover. More recently this has been extended to include the penetration of the Civil Rights Movement in the North which is also subject to increasing Trotskyite influence.'

Oldfield and his colleagues at Gloom Hall had the good luck to find that Andrew Gilchrist, Her Britannic Majesty's ambassador to Dublin at the beginning of The Troubles, was a veteran of the secret world. At one stage, he had served as chairman of the Joint Intelligence Committee (Far East) where he undoubtedly had many dealings with Oldfield.

An Ambassador 'Complicit in Mass Murder'

One of the reasons MI6 and the Foreign Office became so suspicious of Charles Haughey, Neil Blaney and Irish military intelligence, G2, during 1969–70 was because it was their job to view the world through a suspicious and mistrustful prism. A lot of their time was spent dealing with hostile opponents. Inevitably, they came to see the bad, rather than the good, in those on the other side. Andrew Gilchrist, the British ambassador to Dublin was no exception to this malaise. He was a man who had seen more than his fair share of intrigue during a long career and it had coloured his outlook on life.

Gilchrist served as Her Majesty's ambassador to Dublin, 1966–70. Born in 1910, he had served with Force 136, Britain's special force organisation in Siam [Thailand] during the Second World War. Force 136 was the Far East equivalent of the more familiar Special Operations Executive (SOE) that had waged war behind the lines against Hitler on the orders of Churchill 'to set Europe ablaze'. Some of Gilchrist's missions had taken him behind Japanese lines in Thailand.

While many of Force 136's veterans went on to fight in Britain's colonial wars, Gilchrist joined the Foreign Office. He ascended the ranks to ambassadorial status. His last assignment before Dublin was to Indonesia where the British government of Harold Macmillan was involved in a conspiracy to manipulate events in the country and protect Britain's flank in Malaysia. A glimpse at the nature of

Gilchrist's character can be gleaned from Britain's National Archives: in 1965 he informed the FCO that a 'little shooting in Indonesia would be an essential preliminary to effective change'.[1] When the Indonesian machinations were taking place, Oldfield was the deputy chief of MI6.

Gilchrist conspired with the Information Research Department (IRD), a suitably Orwellian euphemism for the FCO's smear machine. Together they planted stories in the media asserting that communists were planning to slaughter the citizens of Jakarta. There was no truth in the allegation that was beamed into Indonesia by the BBC and provided an excuse for the grotesque massacres that would follow. In 1983, Amnesty International declared that the 'government-instigated killings in Indonesia ... rank among the most massive violations of Human Rights since the Second World War. A conservative estimate of the number of people killed in Indonesia is 500,000.' The man in charge of the IRD at this time was Christopher Barclay.

Commenting on Gilchrist's propaganda accomplishments *via* the BBC, Norman Reddaway of the IRD commented: 'I wondered whether this was the first time in history that an ambassador had been able to address the people of his country of work almost at will and virtually instantaneously.'[2]

In November 2021, Kartika Sukarno, the daughter of the deposed president of Indonesia wrote:

> Unfortunately, this dark history of Indonesia remains largely hidden. The European and American history curriculums do not mention their role in the dark periods of colonialism and western imperialism during the cold war. Instead, most textbooks still largely offer self-glorifying roles in this history.

> As the *Observer* [newspaper] story showed, the British were complicit in the mass murders and enabling the thirty-two-year reign of the despotic General Suharto. It is time that the British government apologised to the Indonesian people for the enormous harm it did.[3]

Gilchrist settled into Ireland well and soon found himself mingling with IRA veterans who had fought Britain during the War of Independence. In 1969, he attended a presentation by the author, M.R.D. Foot, to the Military History Society on 'Michael Collins and Irregular Warfare' in Dublin. Foot was the official historian of the SOE. David Neligan who had spied for Michael Collins at Dublin Castle during the War of Independence, and later became the director of military intelligence, accompanied Gilchrist. Neligan had helped set up the garda special branch. Major-General Seán Collins-Powell, a nephew of Collins, was also in the group.[4]

Gilchrist found himself less popular with a new breed of Irish left-wing revolutionary republicans. In June 1968, the Irish special branch ascertained that a Trotskyite republican splinter group, Saor Éire, intended to kidnap or attack Gilchrist and he was placed under heavy armed guard. He accepted the menace with good humour, joking that his imposing bulk made him a good target. He wrote of the branch men that 'though they are much the nicest armed guards I have had in recent years, I would really rather be without them'. During the time he was under garda protection, he developed a first-rate relationship with the head of the Irish special branch, Superintendent John Fleming, whom he deemed highly efficient.

Meanwhile, MI5 had assigned a 'special liaison officer'

(SLO) in Belfast.[5] In 1968, the SLO became an independent source of information about Northern Ireland for London. Some of the information he gathered was channelled to Gilchrist. On 5 August 1969, Edward Peck of the JIC, described the SLO to Gilchrist as a key figure in the 'slightly better intelligence service on Northern Ireland'.[6]

London was less impressed with the weekly summaries emanating from the Stormont Ministry of Home Affairs. Peck advised 'the rumbustious Gilchrist' in Dublin that the reports from the unionists were the nearest Whitehall could get to a 'Belfast dispatch', and, 'you should therefore treat them with the usual caution and destroy them after reading. After a time you may think it worth applying this treatment before reading, but you will realise that there are intelligence pips in this stodgy pudding and they may squeak.'[7]

Later, Gilchrist came to feel he was being left out of the intelligence loop. On 24 July 1969, he complained to Peck about the reports of MI5's SLO: 'We have had little more from London than an out-of-date compilation of information mostly already known from the newspapers.' Worse still, from his perspective, he felt he was being kept in the dark about developments in the Republic. The implication of this is that Oldfield was running the revamping of MI6's apparatus in Dublin tightly in conjunction with the new MI6 Head of Station in the embassy without his direct involvement. Gilchrist wanted to know more:

> … Whatever progress may have been made since we met in developing intelligence work in Northern Ireland *and in respect of the South* [my emphasis], I have heard nothing whatever here of the intended new effort or of any of its products … if communications

from the Irish special branch to London have been suspended, I should like to know. If reports are still coming in, but contain nothing worth passing on to me, I should like to know that too. If there is good stuff available which it is not desirable that I should now see, that is also a matter which it might be useful for me to be aware of ... It is not mere curiosity. If I am to assess correctly the information and gossip I pick up here ... It is important that I should be kept in the picture ... For subversive purposes, Ireland is one island.[8]

Whoever took over the MI6 Station at the Dublin embassy after Peter Carter left for Africa has managed to escape scrutiny from historians. The most likely candidate for the post is Reuben W. Piper who arrived in 1968. He was assigned the post of counsellor and was better known by his nickname, 'Peter' Piper. Carter had served as counsellor before Piper took over the role.

Despite failing to gain entry to Oldfield's inside track, Gilchrist was able to rely on his own resources to find out quite a lot about what was afoot in Dublin.

A DEFENCELESS COMMUNITY

When The Troubles erupted in Northern Ireland, Britain's prime minister, Harold Wilson, and his home secretary, James Callaghan, realised they were not facing an insurrection organised by the IRA. Regrettably, the professional conspiracy theorists in the RUC, MI5 and MI6 were not so discerning. They would soon come to suspect that another revolt against the crown by the IRA was underway; worse still, that the Irish government was involved in the conspiracy. Over time, they would come to believe that Charles Haughey was acting hand-in-glove with the Provisional wing of the IRA that emerged at the end of the 1960s.

The Troubles began in 1968. The IRA was not the cause of the upheaval. On the contrary, militant loyalists launched a series of attacks against nationalist groups who were calling for civil rights, such as one man one vote, a fair allocation of public housing and an end to discrimination in the allocation of government jobs. A motley crew of arsonists and rioters incited by Ian Paisley, John McKeague and others were responsible for the August attacks. Armed RUC officers and their auxiliaries, the B-Specials, joined them. Some of the attackers were members of the UVF. Lenny Murphy, the future leader of the Shankill Butcher gang, was present alongside them.[1] Over the next few years, the ranks of loyalist terror gangs such as the Shankill Defence Association (SDA), UVF and Red Hand Commandos would swell with loyalists blooded that month.[2] Paisley was spurred by a belief that the

Dublin government, the IRA and the Vatican were scheming together to end partition. He saw the Northern Ireland Civil Rights Association (NICRA) as part of this international conspiracy. Paisley was a British-Israelite, and believed that the Protestants of Northern Ireland were one of the lost tribes of Israel.

During the violence, RUC officers took to the streets in Shorland semi-armoured vehicles equipped with Browning 0.30 calibre medium machine guns which had an effective range of approximately one mile. Some of them sprayed bullets into the nationalist Divis flats. One tracer bullet tore into Patrick Rooney's head. He was only nine-years-old. When Paddy Kennedy, MP, visited the flat, he found the boy's father scraping his brains off the wall with a spoon. Hugh McCabe, a soldier with the Queen's Royal Irish Hussars, who was on leave from Germany, was also shot dead in the flats by RUC bullets.

When the loyalist mobs advanced on nationalist/Catholic communities, B-Specials, armed with rifles, revolvers and machine guns, supplied the muscle. In the Ardoyne, the RUC led a violent drunken loyalist mob. A man called Samuel Mc-Larnon was shot in his wheelchair in the front room of his home on Herbert Street.

In Dublin, Haughey warned the cabinet that unless the Dublin government took strong action 'irresponsible groups', i.e., the IRA, might step into the breach and attract substantial public support.[3] The cabinet responded by sending its army to the border to establish field hospitals for refugees. Fearing an invasion, the Stormont government considered blowing up border crossings.

Neil Blaney sent a message to London – as did many others – urging Harold Wilson to send in British troops to protect nationalists. Wilson responded positively and the soldiers managed to put a halt to the loyalist attacks. The British army had never been – and would never again become – as popular with nationalists as it was during the end of 1969 and the early part of 1970.

That August the Dáil voted to make £100,000 available for the relief of distress in Northern Ireland. Later, large amounts of this would be siphoned off as part of a shambolic operation to purchase arms. The weapons were sought by the Citizen Defence Committees (CDCs), not the IRA. They wanted the arms to defend their communities, not to launch a campaign to end partition. The CDCs were made up of civil rights activists, priests, lawyers, and some IRA veterans from the border campaign. The CDCs developed cordial relationships with the British home secretary, James Callaghan, the British army and the new RUC chief constable, Sir Arthur Young.

On 20 August 1969, Patrick Hillery, Irish Minister for External Affairs, attended the United Nations in New York where he attempted to make an appeal to the assembly on the basis that there was a 'threat to peace' in Ireland, but was out-manoeuvred by the polished diplomatic virtuosos attached to the British contingent at the UN. Hillery returned with his tail between his legs. Ambassador Gilchrist later described Hillery's reaction to the experience in a letter to Sir Dennis Greenhill of the FCO.[4] It outlined how, at a dinner party hosted by the ambassador in Dublin, Hillery had acknowledged the diplomatic skills and prowess applied by the British at the UN. After the meal, Hillery had found himself 'closeted' with Oliver Wright, the British government's representative to Northern Ireland (UKREP). 'I think it was quite a useful occasion', Gilchrist wrote. 'Oliver will be writing about it, and one of the points I am sure he will make is the considerable instructional effect on Hillery of his visit to the United Nations, how he was impressed by [Lord] Caradon [in New York], how he was struck by our prestige there and the ability of our machine to mobilise the votes when required'.

Gilchrist then proceeded to described how 'one achieves an occasional smirk of professional satisfaction' at the manner in which Hillery had been side-lined.

The Government Information Bureau (GIB), which answered to Lynch, underwent a rapid expansion so it could engage in an international propaganda offensive. The cabinet appointed George Colley to oversee the campaign. It sought to draw attention to unionist misrule in Northern Ireland, stressing that it was something that had been ignored by a succession of British governments. Denis Kennedy, the diplomatic correspondent of *The Irish Times*, wrote about the GIB campaign on 3 September 1969. He quoted Conor Cruise O'Brien, TD of the Labour Party, as having claimed that there were signs that publicity was allegedly being 'used as a substitute for policy, instead of [as] an arm of it'.[5]

In September 1969, Gilchrist was invited to share his views with the JIC in person. When he did, he emphasised that after the turmoil of the previous August, the IRA was 'a very real menace to [the] stability of Ireland, and therefore ourselves'. His views were met with genteel scepticism. He also argued that the willingness and ability of the Dublin government to deal with the IRA had been affected by the loyalist violence, again something that was met with reservation. Gilchrist felt that London should explore a new arrangement for Northern Ireland with which the Dublin government could be associated and which might be acceptable to all sides.

In September 1969, members of the Irish community gathered an assortment of guns in England. The motive behind the collection was a fear that the British army might withdraw, leaving nationalist communities exposed to the loyalist gangs once again; alternatively, that the military's resources might become so stretched by a sudden large-scale upheaval that pogroms might commence. At this time, nationalists were still hailing Britain's troops as saviours. The weapons collected in Britain were flown to Dublin.[6] Kevin Boland, a member of the cabinet in Dublin, has stated that the importation was carried out with the knowledge of most members of the Irish government. Jock Haughey, a brother of Charles Haughey, was involved. The consignment was brought through customs at Dublin Airport with the assistance of an official who worked there. The Army Council of the IRA knew about the importation and arranged to collect the weapons. However, Cathal Goulding, chief-of-staff of the IRA, ensured that they were delivered to him and he made certain they were not sent to Northern Ireland. This enraged some of his colleagues on the Army Council and news of what had happened became common knowledge within the upper reaches of the IRA. The information about the arrival of the guns reached London within a few months, probably through the garda special branch who had sources inside the IRA, including Seán MacStíofáin who sat on the Army Council.

The garda special branch became fearful that MacStíofáin's role as an informer might be exposed by the information he was furnishing to them about the on-going efforts by nationalists to import arms. They were particularly concerned about one member of the force who was friendly with Neil Blaney. Blaney was one of the driving forces behind the effort to procure arms for the defence committees. The gardaí feared that the officer in question might even have been aiding Blaney in these endeavours. Measures were taken to ensure that the officer did not learn they had a high-level informer inside the IRA.[7]

The supreme irony is that MacStíofáin was not a genuine informer, rather what might be dubbed a 'misinformer' or 'disinformer' who was misleading his garda handlers. His object was to deflect attention from his faction within the IRA and onto Cathal Goulding and his Marxist allies whom he despised. Significantly, MacStíofáin portrayed Blaney and Haughey as allies of the IRA. This sparked MI6's fear about the pair and drove and sustained the campaign of character assassination against Haughey which is the focus of this book.

The mission to procure arms for the CDCs was conducted with the knowledge of Jack Lynch, James Gibbons, Minister for Defence, Blaney and the Haughey brothers. Blaney and Charles Haughey were involved in the operation in their capacity as members of the cabinet sub-committee on Northern Ireland. During a discussion in December 1969, Gibbons brought Lynch up-to-date about the efforts being made by the CDCs, but failed to receive a direction from him as to what he should do. At this point, Lynch was trying to sidestep the machinations which were afoot. When Gibbons relayed Lynch's failure to respond to his cabinet colleague, George Colley, the latter advised him to go back and press Lynch for a clear-cut direction.

In Dublin, Gilchrist became aware that other ministers, including Charles Haughey, were involved in the arms quest. The ambassador was about to come face-to-face with Haughey, a man who would henceforth become of paramount interest to the FCO and Maurice Oldfield at MI6.

HAUGHEY AND THE DIPLOMAT-SPY

In late September and early October 1969, Charles Haughey attempted to open a back channel to the British government. His emissary was Constantine Fitzgibbon, a former British military intelligence officer, who was then living in Killiney, Co. Dublin.[1] Haughey's message to Fitzgibbon, for onward relay to London, was that the British government should drop the pretence that 'Stormont still existed' and talk with Dublin instead about Northern Ireland.

Haughey made little progress with London *via* Fitzgibbon and subsequently concentrated his efforts on Gilchrist in Dublin. He succeeded in luring the ambassador to his home, 'Abbeville', for discussions in early October 1969. At the encounter, Haughey offered 'a firm combative statement of his own position'.[2]

On 4 October, Gilchrist reported to the FCO that Haughey had argued that the reunification of the island was the best solution to the overall problem. He impressed upon Gilchrist that there was nothing he would not sacrifice, including the position of the Catholic church, to achieve a United Ireland; he would even support re-joining the Commonwealth and grant the Royal Navy access to Irish ports; moreover, he would push for the Republic to join NATO.

According to the ambassador, 'It was impossible for me to discuss such a question [i.e. the negotiations which Haughey was suggesting] since I did not know what the Irish government had in mind'. Further, Gilchrist advised London that 'if it came to a planned contact for serious discussion, Haughey's rivalry with Lynch would raise a question'.[3]

Gilchrist detected another fault-line between Haughey and Lynch: he would later advise London that, 'Mr Haughey's passion for Irish unity [was] greater than that of Jack Lynch and Patrick Hillery.'[4]

Blaney, Haughey and others were exasperated at what they perceived as Lynch's inability to handle the crisis. According to Blaney's biographer, on 12 August 1969, the night the violence erupted in Northern Ireland, Blaney had stayed up 'until five o'clock that morning, sitting on the stairs in his Dublin home trying to contact the Taoiseach' by telephone, while others, including the secretary of the taoiseach's department, were also attempting to locate Lynch. Blaney recalled that, 'he just could not be got out of his house by the phone or physically during the hours of twelve midnight and five o'clock on the morning of August 13th'. Lynch's private secretary went out to his house at around one o'clock 'to ascertain whether Lynch was there from the guards who were stationed outside. "And, yes, he was. He had come in, both Maureen [his wife] and himself. That poor Secretary went up to the door, knocked on it, rang the bell. He could hear the two phones ringing. He eventually kicked the door. Maureen and Jack were inside and did not emerge". All efforts to contact Jack Lynch until the morning failed.'[5]

In the morning, Lynch emerged from the house. One civil servant who worked with the Corkman was aware that he was a heavy whiskey drinker and believes he had fallen into a drunken stupor.[6]

Gilchrist found that Haughey was sensitive to any criticism that the Irish government was stirring up trouble. According to Gilchrist, 'Haughey was indignant about boat-rocking: with trivial exceptions recent Irish behaviour had been exemplary; he himself proposed in the Cabinet that no one should offer [an opinion] in public on the North but the Taoiseach and the Foreign Minister, and the position had virtually been held'.[7]

Haughey called upon Fitzgibbon again, a few weeks later, in an effort to forge a link with Anthony Crosland, a member of Harold Wilson's cabinet, but nothing came of that endeavour either. That Fitzgibbon was operating on behalf of the embassy was disclosed much later. Having met with Haughey, Gilchrist sent a communication to London saying: 'After leaving Haughey, Fitzgibbon met me and asked how in the circumstances he could best angle his articles or which points he should emphasise.' This communication was later released by Britain's national archive.

While Gilchrist was open to the possibility that Haughey might have been using Fitzgibbon to fish for information, he gave him the benefit of the doubt, adding that he knew him 'well enough to be sure he is not in the pay of the Irish'.

The intrigues swirling around Dublin soon began to befuddle Gilchrist, who grew less confident about whom he could trust. Soon, he was tempering his faith in Fitzgibbon. On 6 October, he advised London that: 'Though [Fitzgibbon] has so far been of considerable use to me, he is now applying for Irish nationality so that he is an interested party as well as being emotionally involved'.[8]

The 'Concerned' Ex-MI5 Officer at *The Irish Times*

One of the most important strategies in Maurice Oldfield's playbook was the use, manipulation and abuse of the media. He was a disseminator of 'fake news' long before that phrase was invented. He called it 'disinformation'. If he was going to inflict a blow against those he perceived as enemies of the crown, it was going to be crucial to gain some influence over the Irish media.

Oldfield's colleagues at the IRD had enjoyed the co-operation of the Irish government during the 1960s in joint operations directed against the Soviet Union. On 19 November 1969, C. MacLaren of the IRD completed a report entitled, 'IRD Work in Ireland' during which he recommended that going forward the IRD 'may well need to influence Irish opinion independently of the [Irish] government'.[1] In other words, the IRD was already anticipating that it might have to deploy its expertise to manipulate Irish public opinion and, thereby, bring Fianna Fáil to heel.

As luck would have it, one of the most senior figures in the Irish publishing industry came knocking on London's door offering to provide whatever help he could. The approach was not made to MI6 or the IRD, rather the political office at 10 Downing Street. Still, it opened up the possibility that the FCO, MI6 and the IRD could exploit the opportunity to develop contacts once Downing Street had opened the door for them.

The Irish Times was one of the Republic's three leading national newspapers and had once been owned by people with links to the Freemasons. By the 1960s, it was the in-house publication for southern unionists and what were disparagingly described in Ireland – with no small amount of hostility – as 'West Brits' or 'Castle Catholics', i.e., upper middle-class professionals of both religions. Hence, the nationalist mob led by Haughey in 1945 had attacked the offices of the paper in Dublin city before moving to that other bastion of 'West Britain', Trinity College. The editor of the paper since 1963, Douglas Gageby, however, was a modernising influence. He was trying – and succeeding – in widening its readership.

Broadly speaking, *The Irish Independent*, another national newspaper, was read by supporters of Fine Gael. A third publication, *The Irish Press*, had been set up by Éamon de Valera and catered for Fianna Fáil supporters.

The spymasters of the JIC felt Gilchrist should play a part in the recruitment of Irish journalists as sources of information for London. In September of 1969, they invited the ambassador to discuss this possibility with them.[2]

On 2 October, Gilchrist wrote to Kelvin White at the FCO stating that he had '[Major Thomas] McDowell [of *The Irish Times*] in mind in certain conversations I had in London a fortnight ago', about the Irish media.[3]

Maj. McDowell was the tweedy, monocle wearing chief executive and director of *The Irish Times*. Born in Belfast in 1923, he had joined the Royal Irish Rifles and, by the end of the Second World War, had become a captain. He spent some of his time in the Ministry of Defence at the Judge Advocate's department. While his record showed he left the army in 1955, that was only half the story. At some stage during the decade after the war ended, he joined MI5 before returning to civvy street in 1955.

Cecil King, who owned *The Daily Mirror*, was another MI5 asset who had become a newspaper proprietor.[4] King not only knew McDowell, but was aware that he was a former MI5 officer. King's diary entry for Sunday, 23 January 1972, touched upon McDowell's service with MI5. Having enjoyed a lunch with McDowell and his wife, King recorded that McDowell 'asked us to talk about Irish affairs. He is a man with a very varied background – a Protestant father from the North, mother from the South, service in the British Army (Ulster rifles), and had served on the Staff in Edinburgh, and in M.I.5.'[5]

In his book *The Irish Times: Past and Present*, John Martin states that his sources 'within *The Irish Times* have indicated to me that [McDowell] worked for British intelligence in Austria at the end of the war'.[6]

What type of work might McDowell have performed for MI5? At the time, British intelligence was engaged in a de-Nazification programme and the recruitment of former military intelligence and Gestapo officers, some of whom claimed to have access to agents behind the Iron Curtain.[7]

McDowell spent some of his time in London where he was a member of the Naval and Military Club. On 11 September 1969, he called the political office at 10 Downing Street from the club and left a message revealing that he 'could be of some use with regard to the situation in Northern Ireland'.[8] His offer was brought to the attention of Harold Wilson. When the Yorkshire man learned that a number of unsuccessful attempts had been made to catch McDowell before his return to Ireland, he instructed one of his secretaries, Peter Gregson, to get the British embassy in Dublin to contact McDowell. Wilson suspected that 'McDowell's offer of assistance may relate more to intelligence than to journalistic activity'.[9]

Contact with McDowell was established on 2 October 1969, when Gilchrist took the major to lunch in Dublin. The ambassador reported back to Kelvin White of the FCO that same day in a letter marked 'SECRET & PERSONAL' – McDowell was 'one of the five (Protestant) owners of *The Irish Times*, and he and his associates are increasingly concerned about the line the paper is taking under its present (Protestant, Belfast-born) Editor, [Douglas] Gageby, whom he described as a very fine journalist, an excellent man, but on Northern questions a renegade or white n[***]er. And apart from Gageby's editorial influence, there is difficulty lower down, whereby sometimes unauthorised items appear and authorised items are left out.'[10]

Gageby had a background in Irish military intelligence. During the Second World War, he had served as a lieutenant in G2, a post he secured having studied German at Trinity College Dublin. He continued as editor of the paper until 1974.[11] After the Arms Crisis erupted, he was able to avail of his G2 background to find out from Col Hefferon, the director of G2, what had really taken place during the CDCs' quest for arms. Over the ensuing decades, he would prove more sympathetic towards Haughey than most of his colleagues, believing the operation had not been illegal.

Unfortunately, what exactly was 'authorised' by McDowell's board to appear in the paper, and what was not, was not made clear in Gilchrist's memo, nor how the owners exercised control over the paper's content. The ambassador advised that McDowell 'now felt that a certain degree of guidance [from London], in respect of which lines were helpful and which unhelpful, might be acceptable to himself and one or two of his friends on the Board ... His present approach requires rather careful handling and I shall discuss it in London next week. I am writing this letter merely in case you wish to brief No. 10 [Downing Street] and assure them that we will do what we can to exploit this opening. I am destroying the correspondence.'[12]

The courtship of McDowell was conducted by way of a series of 'comfortable' lunches.[13] One of those who played a part in the engagement was John Peck, a senior propaganda specialist, who succeeded Gilchrist as ambassador in April 1970.[14]

On 7 November 1969, Kelvin White brought Gilchrist up to speed about what had been discussed at one of the lunches. The conversation had ranged over 'many Irish matters, and the newspaper world especially, but if I had to sum up very briefly what McDowell really had to say I think it would be that he wants to help and is willing to be used as a link'.

White informed Gilchrist that McDowell felt the 'present situation was so serious and so different he thought he ought to offer his services. His qualifications are his contacts in both capitals, and his acceptability in Whitehall terms through his service in the Judge Advocate General's department.'

Gageby's name cropped up again, but McDowell was not seeking 'ammunition for use against his Editor, but he did, as you forecast, mention rather apologetically that Editor's excessive zeal'.[15]

Overall, White advised that: 'At the moment I think it would be useful, so far as we in the Department are concerned, to keep in touch with McDowell, to keep him briefed in general terms, and to encourage him to forward the moderates' cause in his paper. This is very much what you had in mind. Beyond that I cannot see a go-between role for him, but that would be more a matter for you to suggest if you found doors closed to you.'[16]

Fortuitously for posterity, the McDowell correspondence was not destroyed. The major was alive when it was made public. He acknowledged the contact with the FCO but denied using the words 'white n[***]er'.

The TD who Divulged Military Secrets

Capt. James Kelly and a handful of his colleagues in military intelligence quite literally took their lives into their own hands as they spread out secretly across Northern Ireland gathering intelligence for the cabinet after August 1969. Little did they know that a member of the Dáil, the parliament in Dublin, would soon be revealing some of their activities to the British embassy in Dublin. A stumbling block for the embassy was that the TD was offering a jumble of fact, speculation and fiction.

Capt. Kelly drove about Northern Ireland in his personal blue Renault. He was unarmed and alone during a mission that unfolded over six weeks in August and September 1969. The Renault had southern registration plates which made it stick out conspicuously. His cover, at least when he was near Belfast, was that he was going to visit his brother, a priest in the city. His assignment was to forge contacts in nationalist communities across Northern Ireland. Col Hefferon, the director of G2, was kept awake at night at the thought that his officers might fall into the hands of the RUC or loyalist militants. While the former might detain and question them at a checkpoint, leading to embarrassment for the Irish government, the latter might have beaten them to a pulp, or worse.[1] The difficulty for the colonel was that the cabinet needed to know what was going on across the border but could not rely upon the gardaí or DoJ as neither had any agents in Northern Ireland.[2] By October, the colonel put his foot down and ordered a complete cessation of cross border operations. An office in Monaghan was set up to replace the field operations. By then, a network of contacts had been established and the office was where they would meet.[3] The building masqueraded as a branch of NICRA, to conceal it from British intelligence and loyalist eyes.

Like the colonel, ministers Haughey and Gibbons were eager to conceal G2's activities from British and loyalist eyes. During his evidence at the Arms Trial, Haughey told the court that he and Gibbons were keen for Capt. Kelly to continue his mission, but they were worried and 'wanted to find some post for him inside the public service, where he would be able to continue with his activities. I suggested a good cover for him would be to become a special customs officer with responsibility for pig smuggling, which was then a very serious problem ... I do remember Mr Gibbons telling me of his fears that Capt. Kelly [must have come to the attention] of British Intelligence and that he wanted to get some position for him where he could carry on his valuable work.'[4]

As the weeks passed, Ambassador Gilchrist sought details about 'reports' reaching his ears 'linking [Haughey] with an organisation in Monaghan devoted to trans-border activities'. Conor Cruise O'Brien provided him with some information. O'Brien was a former Irish diplomat who was now an Irish Labour Party TD.[5] He shared information from a document in his possession about G2's activities with Gilchrist. John Devine, the public relations officer of the

Irish Labour Party, had compiled it. The memorandum was entitled *Aspects of the Six County Situation*. An over-arching flaw contained therein was Devine's erroneous assumption that the operation in Monaghan was a 'front organisation for Fianna Fáil' which, he believed, was trying to take over the NICRA and establish a political footing in Northern Ireland.

There were, however, some valuable nuggets in it about G2. Devine described how, 'In the first (and current) issue of the magazine *This Week*, it is reported that Irish Army intelligence officers and British Army intelligence have exchanged visits into each other's territory. Whatever about the British, the Irish certainly have been visiting the North regularly since October 5 last (1968).'[6]

He proceeded to relay how an 'agent' of 'Messrs Haughey, Blaney and Boland, has been conducting ... military intelligence personnel (Captains Doolan and Duggan) on trips behind the barricades'.[7] Devine believed that the officers were co-operating with 'the Republican element in the North', and that 'ammunition and money has been distributed' to them. Although not named, the 'agent' was Seamus Brady. The republicans, Devine believed, who had jumped into bed with Fianna Fáil, were those who had 'more or less broken with the Dublin HQ of the IRA ... The [Goulding faction of the] IRA is highly worried and indignant at the influence which these Fianna Fáil people are having among Northern republicans; the possibility of retaliation is likely from the Dublin end. Fianna Fáil have now established a chain of links from Belfast and Derry, including places like Dungannon, Newry,

Armagh, Coalisland, Omagh and in other places where their sphere of contacts up to now has been negligible. Their aid is being accepted.' In reality, G2 was in contact with various CDC representatives in these areas. In Belfast, Capt. Kelly was talking to Tom Conaty (chairman of the Central CDC and a future adviser to the Conservative party secretary of state for Northern Ireland, William Whitelaw); Jim Sullivan (an ally of Goulding, who also served on the Central CDC); and Paddy Devlin (secretary of the Central CDC and a future SDLP minister). It would be difficult to conceive of a group of nationalists more hostile to the IRA faction that transformed into the Provisionals than the hierarchy of the Central CDC.

Some, if not all, of the information in the Devine Memorandum made its way to the British embassy. On 10 November 1969, Gilchrist sent a confidential telegram to the FCO, describing the mysterious manoeuvrings in Monaghan. He identified O'Brien as his informant. The communication closely mirrored the content of the flawed Devine Memorandum. It described an 'organisation in Monaghan', which was 'quite a small one' and that it had been 'set up by Haughey with party funds'. In reality, the Monaghan operation was being financed in the normal way by funds allocated to G2.

On a more accurate level, O'Brien or Gilchrist, or perhaps both of them, had deduced that: 'It contains an Intelligence Unit, where Irish Army Intelligence Officers brief and debrief visitors to and from the North.'

Gilchrist's interest focused on the allegation that Haughey and his associates had prepared lists of civil rights 'Defence

Units' (*sic*) in Northern Ireland and of their requirements 'for self-defence' should 'further disorders break out'. This was a fair stab at what G2 was up to, save that G2's tendrils were reaching out to the CDCs, not civil rights groups, albeit there was an overlap between the two.

Gilchrist proceeded to explain how, according to O'Brien, the Monaghan organisation was hoping to provide support to the defence units 'by way of weapons, radio sets and personnel'. O'Brien also reported that, 'numerous weapons have already been supplied, not on the responsibility of the [Monaghan] organisation itself but by people who have been given access to its lists'. This however, was unconfirmed, 'being only my own attempt to reconcile conflicting rumours and reports'.

Gilchrist relayed O'Brien's analysis of what was afoot to the FCO. According to the ambassador, O'Brien felt the enterprise was a political stunt which would be brought to 'public knowledge' so it could 'bolster the image of Fianna Fáil as the patriotic party, still fighting for Irish unity'.

But what did Gilchrist himself think? He wrote that O'Brien 'may be right but we should keep our eyes open to this threat on our flanks'.

Having met Haughey at Abbeville, Gilchrist was aware that the minister was interested in moving matters forward at an inter-governmental level and, while he was a 'hard man', he was not a 'wild man'. Had his meeting with Haughey at Abbeville not taken place, Gilchrist might have become more alarmed about and suspicious of Haughey. Gilchrist advised London: 'Mr Haughey's passion for Irish unity being greater than that of Jack Lynch and Patrick Hillery, he is even more certain than they are that the UK government cannot hold the position in the North and that further disturbances will break out.'

Less than a week later, on 4 November 1969, he advised London that there 'has certainly been some very considerable gun-running for the benefit of the Catholics in the North, but it is by no means sure that the IRA as an organisation is responsible for it'. This was an accurate assessment. According to John Kelly, an IRA veteran who later stood in the dock with Charles Haughey and Capt. Kelly at the Arms Trials, 'people all around the Twenty-six Counties contributed weapons at this period, and it was not just Fianna Fáil supporters – people aligned to Fine Gael, traditionally seen as strongly anti-IRA, also helped out. Whatever they had, shotguns, old rifles, Mausers going back to the First World War, were handed over.'[8]

DIPLOMATIC ARM WRESTLING

Conor Cruise O'Brien was also keeping Ambassador Gilchrist up to speed *á propos* what Jack Lynch knew about the arms importation operation. O'Brien told him that Lynch had been 'quite unaware of the range of Mr Haughey's activities' and had been 'much perturbed' by what he had learned about them a few days previously. Yet, since Lynch had done nothing to curb Haughey and G2's association with the CDCs, he cannot have been that 'much perturbed'.

It is likely that O'Brien formed this impression having discussed Haughey's activities directly with Lynch at a private meeting.

On 19 November, Gilchrist had a face-to-face meeting with Lynch. It proved to be an encounter at which two crafty operators tried to size each other up. But who got the better of his opponent?

Lynch spoke first, mentioning a loyalist arsenal on the Shankill Road and pressed Gilchrist to get the British army to dismantle it. Gilchrist returned this serve by revealing that it had come to his attention that there were 'alleged to be activities [i.e. the supply of weapons to Northern Ireland] on this side of the frontier which, if reported back to the people in Stormont … would strengthen them in their suspicion of the Republic … I [told Lynch that I] had no reliable information whatever and … [that] my concern was with the rumours, some of them plausible enough on the surface, and with the political effects which might arise from them'.[1]

Lynch at first denied all knowledge of the gun-running rumours. Gilchrist then 'mentioned the word "Monaghan"' after which he concluded that Lynch 'rather gave himself away by asking if the rumours might relate to activities by a certain member of his cabinet'. But Gilchrist may have under-estimated the wily taoiseach. By the end of the bout, Lynch had ascertained that the British were aware of the G2 base in Monaghan and that at least one of his ministers was participating in a project to import arms; and probably that Gilchrist had been talking to O'Brien.

When Gilchrist's 10 November 1969 telegram emerged from Britain's National Archives in January 2000, O'Brien stated, 'I recognise the Ambassador's report as an accurate record of my views at the time'. No one, however, seems to have asked him why he had felt it had been appropriate to inform the British government that there was an office in Monaghan which contained an 'Intelligence Unit', where Irish Army intelligence officers debriefed visitors from Northern Ireland. No one asked him if he had passed on the document that named Captains Doolan and Duggan to Gilchrist.

Gilchrist had a few other tricks up his sleeve. He had been able to direct certain TDs to ask questions for him, in the Dáil, about Fianna Fáil's anti-British propaganda campaign. It had been launched after the eruption of violence in August 1969. George Colley, with full cabinet approval, had supervised a team of press secretaries, which had been dispatched around the globe with briefs, which were critical of Britain's record in Ireland. Gilchrist's view of Colley, as expressed at the end of September 1969, was that he was part of a group of 'hawkish' ministers, including Blaney and Boland.[2] He described the propaganda offensive to UKREP Oliver Wright, as a process of 'emitting poisonous propaganda'. On 7 November 1969, Gilchrist boasted, that: 'There is a general tendency in Dublin to regard the whole thing as a mistake, a concession made at the time to hot-heads, something best forgotten. The newspapers on the whole have been critical, sometimes scathing; and there have been questions in the Dáil (some of them stimulated by your humble servant – tell it not in Gath[3] publish it not on the streets of Belfast) which have made the Government decidedly uncomfortable.'[4] Gilchrist was referring here to questions, which had been raised in the Dáil, on 22 October 1969, by Gerry L'Estrange of Fine Gael who had asked why there was a need for the new Government Information Service.

Despite his abhorrence of the IRA, O'Brien enjoyed a lunch with Ruairí Ó Brádaigh, the leader of the breakaway Provisional IRA movement, on 2 July 1970. Ó Brádaigh was a former abstentionist TD who had served as IRA chief-of-staff during the border campaign, a fact well-known to O'Brien. The lunch proved to be a cordial affair at the National Gallery in Dublin. O'Brien used it to discuss the state of the IRA with Ó Brádaigh. He recorded in his diary that it appeared as if the 'Belfast Provisionals [were] less under [Ó Brádaigh's] control than the Derry ones'.[5] It is not known if O'Brien relayed these observations to Gilchrist too.

Meanwhile, a plot was afoot to lure Neil Blaney, a member of the cabinet sub-committee on Northern Ireland, and his associates, into a trap in London. The mission almost cost the life of a British spy.

The Plot to Assassinate a British Spy in Dublin

In November 1969, British Intelligence launched an operation to penetrate the on-going efforts of the CDCs to acquire arms.

British intelligence – probably a combination of MI5 and MI6 with local special branch support – had already penetrated a gun smuggling operation run by Saor Éire. Frank Keane, a former senior IRA commander, was involved. British agents masquerading as arms dealers had managed to win the trust of Keane. Keane or some of his republican colleagues made contact with people who knew Jock Haughey, a brother of Charles Haughey, who was looking for arms for the defence committees. Soon, Neil Blaney was involved. 'The first meeting I had with Pádraig Haughey, Jock as he was known, was through Neil Blaney who told us he had a contact in London who was prepared to supply arms', John Kelly revealed in 2005. Kelly was the National Organiser of the CDCs. He was also in the IRA. Blaney told Kelly that he had been led to believe that a London contact 'was equipped to buy arms within 48 hours. Arrangements were set in place with the banks and whatever else had to be done'.[1]

All told, Jock Haughey made two trips to London in November 1969. Martin Casey, a member of Saor Éire, went with him on the first one. His role was to introduce Haughey to 'Hyman Godfrey' an associate of 'Capt. Peter Markham-Randall' at 299 Oxford Street.[2] Markham-Randall did not attend the Oxford Street meeting in person, but made himself available *via* telephone.

The second trip involved Jock Haughey and John Kelly. The Irishmen were followed from the moment they arrived in the city. Photographs were snapped as they left Oxford Street tube station near Markham-Randall's office. Kelly spotted a man at a bus stop, 'standing on his toes looking after them, with a radio to his ear'. Further down, he saw a woman standing at the tailgate of a station-wagon. When they passed, she drew a radio from her bag 'and seemed to say a few words before replacing it'.[3]

Jock Haughey returned to Ireland, while John Kelly went to meet the mysterious Markham-Randall. The encounter only served to increase his suspicion and he hightailed it back to Dublin, where he joined Capt. Kelly at Buswells Hotel, across the road from Leinster House.[4] John Kelly told the captain of his suspicion that they were being 'set-up'. Behind the captain's back, John Kelly and some of his associates were scheming to assassinate 'Markham-Randall'. In furtherance of the plot, John Kelly rang the spy in London and informed him that he had returned to Dublin. 'I invited [Markham-Randall] to Dublin to meet us along with [Capt.] Jim Kelly in the Gresham Hotel. We were going to assassinate him; that is why we arranged the meeting.'

Despite the danger, the prospect of meeting Capt. Kelly was too tempting for Markham-Randall and he agreed to take a flight to Dublin and rendezvous with them at the Gresham Hotel. On the appointed day, Capt. Kelly ventured out to Dublin Airport to see if Markham-Randall would disembark from a passenger flight from England. He proved a no-show at the arrivals gate. Yet, when Capt. Kelly reached the Gresham, he had already checked in. The captain deduced that he had taken a military craft to Northern Ireland, confirming he was indeed a spy.

At the hotel, John Kelly and Markham-Randall went upstairs to negotiate. According to Capt. Kelly:

> When the small, dark-haired, goatee-bearded man [Markham-Randall] finally got down to talk with John [Kelly] in an upstairs bedroom, he claimed to be a former British army officer, introducing himself as Captain Markham-Randall. Whatever he was, he turned out to be very well informed on behind-the-scene events in Ireland, throwing around the name Kelly in an obvious manner, which John took to refer to me. He was also very interested in Ministers Haughey, Blaney, Boland and Gibbons, whom he intimated were strong supporters of Northern nationalism.

Capt. Kelly proceeded to describe how the reference to him 'on which Markham-Randall harped, also indicated inside knowledge which could only have come from an Irish source'. Markham-Randall tried to convince John Kelly that he felt, 'like an Arab, [thought], like an Arab. My father may have been an Englishman, but I am one of my mother's people. I served with the British army. So did many Irishmen. That does not make them any less Irishmen, as it does not make me any less an Arab ... I trust you understand me. There are many Irish and many Arabs who do not like the English. I am Captain Markham-Randall and I am here to help you.'[5] Clearly, Markham-Randall believed he was talking to a member of the IRA. Ostensibly, John Kelly was a representative of the CDCs, but his true hidden allegiance was to the IRA, so the spy was actually on the right track. Markham-Randall's mission was to infiltrate the IRA, if he could. He proceeded to tell Kelly that he was an expert in guerrilla tactics and had completed many courses in counter-revolutionary warfare. 'I could be a big help to you people,' he declared. 'If I visited one or other of your training camps I would be very useful: small arms, fire and movement, tactics and that sort of thing.' Had Markham-Randall succeeded in gaining access to the camps he assumed had sprung up, he would have been able to ascertain the identities of those attending them. John Kelly insisted he was only interested in arms: 'Arms, okay, okay,' he shrugged his shoulders. 'A consignment of automatic weapons, grenades and LMGs for thirty thousand [pounds]. It's cheap. It's the market price. But I am on your side. You may have the lot for three thousand.'

At this, John Kelly could contain himself no longer and accused the man of being a spy. 'Maybe I am,' Markham-Randall conceded, 'but what difference does it make to you? You get the guns and you can keep the money. All I want is access to the training camps.' The fact that the Irish Army had provided instruction in the use of arms to a group of CDC men from Derry at Fort Dunree, Co. Donegal, should have been, but was no longer, a secret. On 24 October 1969, *Private Eye* magazine in London had revealed what was occurring at the base. The activity was taking place on the orders of Jim Gibbons, the Irish defence minister.

There were two possible sources for the *Private Eye* article. First, it might have reached Paul Foot, a left-wing journalist, who wrote for the magazine, through his contacts in Derry.

Second, a garda or DoJ mole might have alerted MI6. Larry Wren, the chief superintendent in Letterkenny, let G2 use his office and phone during the course of the training. Once he knew, the information would have reached the DoJ quickly. After that, news of it could have been relayed to Oldfield by one of MI6's sources. If so, Oldfield's motive in alerting *Private Eye* would have been to sabotage the programme. As it transpired, G2 shut it down once its integrity was breached. A second course at Finner Camp was not known to the gardaí or the DoJ at this time but the CDCs knew about it. *Private Eye* did not expose it. This makes it more likely that a garda or DoJ mole leaked the details about Fort Dunree to *Private Eye*, rather than a CDC source.

Capt. Kelly and three men from Northern Ireland were downstairs in the lobby of the Gresham, awaiting news of the discussions taking place upstairs with Markham-Randall. John Kelly descended and told them he was convinced that the visitor was a spy. There then followed a discussion about killing him. According to John Kelly, the captain put his foot down and said 'no to it' and Markham-Randall was left unharmed.[6]

While Markham-Randall was busy in Dublin, British agents in Derry were trying to ingratiate themselves with Paddy Doherty, one of the CDC men who had received instruction from the Irish army at Fort Dunree. Doherty was a friend of John Hume and an opponent of the IRA.

A concerned Capt. Kelly kept a protective eye out for Markham-Randall while he remained in Dublin. His notebook recorded that the man continued as a guest of the Gresham between 25–28 November, before he moved elsewhere for a few days. On 30 November, the spy sent a letter addressed to 'G. Dixon' at the Munster and Leinster bank in Baggot Street. This demonstrates significant inside knowledge of the CDC operation, for 'G. Dixon' was the fictitious name employed by the CDCs for the account they were using at the bank to fund the arms quest. It had been opened for them by G2.[7] Once the letter was posted, it was possible that someone would go to the bank to collect it. This possibility implies that Markham-Randall had a team with him in Dublin, large enough to keep the bank under surveillance. Such a group would have been supplied with photographs of people such as Jock Haughey and John Kelly who had visited London earlier in the month.

While he was in Dublin, Markham-Randall also had a meeting with two men from Saor Éire at the Shelbourne hotel. One was Frank Walsh, who developed the impression Markham-Randall was a spy and considered having him shot too.

Markham-Randall spent a number of weeks in Dublin. He may have returned to London and made day trip returns. During his time in Dublin, he tried to make contact with Jock Haughey who decided that he wanted to have nothing to do with him.

Capt. Kelly became so concerned about the safety of the British spy that he drew on official funds to expedite the man's departure from the country on a flight from Dublin Airport. He reported the assassination bid to Col Hefferon.

Markham-Randall's knowledge of Irish affairs is a strong

indication that there was an individual inside the Irish state security apparatus with access to sensitive intelligence who was prepared to share it with MI6. This figure knew that Capt. Kelly, Haughey and others were involved with the CDCs in their quest for arms. While some peripheral information could have emanated from a person such as Conor Cruise O'Brien, he did not know about the secret private bank account held in the fictitious name of 'George Dixon'. The list of realistic suspects includes members of the gardaí and officials of the DoJ. There may even have been a leak from inside the CDCs.

The question arises: what did Jack Lynch make of all of this?

THE CAT JUMPS OUT OF THE BAG

There are several reasons to believe that Jack Lynch was kept abreast of what was happening, realised that matters were spinning out of control, and took a few deft steps to regain control of events.

Capt. Kelly reported all that he knew about the Markham-Randall affair to his superior, Col Hefferon, who undoubtedly relayed it to Jim Gibbons, the Minister for Defence. In turn, the minister should have relayed the astonishing news of the near killing of a British spy to Lynch. Even if Lynch was kept in the dark about the attempt to kill Markham-Randall, he still had enough information at his disposal to realise that his government's nod and wink arrangement with the CDCs was no longer a secret from London. Moreover, he already knew from his meeting with Ambassador Gilchrist on 19 November 1969, that the embassy was aware that Haughey and others were immersed in some sort of an operation linked to the supply of arms to Northern Ireland.

Patrick Hillery, the Minister for Foreign Affairs, should have been brought up to speed about the Markham-Randall affair by the London embassy. Its press attaché, Con Houlihan, had joined John Kelly and Jock Haughey at the Irish Club in Eaton Square in London after the first phase of the Markham-Randall débâcle. Gerry Fitt, MP, who became leader of the SDLP the following year, had also been present. The group sat and 'talked about what had happened and they knew all about it. Gerry [Fitt] was aware of [the quest for arms] from a meeting in his house with [Capt.] Jim Kelly, which was the first meeting we had with the Irish government [in August 1969. Gerry had] asked for guns very histrionically. My brother Billy was [at the meeting in Fitt's house] so was Tom Conaty [chairman of the Central CDC].'[1]

Con Houlihan, like any diplomat, was in the business of gathering useful information and reporting it to his principals. He would hardly have withheld from them details of the discussion at the Irish Club.[2] Indeed, he may have been at the rendezvous by appointment, with a full report being expected by his superiors. Even if he was there by happenstance, it is likely that he would have furnished the embassy with a report destined to land on Patrick Hillery's desk within days, if not hours. Unless there was a monumental breakdown in communications, Lynch should have been told about the development by both Hillery and Gibbons.[3]

Clearly, Neil Blaney knew what was afoot. According to John Kelly, when 'we questioned Blaney [afterwards] about Markham-Randall he said, "It was a mistake, I'm sorry John but we were put on a bum steer." He didn't go into too much detail ...'

It is inconceivable that Jock Haughey would not have told his brother Charles what he knew too.

The gardaí soon learned about the escapade. Col Hefferon made inquiries about Markham-Randall with garda intelligence. 'Word came back that Markham-Randall was a person of ill-repute; some type of underworld figure, who was not particular how he made his money; just the type of person who would involve himself in selling arms or any other underhand activity for that matter,' Capt. Kelly wrote.[4]

In February 1970, Capt. Kelly learned that a large dossier on the London farce had been sent to Garda HQ and he was given an opportunity to inspect it. Among the papers, he found a photograph of John Kelly and Jock Haughey climbing up the steps of the Oxford Street tube station. Jock Haughey was instantly recognisable as he was a star player on the 1958 All-Ireland winning Dublin GAA football team. According to Capt. Kelly, 'obviously, the Irish police had been briefed on the affair by their British counterparts. Interestingly, while the gardaí recognised [Jock Haughey], they did not identify John Kelly. Presumably, neither did the British. Apart from filing the information, the security agencies here took no action on the matter, but the file confirmed that Markham-Randall was a British agent.'

Jack Lynch can have reached no conclusion other than that the G2-CDC cat was now well and truly out of the bag. It was against this background that a crucial development took place: in late December 1969, the CDCs asked Capt. Kelly of G2 to request his superiors to take over the task of procuring the arms for them. The entreaty was passed to Gibbons. G2 was given the green light to proceed by January 1970. The plot to kill Markham-Randall must have been a significant factor in convincing Lynch to accede to the appeal. From this point on, the revised plan became one whereby G2 would import a consignment of weapons, which would be held under lock and key by the Irish Army, and only be released in the event of a doomsday situation. Presumably, Lynch hoped the British Army would maintain the peace, while the weapons would do no more than gather dust.

While Capt. Kelly was arranging to import a consignment of arms, the Irish Army put aside a supply of surplus army rifles in case a 'Doomsday' emergency erupted in Northern Ireland. The memorandum directing this operation came into existence on 6 February 1970. Then, on 10 February, an addendum was written in the Department of Defence that was sent to the chief-of-staff of the Irish Army. It stated that the 'Taoiseach and other Ministers have met delegations from the North. At these meetings, urgent demands were made for respirators, weapons and ammunition the provision of which the Government agreed. Accordingly truckloads of these items will be put at readiness so that they may be available in a matter of hours.'[5] Gibbons withheld the existence of this document from the Arms Trial.

The Hamburg Con Artist and MI6

The CDCs made contact with an arms dealer based in Germany called Otto Schlueter or 'Waffen-Schlueter' as he was known in Hamburg. They were walking into a trap.

Schlueter had fought in the Second World War and had been wounded three times on the Russian front. Albert Luykx, a former Flemish SS soldier who was living in Dublin, made the introduction.

Schlueter was a notorious con man. He had been charged in 1964 with defrauding three customers – two of them from small Arabic countries – of a total of almost £11,000 in connection with an arms deal. He had also run an arms factory in the town of Moelln which had gone bankrupt to the tune of £36,000. After that he had started Schlueter GmbH, the company with whom the CDCs and Capt. Kelly would negotiate.

In the 1950s, Schlueter had supplied weapons to the National Liberation Front (FNL) during the Algerian war of independence, something which had drawn the wrath of the French Secret Service down upon him. French agents masquerading as 'La Main Rouge' were assassinating FNL suppliers. Schlueter was put on their death list. On 28 September 1956, French assassins bombed his Hamburg office, killing his deputy, a Mr Lorenzi. On 3 June, Schlueter's mother was killed and his daughter injured, when a French bomb exploded in her car. A passer-by also perished.

Schlueter, who visited his mother's grave every day, knew better than to cross the French again, or take a risk by vexing MI6. He decided to take as much of the CDC money as he could, while secretly betraying them to MI6. Whether he dealt with German intelligence or MI6 directly is not clear. In any event, all the necessary information was being relayed to London. MI6 did not pounce at this stage. 'Dealing with something like this is like cutting a growth', a British intelligence officer has explained. 'If you cut it out too soon, it will grow back again and you may not get at the root. Sometimes it is better to let the growth swell until the last minute, and then apply the knife, but we knew every move involving Schlueter.' While MI6 did not yet want to 'apply the knife', they did not want to risk any chance of the guns reaching Ireland either. Hence, steps were taken to ensure that the paperwork in Antwerp was scrutinised and it was 'discovered' that there was no 'end user certificate', a necessary document which proved that the intended recipient of the consignment was a legitimate party. As a veteran arms dealer, Otto Schlueter should have ensured that such a certificate was in place, but he did not. The result was that the arms cargo was not allowed onto a ship called the *M.V. City of Dublin* which was waiting to carry it to Dublin.

Schlueter could have betrayed his Irish clients directly to German intelligence. Alternatively, he could have contacted MI6 through Tony Divall, another arms dealer who lived in Hamburg. Divall had served in MI6 until the 1950s.[1] Schlueter and Divall occasionally worked together.

Capt. Kelly was now adrift inside the world that James

Jesus Angleton of the CIA once described as a 'wilderness of mirrors'. He had no inkling either that John Kelly was working to another agenda: he was a Provisional IRA die-hard, who fully intended to hijack any cargo that might reach Ireland. The arms were meant to arrive on board the *M.V. City of Dublin*. When the ship reached Dublin Port in March 1970, John Kelly went to collect it with Capt. Kelly. Unknown to the captain, a group of four IRA gunmen was lurking in the shadows intent upon seizing the arms. The IRA unit consisted of Paddy O'Kane, Michael Kane, Harry Canavan and Billy Kelly, a brother of John. When it became apparent that there were no arms on the ship, the IRA unit remained hidden in the shadows.

Subsequent press reports in *The Times* of London stated that MI6 agents working on the Continent had acted to ensure that no arms were loaded onto the *M.V. City of Dublin*. The story was probably based on a leak from Oldfield. While the report reflected well on MI6, it placed Schlueter in a precarious position. The German subsequently tried to distance himself from his betrayal of Capt. Kelly, in negotiations he had with Aidan Mulloy, Ireland's consul-general in Hamburg.[2] Mulloy made contact with Schlueter in an attempt to recover the money handed over to him by the CDCs. During the discussions that ensued, Schlueter described how an offer to charter a 'British plane' at a special low rate for transporting freight, had been brought to his attention and that he had suspected it was a trap. 'Why should a British air freight company have offered to ship the goods at a rate less than half the standard rate, except that the British Government had hoped to grab the lot?' he suggested in an effort to make it look like he had not betrayed his clients to MI6.

In April 1970, John Peck, a former wartime aide to Winston Churchill, replaced Gilchrist. Peck was yet another diplomat with multifarious connections to the clandestine world of British intelligence. He was no stranger to the Republic either, having been involved in the courtship of Major McDowell of *The Irish Times*. Like Gilchrist, he had more than a few traces of blood under his fingernails.

THE DIRTY TRICKS BRIGADE
DESCENDS UPON DUBLIN

In November 1969, Ambassador Gilchrist had advised the FCO of what he had learned about Charles Haughey's activities in Monaghan, some of which were associated with clandestine gun-running. As noted earlier, he had warned London: 'we should keep our eyes open to this threat on our flanks'.

That same month, the FCO decided to move one of its more dangerous pieces onto the Anglo-Irish chessboard to deal with the 'threat' in Dublin: John Peck was earmarked to replace Gilchrist. He was the first choice of the intelligence mandarins, who were in the ascent at the King Charles Street headquarters of the FCO. The recently retired chairman of the JIC, Dennis Greenhill, was now head of the FCO, while Edward Peck (not related to John), was running the JIC. Edward Peck was a MI6 veteran. Both of these men were instrumental in John Peck's appointment, which was to commence the following April.[1]

For his part, Maurice Oldfield dispatched Peter Evans from among the ranks of his troops to Dublin. He took up his post in March 1970. Like Oldfield, Evans was an old Singaporean hand.[2] Born in September 1925, his cover in Dublin would be that of 'information officer' at the Dublin embassy.

John Peck was a diplomat-black propagandist, an individual who had long since learned how to bend the rules.

By the time he took up residence in Dublin, he had become an accomplished exponent of the complementary arts of deception, misdirection and vilification; perhaps even the most accomplished practitioner of these skills then available to the FCO. Peck and Evans would soon form a partnership that would target Charles Haughey for denigration.

No less a figure than Winston Churchill had provided the new ambassador with an early lesson in bending the rules. It happened during the Second World War while Peck was serving as one of the politician's private secretaries. One day, the young Peck had prepared 'ten or a dozen cheques and photographs' for Churchill to sign. As he recorded in his memoirs:

> Churchill looked at them with some gloom and then said, 'Sign these for me.' I gulped.
>
> 'You mean, sir, that I am to forge your signature?'
>
> 'Yes, can you? Let me see.'
>
> 'May I borrow your pen? The one you always use?' [Churchill] scrutinised the sample. 'Hm Hm Hm Hm. All right, do them.' So I forged the Prime Minister's signature on cheques and photographs. I was privately rather proud of my rendering of his signature ...[3]

After the war, Peck was instrumental in setting up the Information Research Department (IRD), the Foreign Office's black propaganda and forgery directorate. Peck's one-time IRD colleague and obituarist, Michael Cullis, has described how, 'I was well placed to admire what [Peck] did (perhaps occasionally overdid) by way of getting this whole, very necessary, operation off the ground at an important juncture in world affairs'.[4]

Peck served as the assistant director of the IRD from its inception in 1948 until 1951 when he was promoted to head it up. The IRD worked hand-in-glove with the various branches of British intelligence, particularly MI6.[5]

The IRD was every bit as pitiless as MI6. During its early incarnation, it had attempted to stem the flow of Holocaust survivors from the Soviet Union to Palestine. Some of the refugees, who reached the Balkans, managed to secure the use of US military vehicles for transport en route to the Middle East. The British protested about this to Washington in October 1947. When they were met with deaf ears, they turned instead to deception to achieve their goal. Oliver Wright of the Foreign Office furnished the US State Department with fabricated yet 'convincing evidence' that the 'Romanian government, with the approval of the Soviet authorities, was sending 10,000 hand-picked communists to Palestine'.[6] Wright, who spent at least a year with the IRD, subsequently became the first 'UK Representative' (UKREP) to the Stormont government in Belfast, arriving in August 1969. He had just left Belfast when Peck arrived in Dublin.

In yet a further twist to the Palestine operation, MI6 spread rumours that British agents were among those trekking across Soviet-controlled territories in the hope the KGB would block the routes. This did not stem the flow, but may have exposed entirely innocent people to interrogation at the hands of Stalin's secret police.

These activities were part of a wider campaign that included bombing the ships which the Holocaust survivors had chartered in the Mediterranean. If this sounds far-fetched, it should be noted MI6 has officially acknowledged it happened. It was part of Operation Embarrass. During the project, some of MI6's bombs were discovered on the ships. MI6 deflected the blame for this, by laying it at the feet of the fictitious 'Defenders of Arab Palestine'. At a later stage, they tried to implicate the Soviets by forging documents using typewriters of a brand that were known to be used by them.

Both Peck and Oldfield had contributed to the MI6–CIA *coup d'état* which toppled Muhammad Mosaddegh, the democratically elected prime minister of Iran in 1953. Mosaddegh was a secularist who favoured advancing women's rights. That plot was codenamed Operation Boot. Oldfield's passport stamps establish that he visited Cyprus and Beirut at the time of the key planning meetings for the overthrow of the Iranian leader.

During the coup, Peck performed his standard party piece: Muhammad Mosaddegh was a Communist bogeyman who was trying to hand the country over to the Soviets. Mosaddegh's real crime in the eyes of the FCO was that he had nationalised his country's oil reserves at the expense of British owned companies. The IRD used the BBC's Persian service to attack Mosaddegh. The sheer volume of the venom pumped through the BBC drove the Iranian staff at its Persian station to walk out on strike. These and other libels, along with the bribery of officials, the employment of organised criminals, and the use of rent-a-mobs, eventually toppled Mosaddegh. This short-term success turned into a long-term nightmare. After the dust settled, the Shah of Iran was firmly placed in control of the country, something that ushered in decades of torture and repression, ultimately sparking a revolution that placed the clerics in charge of Iran. On the anniversary of the *coup* on 18 August 2011, the BBC finally confessed its role in the affair. Moreover, a document emerged which showed that the Foreign Office had thanked the then British ambassador to Tehran for the ideas he had supplied to it about those who might be targeted for vilification. The BBC had castigated those pinpointed during the operation.

Oldfield's friend, Anthony Cavendish, confirmed that Mosaddegh was 'removed through skilful planning by SIS [i.e. MI6], with some little help from the CIA, although Kermit (Kim) Roosevelt, in his book *Counter Coup* (1979), claimed virtually all the credit'.[7] Cavendish felt George Kennedy Young of MI6 deserved acclaim for the success of the plot, one which was 'two years in the planning' and that it was MI6's 'encouragement and persuasion [that] contrived to arrange for this demonstration, and the help they immediately gave to the Shah's supporters, that returned the Shah – in temporary exile from the capital – in triumph, and ensured Mossadeqh (*sic*) was brought to trial'.[8] Young was a veteran of regime change operations. He had participated in the failed conspiracy against Albania. He was also the driving force behind the anti-Nasser machinations in Egypt at the time of the Suez Crisis and yet another regime change scheme, Operation Straggle, in Syria, also in 1956.

At street level, the Iranian coup was managed by Norman Darbyshire of MI6 who marshalled mobs of Mosaddegh's opponents to generate violence and chaos on the streets of Tehran. Soldiers, police officers and civil servants were bribed to turn against the government. Darbyshire recruited a motley collection of thugs, criminals – and even a bevy of prostitutes – as part of a rent-a-mob to swell the street protests.[9] Mosaddegh was arrested and put on trial. While he was in the dock, some of his closest supporters were killed by the new regime.

Alan Hare, the son of the fourth earl of Listowel likewise played a part. He operated from the MI6 planning base in Cyprus. Previously, Hare had been involved in MI6's failed regime change projects against Enver Hoxha in Albania, 1949–53.[10]

Oldfield enjoyed a twenty-five-year relationship with the Shah after the coup. Throughout that time the latter's intelligence service, Savak, murdered and tortured dissidents at will.

The IRD assisted the CIA in their conspiracies against Jacobo Arbenz in Guatemala in 1954, and Joao Goulart in Brazil in 1964.

Another of Peck's tactics was to use the BBC's overseas broadcast service to encourage Soviet officials to defect to the west.

The nadir for the IRD was when it acted as cheerleader for the slaughter of 500,000 'communists' in Indonesia in the 1960s, again with the aid of a compliant BBC. Peck was no longer running the IRD at that stage, but his predecessor as ambassador to Dublin, Andrew Gilchrist, was deeply involved in the atrocity.

Peck's account of his time with the IRD in his memoirs was not at all revealing. All he disclosed was that having been assigned to The Hague, he returned to the Foreign Office where he was 'posted first as Assistant and then as Head of Information Research Department', and thus 'became, at thirty-eight, one of the youngest counsellors in the service. This department, having world-wide interests, gave me world-wide perspectives which later made me very receptive to a precept of that astute philosopher-politician Leopold Sedar Senghor, the President of Senegal: "When a problem is insoluble, start by placing it in a broader context" – advice which is as valid for Ireland today as it was for West Africa fifteen years ago'.[11]

THE AMBASSADOR WHO KNEW NOTHING

John Peck arrived in Dublin on 9 April 1970 and took up the reins as ambassador on the 17th.

Peck developed a high regard for Peter Evans and the team he found at the Dublin embassy. In his book, *The View From Downing Street*, Peck explained:

> The Foreign Office … had fortunately decided to satisfy their interest in the Republic by posting two officers of the highest quality – Peter Evans as Information Officer and David Blatherwick as Second Secretary in Chancery. They preceded me by a few weeks and it was immediately obvious that we three were on the same wavelength and could work together as a closely-knit team. The Counsellor, Peter Piper, was of the old school and within a few months of retirement – a well-known and well-liked figure in Dublin, in whose house we first met many of our subsequent friends.[1]

As Evans and Peck were settling in, Capt. Kelly, undaunted by the failure to bring in arms by sea, travelled to the continent to arrange for a consignment to be flown to Dublin airport from Vienna. Garda special branch learned what was afoot from Seán MacStíofáin and, independently, from officials at Dublin airport. According to a British intelligence source, the branch also knew what was taking place because Otto Schlueter was co-operating fully with MI6 and the British spies had alerted the gardaí. Spoiled with all of this information, special branch officers surrounded the airport on Friday 17 April. Minster Brian Lenihan was informed and alerted G2.[2] The chartered flight from Vienna was cancelled before it took to the air. The ministers who knew about the fiasco by the morning of Monday 20 April included Gibbons, Lenihan, Haughey, Blaney and Ó Moráin.

Peter Berry of the DoJ met Lynch on the afternoon of Monday 20 April to inform him about the attempt to land arms at Dublin Airport.[3] Lynch claimed that this was when he first found out about the endeavour to import arms.

Before he had the chance to go inside and talk to Lynch, Berry was left outside the taoiseach's office while Lynch conducted a meeting with the new ambassador. Peck has described the visit as one during which he had 'an informal, wide-ranging chat of some forty-five minutes, in which Jack Lynch mentioned problems that had arisen over settling some of that group of nomads known variously as tinkers, itinerants or travelling people, in which a small Galway town called Rahoon had figured prominently'.[4] If we are to believe Peck, the embassy and its array of diplomats and spies knew nothing about the arms importation at this juncture. In his book, he described how it was not until 6 May, that he was awoken by Peter Evans, at 7.15 a.m., to be told the news which allegedly shocked him, namely that Haughey and Blaney:

> had not only been sacked from the government by the Taoiseach, Jack Lynch, but had actually been arrested on charges of illegally financing and trafficking in arms, and a third Minister, Kevin Boland (Local Government), had resigned in sympathy ... The British government naturally had to be told what was going on and what was likely to happen, particularly as the arms, if any, were presumably destined for the Catholic minority in Northern Ireland. We had a major political crisis on our hands.[5]

In order to believe what Peck wrote, one has to discount the fact that his predecessor, Ambassador Gilchrist, had been aware of Haughey's involvement in gun-running intrigues connected to a G2 base in Monaghan; moreover, that MI6 knew about the secret 'Dixon' bank account in Dublin which was being used to finance the arms purchase. In addition, that while Otto Schlueter had been keeping MI6 abreast of what had happened in April, no report had reached Peck and Evans at the Dublin embassy by 6 May.

Once the existence of the arms importation became public knowledge, the Irish and UK governments had to decide how they would deal with what was a volatile issue. The Irish ambassador in London, Donal O'Sullivan, invited George Thomson, chancellor of the Duchy of Lancaster, to a lunch at the Irish embassy the day the crisis erupted. O'Sullivan warned the chancellor that the more militant elements inside Fianna Fáil had been challenging Lynch's increasingly moderate policies on Northern Ireland for some time. O'Sullivan's task now became one of ensuring London would not cause any additional trouble for Lynch.[6]

The following morning, Thomson reported to the British cabinet that the removal of Blaney and Haughey had left their colleagues 'badly shaken'. His concern was that by having those he perceived as hardliners outside the door, it might prove more difficult to control them. He may have had a point insofar as Blaney was concerned, but Haughey was a far more complex individual, as his history of crushing the IRA's border campaign, his support of rapprochement with

Stormont, and his more recent discussions with Gilchrist testify. Irrespective of this, Thomson's concern was that the 'relatively moderate' policy, which Lynch had adopted to the relief of London, might now be in danger.

Harold Wilson was determined to quash any rumour which suggested he had demanded the dismissal of Blaney and Haughey. He instructed his officials to counter any such gossip.[7] He was also concerned that Lynch's administration might weaken or, worse still, collapse.

Dublin sought to find some silver lining amidst these dark clouds. Eamonn Gallagher at the Department of External Affairs in Dublin told the British embassy that since the civil rights reforms in Northern Ireland had failed, Lynch's moderation was becoming a political liability for him. Gallagher argued that since Lynch had faced down his hardliners, despite the political danger this posed to him, it was now time for London to do the same with the unionists. David Blatherwick, a diplomat at the British embassy (and future ambassador to Dublin) reported to Maureen McGlashen at the FCO that as a result of the turmoil caused in part by the Arms Crisis, the Dublin Government 'may continue to press the line that in order to preserve a government in the South sympathetic to H.M.G.'s policies in the North, we will have to take account of their views'.[8]

As the tumultuous month of May 1970 ended, Peck found himself saying to London that he felt that the survival of Lynch was 'an absolute priority' for the security of Northern Ireland although his fate was in the hands of the Irish and 'London could not control events'.[9]

Oldfield and the FCO also had the benefit of the intelligence-gathering skills of a team of diplomat-spies who were dispatched to Northern Ireland to gather information about what was happening there. Little or nothing has ever emerged to indicate that British agents in Northern Ireland had a realistic appreciation of what the CDCs were doing. London had developed a small quasi spy base of its own in Northern Ireland, one separate from the RUC. It was led by the 'UK Representative of the British Government to Northern Ireland', who became known as the UKREP. As a constituent part of the UK, Harold Wilson could not send an ambassador there, hence he sent the UKREP, a hybrid diplomat-civil servant-spy. The first UKREP, Oliver Wright, was a FCO diplomat who had extensive dealings with the British Intelligence community.[10]

The Arms Crisis severed the links between G2 and its network of CDC contacts across the border. Col Hefferon, having reached the age of retirement, had stepped down from his post at G2 in April 1970. His successor was Col 'Bud' Delaney. He started sending officers back across the border to find out what was happening in Northern Ireland. Their efforts soon came to the attention of the British government. On 17 June 1970, Ronnie Burroughs, the second UKREP, wrote to the FCO, referring to a delicate 'source' who had supplied information about G2 activities in Northern Ireland:

> If the function of these [Irish military intelligence] Officers is as innocent as is suggested [their work] can be carried out by ordinary political observers operating quite openly. If there is a clandestine element then I do not see how we can tolerate them. We certainly would not do so in any other part of the UK …

Owing to the delicacy of the source it would of course not be possible to reveal to the Irish their own acknowledgement of the presence of these Officers.[11]

The use of the word 'delicacy' about the source of the information about G2, raises the prospect that the individual in question was the holder of a senior position within the Irish state security apparatus and had confirmed the deployment of Irish officers across the border.

The next day, 18 June, Peck and his wife Mariska gave their first formal dinner party. It was one 'in honour of Dr Hillery'. It gave Peck an opportunity to gauge Hillery's attitude towards the political parties which were fighting for power in the British general election that night. Peck assumed that Fianna Fáil favoured Wilson's Labour Party: 'The evening passed pleasantly enough and Dr Hillery was just showing signs of preparing to leave, when I suggested that Peter Evans, who was among the party, should go to the television room and see if there was any news. He came back a few minutes later to say that on the evidence of the first seven returns, there would be a Conservative majority of around sixty.' This gave Peck and the MI6 man an opportunity to gauge Hillery's response. Peck's conclusion was that the 'Irish guests courteously concealed most of their dismay while I spoke my consoling words, and they went their way. But the result, so far as they were concerned, was that instead of a Prime Minister with a large Irish element in his constituency, and a Minister called Callaghan and a Minister called Healey, they would be dealing with a tough Unionist from Kent, the 14th Earl of Home and the 6th Baron Carrington.'[12]

On 29 June 1970, Hillery flew to London where he met Sir Alec Douglas-Home, Britain's new Foreign Secretary. It was resolved that, despite London's desire to help Lynch, such help was potentially poisonous and the best course of action was for the British government to avoid singing any of his praises in public.[13]

The potential for Peck, the IRD and Oldfield to manoeuvre at a subterranean level with 'sibs' and other actions to influence political events in the Republic was altogether another matter.

THE POLITICS OF THE BEAR PIT

A lifetime fighting the IRA took its toll on Peter Berry. Des O'Malley, who became Minister for Justice in May 1970, wrote how 'Berry displayed the siege mentality that afflicted so many of those who worked for prolonged periods in the Department of Justice ... He was keen to be informed about every detail of security policy and activities; in fact everything went through him. He had a close relationship with the Gardaí.'[1] Garret FitzGerald described him as a 'strange' man.

Berry had been shaken by Lynch's initial decision not to dismiss Haughey and Blaney after Berry had informed Lynch of the arms importation attempt on 20 April. When he spoke to Lynch shortly after this, Berry asked him who would now protect him from the wrath of the two ministers. Lynch promised that he himself would. Berry was hardly convinced by the promise. It was after this that details of the importation were leaked to the opposition and the Arms Crisis, together with all that followed it, erupted. One of those responsible for the leak to Liam Cosgrave, leader of the opposition, was Philip McMahon, the former head of the special branch, who worked hand-in-glove with Berry. Berry undoubtedly encouraged McMahon to approach Cosgrave, a move that would help to preserve his – Berry's – career by exposing Haughey and Blaney, who were arrested and placed on trial for the allegedly illegal importation of arms to the Republic. The charges against Blaney were soon dropped for lack of evidence.

On 22 September 1970, Haughey, Capt. Kelly, John Kelly and Albert Luykx, were put on trial in Dublin.[2] James Gibbons was not charged. Lynch had twisted Gibbons' arm, forcing him to turn state's evidence against his colleagues for the good 'of the party'. Gibbons never forgave Lynch for this, as it changed his life, and not for the better.

Gibbons, however, had left a trail of evidence in his wake, revealing his involvement in the operation. On 6 February 1970, he had called Lt Gen. Seán Mac Eoin, chief of staff of the Irish Army, and Col Hefferon, to his office. He told them he was about to say something that was for their ears only. He then proceeded to issue a verbal directive, which caused them to look at each other in astonishment. After they left the room, General Mac Eoin turned to Col Hefferon and advised him to go back to his office straight away and write down the order exactly as they had heard it. Mac Eoin had the directive recorded by the Plans and Operations Officer. It read:

> The Government directs the Army (1) prepare for incursions into Northern Ireland, (2) to make weapons available and (3) make gas masks available.

The reference to making 'weapons available' was not and could not have been a directive to furnish the Irish Army with weapons, since it not only possessed an adequate supply, but a surplus.

Four days later, a second document addressed to the chief of staff or ceann foirne (CF) of the Irish Army was prepared. It referred specifically to the taoiseach and was entitled *Addendum to the Memo of 10/2/70, Ministerial Directive to CF*:

> The Taoiseach and other Ministers have met delegations from

the North. At these meetings urgent demands were made for respirators, weapons and ammunition the provision of which the Government agreed. Accordingly truckloads of these items will be put at readiness so that they may be available in a matter of hours.[3]

A military intelligence record marked 'secret' reveals that on 18 February 1970 the following items were assembled in Dublin and Athlone:

500 rifles;

200 Gustav machine guns;

3,000 respirators;

80,000 rounds of 303 ammunition;

99,000 rounds of 9 mm ammunition.[4]

After the Arms Crisis erupted, the written version of the directive, which had been filed at the ministry for defence, disappeared. A forgery was manufactured to replace it. Jack Lynch concocted the forgery during a telephone conversation with his new minister for defence.[5]

The state engaged in other dirty tricks. Berry altered Col Hefferon's witness statement, before it was put in the book of evidence for the proceedings, by removing key tracts that demonstrated Gibbons' knowledge of the operation.[6] The alleged basis for the erasure of key tracts was that they were 'hearsay', i.e. second hand evidence, of which Col Hefferon did not have direct knowledge. But the key deletions were not all hearsay. Ultimately, two high court judges would allow Col Hefferon present evidence, which Berry had excised from the written statement, when he reached the witness box.

Des O'Malley, the Minister for Justice, read the doctored statement. It contained the deletions which were marked by hand. O'Malley signed off on them, before it was retyped and put into the book of evidence. O'Malley had been a practising solicitor and – unless he had no grasp of the basic rules of evidence, including hearsay – must have appreciated the impropriety of what Berry was doing.

James Gibbons rang Col Hefferon at his home in the run up to the trial, and put him under pressure to lie about the legality of the importation.[7]

On the morning of the trial, Col Hefferon visited a church where he contemplated the evidence he would give later. The script Berry and Gibbons hoped the colonel would follow was the doctored version of his witness statement. When he reached the Four Courts, he told the solicitor acting for Capt. Kelly that he was not going to commit perjury on behalf of the state. His testimony unravelled the elaborate tissue of lies that Berry and others had spun for the hearings.

The proceedings collapsed after a few days. Cynically, the state decided not to call the colonel when a fresh trial commenced in October 1970. After a legal wrangle, the judge in the second prosecution called him as a 'bench witness'.

The exertions of Berry and Gibbons were for naught. The jury unanimously acquitted all of the defendants. The shambolic evidence of Gibbons, compared to the well-ordered testimony of Col Hefferon that Gibbons had known about and supported the importation attempt, was the decisive factor in the exoneration of the accused.

John Peck was at the Wexford Opera festival, with his wife when news of the verdict came through:

> We were in our hotel in Wexford changing to go to the opera when the radio announced the verdict in the Arms Trial: Mr C. J. Haughey had been acquitted. Mr Heath and Mr Lynch were in

New York, attending the Assembly of the United Nations, where incidentally they met face to face for the first time. The Foreign Office was obviously going to need to know whether the acquittal precipitated another crisis in the Irish government, and equally obviously I should not show too much concern about a domestic matter. I telephoned to Peter Piper to lay on a staff meeting at 10.00 a.m. the next morning, which was a Saturday. At 9.30 a.m. I slipped out of Wexford in the police escort car, leaving Mariska to be seen around in the embassy Daimler. A discussion, a few telephone calls, the drafting and approval of some telegrams, and so back to Wexford for lunch at 1.30 in the hotel restaurant. The acquittal was obviously a blow to the Lynch government, but again we prophesied confidently that the Taoiseach would survive. The government and the Fianna Fáil party gave Jack Lynch a huge welcome at the airport on his return, party solidarity was manifest and one more political hurdle was safely cleared.[8]

For some reason, Lynch felt it necessary to criticise Gibbons behind his back during a conversation with Peck in the wake of the acquittal. After the discussion, the ambassador reported to London that Lynch 'was much perturbed by Gibbons' performance in the witness box' and that Gibbons had 'emerged as either a fool or a liar, and a considerable embarrassment to Lynch'.[9] Yet, if Gibbons had become an embarrassment, it was because Lynch had placed him in that position in the first place. In public, Lynch never behaved as if he had lost faith in Gibbons. On the contrary, he promoted him by making him minister for agriculture.

Haughey's acquittal was a humiliating blow for Berry, his deputy Andrew Ward and their subordinates.

Two antagonistic factions now emerged inside three key Irish organisations: Fianna Fáil, the gardaí and the army. On one side stood those who believed – or pretended to believe – that Haughey and Blaney had tried to import arms illegally for the IRA, with misdirected public money, aided and abetted by treacherous military officers, and had done so behind the backs of Lynch and Gibbons, neither of whom had an inkling of what was afoot. On the other side of the fence were those who argued that the arms importation attempt had been a legitimate government operation and that Haughey should never have been put in the dock.

Kevin Boland, a cabinet minister who had resigned in protest at Haughey and Blaney's sacking, asked Haughey to join a new political party which he had formed called Aontacht Éireann. Haughey turned him down, opting instead for rehabilitation inside Fianna Fáil, and a more realistic chance of becoming taoiseach, despite the internal feuding. The public caught a glimpse of the acrimony that was gripping the party, at the funeral of Seán Lemass in May 1971, at Deansgrange Cemetery, Co. Dublin. When Jack Lynch and George Colley turned up at the funeral, the Lemass clan snubbed them.

In *Up Dev*, Boland described how, after his father, Gerry died, 'the Fianna Fáil people, who knew my father, had the sensitivity to stay away, but numbers of those, who didn't know him, affronted the family by attending.[10] When Tánaiste [i.e. Childers], after being told the previous night in no uncertain terms by myself and other members of the family that his attendance was most unwelcome, took his place at a *prie dieu* at the funeral Mass to represent the Taoiseach – of all people – it was too much for my sister Maire, who stood beside him and offered two words "Get Out". Fortunately he did so and the Mass was able to proceed.'[11]

A Mouth-watering Stockpile of Intelligence

The Republican Movement was made up of Sinn Féin and the IRA. The events of 1968–69 handed the militants in the IRA an opportunity to regroup and launch a new campaign dedicated to the reunification of Ireland through military action. The fracture in the IRA took place in December 1969. The militants became known as the Provisional IRA and the Marxists became the Officials. Cathal Goulding, Seán Garland and Tomás McGiolla led the Officials, while Ruairí Ó Brádaigh, Seán MacStíofáin and Dáithí Ó Conaill set up the Provisionals.

Sinn Féin, the political wing of the republican movement, split the following month into 'provisional' and 'official' wings. On 12 January 1970, Gilchrist relayed the names of the new leadership of Provisional Sinn Féin to London, only hours after the organisation was founded.[1] It is more than likely that he obtained this information from journalists, police officers or officials at the DoJ, as opposed to agents inside the IRA.

In the early stages of The Troubles, most of the state's resources were directed towards monitoring the Officials who were seen as the greater threat. Initially, the Provisionals were perceived as a splinter group.

An item high on Maurice Oldfield's list of Irish priorities was to secure an improved flow of intelligence from garda special branch sources about the IRA and the political response to the events engulfing the Republic. For a start, the gardaí had access to IRA informers living in the Republic. Secondly, they drove government ministers in 'state cars' and were privy to their movements, meetings and the discussions which took place behind the closed doors of the ministerial fleet.

The special branch knew more than about Charles Haughey than other politicians because, in the autumn of 1970, a small garda unit masquerading as officials from the Department of Post & Telegraphs (P&T) had visited his home, Abbeville, at Kinsealy. When they arrived, they announced that they were from the P&T and needed to adjust the family's phone. Once inside, they entered Haughey's private office and planted a listening device in it. It was not placed in his phone, which was undoubtedly already tapped.

The gardaí had no legal entitlement to enter Abbeville on such a false pretence to plant a listening device. According to Vincent Browne, who broke the story in 1984, the device 'was left in [Haughey's] house for a considerable time – it is believed that the device was placed in a small study used by Mr Haughey. The name of at least one of the gardaí who participated in the Haughey bugging operation is known to this reporter.'[2]

A garda officer, familiar with the type of bug that was available to the gardaí in 1970, believes it would have been 'of poor quality [and] run on [a] battery. The type of batteries we used back then were commercially available and did not last very long. The range would have been very short. They would not have been connected to electricity. The battery would have needed replacing. The device would have been quite big compared to what one has nowadays.'[3] Hence, the device would have broadcast a signal to a listening post nearby, probably a van with recording equipment, which drove up to Abbeville when Haughey arrived home. The bugging of Abbeville was not a unique event. At this time, the gardaí were bugging rooms in garda stations around the country, so they could eavesdrop on privileged conversations between lawyers and their clients. Vincent Browne also disclosed that: 'Two of our sources state that the [Haughey] device was removed some time later, following another entry to the house, again under the P&T guise'.[4]

The information obtained from Haughey's home was only the tip of the iceberg. Many other politicians were placed under surveillance by the special branch. James Downey recalls in his book, *Lenihan, His Life And Loyalties*:

> For the Lenihan family, this was a terrible time. ... Telephones were tapped (this practice was common long before [Haughey] would come to power, but it was exceptionally prevalent at the time of the Arms Crisis. According to a senior official of the Department of Justice, the Special Branch filled an entire room in Dublin Castle with tapes of taped conversations, mostly involving ministers). Men, presumably from the intelligence services, lurked outside Lenihan's house. He was 'shadowed' on his way to work and social functions. Ministers would appear suddenly at the house late at night and disappear as quickly and mysteriously as they had come. Their movements were undoubtedly logged, thus bringing Lenihan under unfounded suspicion.[5]

If Lenihan was placed under this level of scrutiny, other ministers must have been too, including Blaney and Boland. In addition, the phones of people such as Capt. Kelly were tapped.[6] The knowledge collected by these drift net surveillance operations was precisely the type of information to which Oldfield coveted access. However, one of the challenges facing the spymaster in 1969–70 was that intelligence sharing between Dublin and London raised the spectre that some of it might wind its way to the RUC. Public opinion in the south was largely opposed to co-operation with the RUC. The force was seen as the oppressor of the minority in Northern Ireland. Harold Wilson, his home secretary, James Callaghan, and their colleagues, were just as appalled by its behaviour and, in October 1969, the B-Specials were disbanded while the RUC was disarmed.

In October 1969, Michael O'Leary TD of the Labour Party, and for a brief time a future tánaiste, probed the Minister for Justice, Mícheál Ó Moráin, about the gardaí's dealings with the RUC. He wanted to know whether there was contact between the RUC and the gardaí and whether it was 'confined to co-operation in cases of criminal offences'. He asked the minister to make a statement on this and the 'general area of co-operation' that existed. Not surprisingly, Ó Moráin was coy in his reply, but did acknowledge there was contact: 'Garda Síochána co-operate with other police forces, including the RUC, in the prevention and detection of crime'. He was not, however, 'prepared to be specific' about the extent and limits of 'co-operation with other police forces, as such information that would assist those whose activities call for police attention'.[7]

The RUC–Garda grapevine that grew along the border would survive and, in time, flourish. Patrick Crinnion, who had worked with the gardaí's ultra-secret C3 intelligence directorate until the end of 1972, provided a flavour of how the system operated in the early 1970s. He did this in a letter he wrote to Garda Commissioner Patrick Malone, his former boss at C3, on 23 June 1973. He pointed out that along the border 'every detective with an interest in his job has discreet contact with his opposite number in the Royal Ulster Constabulary and this personal conduct is not discouraged by Garda HQ although it is not specifically authorised'. Secretly, Crinnion was in contact with MI6.

Robert Armstrong, who served as private secretary to Ted Heath in the early 1970s (and as Thatcher's cabinet secretary in the 1980s), confirmed the existence of these sorts of links in a memorandum he prepared for Heath on 23 December 1972. It was prompted by a meeting he had with the Irish ambassador, Donal O'Sullivan, after the arrest of Crinnion and a MI6 officer called John Wyman in Dublin. Armstrong's memo alluded to a level of co-operation between 'other agencies' which was taking place 'elsewhere'. Unfortunately, Armstrong did not elaborate. What the memo reveals is that he had asked O'Sullivan:

> specifically whether we could take it that there was no intention that the contacts between British and Irish security forces *and other agencies* [my emphasis], across the Border *or elsewhere*, [my emphasis] should be reduced or interfered with. The [Irish] Ambassador assured me that this was the case: there was no intention or desire that these contacts should in any way be impaired.

THE SMEAR CAMPAIGN AGAINST JOCK HAUGHEY

Jock Haughey, the brother of Charles, was another object of intense MI6 scrutiny. He was of interest to them for a number of reasons. Firstly, he had helped smuggle a consignment of arms through Dublin airport in September 1969; and secondly, a British intelligence surveillance team in London had monitored him in November 1969 during the 'Markham–Randall' fiasco. However, there are grounds to believe that in October 1970, Oldfield was looking for an opportunity to manufacture a link between Jock Haughey and a gun which had killed a garda officer, Richard Fallon, in Dublin the previous April. Oldfield's motive in linking the Irishman to the weapon was to deflect attention from the fact that British intelligence had let pistols from an armoury in Birmingham slip into Ireland. The 9mm Star semi-automatic pistol, which killed Garda Fallon, emanated from the armoury. It had no connection to Jock Haughey.

The gardaí have long since concluded that Jock Haughey had nothing to do with the Star pistol which was used in the Garda Fallon killing. In 2007, Michael McDowell, the then minister for justice, stated that 'the gardaí were aware of the source of the firearms in question ... low-life Dublin gangland people who sourced the weapons in Birmingham'.

Jock Haughey had booked a break in Portugal for himself and his wife Kitty during October 1970. The couple had calculated that the trial of Jock's brother Charles would be over by then. The proceedings, however, collapsed in September, and a fresh prosecution was scheduled for the following October. The Haugheys decided to take their holiday, despite the clash of dates with the new trial. The outward leg of the journey to Portugal took the couple through Britain, where they picked up a tail, a British man who shadowed their every move. As this was an overseas operation, the spy was most likely working for Oldfield.

Each morning the man sat at the table next to the Irish couple while they ate breakfast and then shadowed them during the day. At night, he would sit next to them again. While he had unsettled the Haugheys at the start of their holiday, they soon found his behaviour amusing, especially his habit of ordering lobster – and no other item on the menu – for his evening meal. On at least one occasion, they attempted to engage him in conversation much to his embarrassment and without success. He must have realised that the game was up. On their return to Britain, the spy skipped the passport control queue and went directly to talk to the officials ahead of them, while the other passengers were forming an orderly line. Clearly, he was not a 'normal' passenger.

The surveillance of the Haugheys indicates a high-level of co-operation between the gardaí and MI6. Plainly, the British knew about the couple's holiday plans in advance. To achieve this, they must have had access to at least some of the family's phone conversations with their travel agent. In 1970, phone-tapping was carried out by making a physical connection to a phone line, something that could only be achieved near a junction close to the target's phone. It is possible – though unlikely – that Oldfield deployed a tapping unit to Dublin in 1970. It is more likely that the information was furnished to them by a senior figure with access to the transcripts generated by garda listening devices. In those days, conversations were physically recorded on spools of tape in the GPO in O'Connell Street. A motor-cycle courier then collected and conveyed them to the transcription department of C3 at Garda HQ in the Phoenix Park. They often reached Berry at the DoJ. MI6 could have obtained them from anybody positioned along the distribution pipeline who had time to copy them or make notes based on their content.

Saor Éire gunmen in Dublin perpetrated the killing of Garda Fallon on 3 April 1970. A gang of three men burst into the Royal Bank of Ireland at Arran Quay that morning. Three unarmed gardaí, Richard Fallon, Paul Firth and Patrick Hunter, were on patrol in a garda car. They were told to go to the bank. Garda Hunter, the driver, raced towards it. As they arrived, the raiders, all armed with pistols, were making their escape through the front door. Fallon and Firth confronted them, only to be fired at repeatedly. Ignoring the bullets tearing at him, Fallon advanced to grab one of the gunmen, but was shot in the neck and shoulder. Bullets from a Star pistol killed him. His father later described him as 'fearless'. Fallon was afforded a state funeral. 1,000 gardaí attended it. He was posthumously awarded the Garda Síochána's Scott Medal for heroism in the line of duty.

Saor Éire issued a grotesquely crass public statement: 'We deny that Garda Fallon was killed, as the Government and the anti-socialist press suggest, in the course of protecting the public. He died protecting the property of the ruling class, who are too cowardly and clever to do their own dirty work.'

The slaying engendered a sea change in the attitude of the force against republican paramilitaries. 'The honeymoon is now over' a special branch officer declared in the newspapers. 'One of our men has been killed, a father of five who never did harm to anybody.'

In the shadows, a rupture between British intelligence and the gardaí was also on the cards.

Saor Éire was active in England, where British Intelligence was monitoring its efforts to procure arms. The Irish group had a contact in Birmingham, a 'proofer', who tested 9mm Star pistols for the Star munitions factory in Spain. He would condemn perfectly good instruments as flawed and smuggle them out of the armoury in a bag. In 2001, Liz Walsh described the process:

> When he got home he placed [the pistol] into a larger carton, about twelve inches by twelve, sealed it and wrapped a colour code around it. It was now ready for transportation by plane to Dublin Airport. Thirty years ago, it was relatively easy to get metal objects onto an aeroplane: x-ray machines and metal detectors were to come later. The proofer was being paid for his trouble by Saor Éire, an outlawed Republican group that was behind a spate of armed robberies in Ireland in the late 1960s. The payments were made through a notorious Dublin criminal who acted as go-between for Saor Éire and the armoury contacts for a certain cut.

> When the plane landed at Dublin Airport, an airport worker went out to the hold. He had been told to watch out for a box with a certain colour code. He found what he was looking for, tipped it to one side and later put it into the boot of his car. A day or two after, he met a member of Saor Éire and handed him the carton, and the republican paid him … In that way, members of Saor Éire had been arming themselves for years.[1]

'Capt. Markham-Randall' spearheaded the assignment to penetrate the Saor Éire gun-smuggling network. He was the same individual who had attempted to infiltrate the CDC arms procurement operation during his visit to Dublin in November 1969. In *Orders for the Captain* James Kelly described the British spy, who had stayed at the Gresham hotel in Dublin, as a 'small, dark-haired, goatee-bearded man'. This description bears a striking resemblance to the arms dealer described by Seán Boyne in his book, *Gunrunners*, as having helped Saor Éire. He too was a 'small man with a goatee beard'. He used the name 'Randall'. According to Boyne's source, Randall had made contact with a person linked to Saor Éire in the UK in the late 1960s and the:

> 'arms dealer' gave his name as Randall, although other versions of the name were also reported. The Saor Éire-linked individual in the UK, in good faith, passed on this contact to his friends in the organisation back in Ireland, who were equally unsuspecting. In retrospect, the possibility opens up that British intelligence somehow detected Saor Éire activities in the UK and decided to infiltrate the subversive group by using an agent or a 'front' man, the mysterious Mr. Randall.[2]

The gardaí concluded that one of the Birmingham pistols was used to kill Garda Fallon. After the slaying, the police began to come down heavily on republicans of every hue. Three members of Saor Éire stood trial for the murder of Garda Fallon, but were acquitted by a jury.

The gardaí could have vented their fury at British intelligence in equal measure had the knotty details of Markham-Randall's assignment to infiltrate Saor Éire been known to them. Put simply, British intelligence could have ordered the seizure of the Star pistols from Birmingham before they had reached Saor Éire. If they had, Garda Fallon might not have been killed, at least not by one of the Birmingham weapons. Instead, the British let the operation proceed, thereby preserving Markham-Randall's cover so he could develop further leads. One of these threads led to Jock Haughey.

The contact between Jock Haughey and Markham-Randall, described in an earlier chapter, was set in motion by Richard Timmons. Timmons had been involved in the IRA's 1939 bomb campaign in England along with Brendan Behan, both of whom had been arrested. Timmons was sentenced to thirteen years in prison while Behan was sent to borstal.[3] Timmons escaped from Wakefield prison after ten years and made it back to Ireland. Timmons knew people in Saor Éire, including Frank Keane, a former officer-in-command of the IRA in Dublin. Keane and his circle had become entangled in Markham-Randall's sting operation. Martin Casey of Saor Éire agreed to introduce Haughey to Markham-Randall. In normal circumstances these men would have been antagonistic towards Fianna Fáil, yet were prepared to put aside their hostilities to help Jock Haughey acquire weapons for the defence committees in Northern Ireland.[4] At the time, figures from across the political spectrum were helping to supply guns to Northern Ireland for defensive purposes, including people in Fine Gael.

Casey took a boat to London on 2 November while Haughey flew over and met him at the Marble Arch in London the following day. Casey brought Haughey to meet a certain 'Mr Godfrey', an associate of Markham-Randall of the Savoy Finance Company, on the sixth floor of 299 Oxford Street. Jock Haughey returned later in the month with John Kelly, as described earlier. Aside from making the initial introduction, Casey had no further involvement in the affair.

A retired garda special branch officer familiar with Saor Éire has revealed that the gardaí had two informers inside the organisation and developed a shrewd idea about what had been going on there. He is adamant that Jock Haughey had 'nothing whatsoever – absolutely nothing – to do with Saor Éire' or the Birmingham pistols.[5] No weapons made it to Ireland as a result of Haughey's November 1969 trips to London. The cargo he had helped fly to Dublin, the previous September, was a mixum-gatherum collection of second-hand weapons. There was no inventory of them for the gardaí to inspect. All of the September guns had been taken by Cathal Goulding of the Official IRA and were kept under lock and key by him for months – most likely until after April 1970 when Garda Fallon was shot. Goulding did not supply any of them to Saor Éire. On the other hand, the Star pistols from Birmingham were freshly minted and traceable. They reached Saor Éire without any assistance from Haughey. Since the gardaí were able to trace the pistol which shot Garda Fallon to the factory in Birmingham, it rules out any possibility that it was one of those imported by Jock Haughey.

After the killing of Garda Fallon, Oldfield, Peck and Evans desperately needed to keep their entanglement in the Birmingham quagmire concealed. Luckily for them, rumours were soon making the rounds that Jock Haughey and his associates were somehow connected to the murder weapon. Shortly after the arrest of Capt. Kelly in May 1970, Chief Superintendent John Fleming and Inspector Doocey interviewed Capt. Kelly at the Bridewell. As the captain recounted in *Orders for the Captain*, the first question put to him by Doocey had been: 'What do you know about the Garda Fallon murder?' When Capt. Kelly responded with purple veined outrage, the question was withdrawn.

By 1971, the truth about Markham-Randall's links to Saor Éire was only a short step away from exposure and therefore disaster for Anglo-Irish security and intelligence co-operation.

In his book on the Arms Crisis, *Arms & The Men*, published in 1971, Seamus Brady described how unnamed individuals had gone to London seeking arms, i.e., Jock Haughey's second trip to London, the one with John Kelly. To the undoubted relief of Oldfield, Peck and Evans, Seamus Brady neither named nor described Markham-Randall.[6] Brady merely revealed how Haughey and John Kelly had been placed under surveillance and that an 'arms agent' had followed them to Dublin 'where he stayed in the Gresham Hotel. He invited them to introduce him to "their principals", and later offered one of them a bribe. He was advised for his own safety to return forthwith to Britain. An interesting sequel is that a few weeks later, the British Special Branch forwarded photographs of the two Irishmen, taken surreptitiously in London's Oxford Street, to the Special Branch in Dublin.'

Capt. Kelly decided to write his account of the Arms Crisis. News of Capt. Kelly's decision percolated through the grapevine to Jack Lynch. Before Christmas 1970, Lynch told Ambassador Peck about Kelly's initiative. After the meeting Peck informed Kelvin White of the FCO that: 'When I saw the Taoiseach just before Christmas [1970] he mentioned casually that Capt. James Kelly was trying to produce in double quick time, a book about the arms trial which, he claimed, was going to be full of damaging material about the involvement of the whole Irish government.'

Why Lynch passed on this information to Peck is a mystery, but the result is certain: the tip-off lit a fire under Peck and the FCO who set about thwarting its publication. Capt. Kelly secured a contract with the British publisher Collins. They began to promote it as the 'most explosive book for some time' in the London media. The proposed title for the book was *Orders for The Captain*. Peck suggested to the FCO that they frighten Collins by telling the company that the book was libellous. Somehow the FCO managed to persuade Collins to abandon the publication. A FCO diplomat, A.C. Thorpe was well pleased with the result and commented, on 3 February 1971, that Kelly's search for a publisher would now 'have to start again from scratch'.[7]

The FCO and MI6 were right to be concerned about the book. A passage in it read:

The quest for arms by Northern representatives continued, and in November a suspected British agent was lured to Dublin. After three or four days' negotiation in the Gresham Hotel, the supposed arms salesman offered a bribe to one of the Northerners. Negotiations were immediately broken off and an agent, who was using the name of Peter Markham-Randall, presumably returned to England. I reported the affair to Colonel Hefferon and he initiated enquiries with Garda Headquarters.

Equally, Capt. Kelly's description of Markham-Randall in the book as a 'small, dark-haired, goatee-bearded man' threatened to unravel Markham-Randall's connections to Saor Éire.

While there was no reference in the book to Markham-Randall's meeting with Saor Éire in Dublin, it was entirely possible that it would emerge during interviews conducted with the captain when his book went on sale.

The effort of the FCO to thwart the publication of the book turned out to be a waste of time because Dick Walsh produced a report in *The Irish Times*, on 10 February 1971, in which he described the English spy as 'Peters, an ex-British Army officer'; also that, 'Accounts vary about the name he used – some say Peters, other Captain Randall'.[8] The article also referred to the involvement of Frank Keane, Liam Walsh and Martin Casey of Saor Éire in setting up the meeting with Markham-Randall.

Capt. Kelly did not intend to abandon his book. Michael Gill, managing director of Gill and Macmillan, stepped into the breach with an offer to publish the work. Plates were made up and sent to a printing firm called Cahills. At this juncture, George Colley took up the cudgels against the author. Cahills were told that their 'valuable government printing contracts' would be cancelled if they went ahead with the book.[9] They too abandoned the project.

Capt. Kelly was left with no option but to self-publish

and towards this end approached a series of printers but 'the word had got out' and they were 'not prepared to print in the face of official opprobrium'. He eventually succeeded with the support of a mystery man – probably an associate of Charles Haughey or Neil Blaney – who procured a printer for him on Abbey Street and the book finally saw the light of day in the autumn of 1971.

Despite the publication of the two books and the newspaper article, the gardaí failed to make the connection between Markham-Randall, British intelligence and the Birmingham murder weapon. It did not help their inquiries that the police in London misled them. This became apparent after Col Hefferon, the Director of G2, learned that the gardaí had been told by London that Markham-Randall was merely a person of 'ill-repute' as opposed to one of their agents.[10] It is difficult – though not impossible – to accept that the gardaí were gullible enough to swallow this portrayal of Markham-Randall. The gardaí did not know that he had sought access to what he perceived were IRA training camps, nor that he wrote a letter to the bank at which the 'Dixon' bank account was held.

The gardaí certainly gave credence to the rumours linking Jock Haughey to the Garda Fallon murder weapon; hence, the question to Capt. Kelly after his arrest at the Bridewell.

The rumours did not go away. On 4 November 1971, Gerry L'Estrange, a Fine Gael TD, raised the killing in the Dáil. L'Estrange was one of three TDs who had asked questions in the Dáil about George Colley's anti-British propaganda campaign in November 1969.[11] Ambassador

Gilchrist had boasted of prompting them. Now, L'Estrange was fed misleading information about Garda Fallon's murder, which he raised in the Dáil. He declared: 'One of those men who murdered Garda Fallon was brought down to Greenore [Co. Louth] ferryboat in a State car and if you want to know who owned the car I can also tell you.' L'Estrange was deemed by the media to have had Blaney's car in mind. On 16 December 1971, L'Estrange regurgitated the allegation: 'The Government did nothing about the murderers of Garda Fallon. One of them was brought in a State car to get away on a boat to Ostend.'[12] The notion that a state car – driven by a garda – would have been used to transport the killer of Richard Fallon, and that this had remained a secret until L'Estrange revealed it, is so absurd that it does not merit rebuttal. He did not name the driver or name the passenger.

L'Estrange could not have obtained this information from an informed and honest garda source, as a knowledgeable garda would have known that the story was not true. Similarly, it could not have emanated from an honest DoJ source. So who fed these deeply dishonest and misleading lies to L'Estrange? The list must include people like Peck and Evans, or a dishonest garda or DoJ official working in league with them.

As indicated earlier, the gardaí and the DoJ have known since the early 1970s that Jock Haughey had 'nothing what-soever' to do with Saor Éire. Nonetheless, Garret FitzGerald raised the issue of Jock Haughey's alleged links to Saor Éire and the gun that killed Garda Fallon, under privilege in the Dáil as late as 1980. Des O'Malley was another politician who banged this drum. In 2001, he alleged, 'there is some reason to believe Garda Fallon may have been murdered in April 1970 with a weapon which had been part of earlier illegal arms shipments into the State ... There is also reason to suppose that some senior gardaí suspected that a prominent politician was fully aware of this earlier importation and had turned a blind eye to it.' Yet, O'Malley, as minister for justice, 1970–73, must have known that the murder weapon emanated from Birmingham.

To add to O'Malley's muddle, Liz Walsh has described in her book, *The Final Beat*, that O'Malley 'has confirmed that, while aware of the rumours, he never found anything to substantiate them.'[13]

Although O'Malley acted as if he wanted to get to the truth about the gun used to kill Garda Fallon, he never spoke to Sean Boyne, the highly regarded author and journalist. Boyne had published details about the link between Markham-Randall and Saor Éire in his 2006 bestselling book, *Gunrunners*.[14]

In 2007, Michael McDowell explained that he had studied the files at length and he was satisfied there was 'no conspiracy involving any person at the political level'.

O'Malley did not repeat the innuendoes he had disgorged during his career about the killing of Garda Fallon in his 2014 book, *Conduct Unbecoming*.[15] Similarly, Garret FitzGerald failed to address the issue in his 1991 and 2014 memoirs.

The focus on Jock Haughey's alleged role in the events surrounding the killing of Garda Fallon has deflected public attention for decades from MI6's role in allowing Saor Éire weapons to enter the country.

Dublin gangsters involved in the heroin trade also benefitted from Oldfield's decision to ignore the Birmingham swindle, as they too acquired guns from the Star factory. The 'proofer' was probably recruited as a British agent, as it does not appear that he was ever arrested or charged with illegally supplying arms to Irish customers.

Had there been the merest suspicion that the Birmingham pistols had reached Ireland with the connivance of MI6, albeit as part of a sting operation to assist the service penetrate and undermine Saor Éire, the gardaí would have vented their fury on MI6. 'If we had established that [i.e. the link between Saor Éire and Markham-Randall] as a fact, there would have been no cooperation for at least a decade', one senior Garda intelligence officer has commented.[16]

What lesson did Oldfield draw from the killing of Garda Fallon? In 1972, he retained two criminals, Kenneth and Keith Littlejohn, who carried out a series of armed bank robberies in the Republic and attacked garda stations as part of a campaign to frighten the Irish public and create an atmosphere in which Jack Lynch would be able to introduce stern anti-IRA legislation.

'Winning Acceptance and Confidence'

Her Majesty's spies and diplomats left no stone unturned in their efforts to find out what was going on behind Dublin's closed doors. The diplomat-spies at the Merrion Square embassy in the early 1970s are a good example of the elasticity of Britain's information-gathering skills. Among their targets were the politicians of the larger parties in the Republic, business leaders and influential media figures. Clearly, these pillars of society had to be treated differently to working class nationalists in Northern Ireland, who could be treated roughly when the need arose. In Dublin 'white noise' was replaced by flattery; beatings with backslapping; and prison gruel with five-course meals. The diplomat-spies assiduously collected gossip, speculation and, whenever possible, hard facts about what was going on behind the scenes in Dublin. Over time, the embassy grew into a glorified nest of spies, possibly the largest of its kind in Western Europe. Ambassador Gilchrist had specifically referred to the collection of 'gossip' in a communication he sent to Edward Peck, chairman of the JIC, on 24 July 1969. For his part, Ambassador Peck provided a masterful summary of the wider information-gathering task in his memoirs, asking:

> does an Ambassador know [what is going on]? How does he find out? How can he be sure that what he reports to his Foreign Secretary will not be proved next week to be utter rubbish? The

short answer is that the information he needs comes from all over the place, and part of his job is not only to know what to look for, but also to make sure that all the members of his staff, no matter how junior, know what to be curious about. Government Ministers, politicians of all parties in and out of office, the Press (which means not only what is printed but what editors and political correspondents know or think they know and can discuss but cannot print), civil servants, other Embassies – the list is endless ... But there remains the question of how an Ambassador and his staff get to know this necessary multitude of informants. The answer is by getting out and about, being as sociable and hospitable as purse and liver permit, merging into the social landscape and winning acceptance and confidence. When you come home at six in the evening from a heavy day in the Embassy, the day's work may be less than half done ...[1]

The tánaiste and future president of Ireland, Erskine Childers, was one of the embassy's established contacts. As Gilchrist recorded the 'three Irishmen with whom I can talk most freely and frankly about Irish politics are moderate men, and they know very well what side they are on. They are General Collins-Powell, Mr David Neligan, & Mr Erskine Childers.' Neligan had set up the special branch, but was enjoying his retirement in Booterstown, Co. Dublin. General Collins-Powell, also retired, understood the thinking of the Irish Army.

Childers, who served as tánaiste in Jack Lynch's first cabinet, was born in London in 1905, educated at the University of Cambridge and became an Irish citizen in 1938. His father – once a British naval intelligence officer – had been executed in November 1922 by the Provisional Government. Such was the son's abiding resentment of the Irish Army, when he became president in 1973, he attempted to dismiss his military aide. Childers also developed an animosity towards Haughey. He once offered cigarettes from an open package to each one of his cabinet colleagues while clutching it firmly in his hand as he went from one to another. He pointedly ignored Haughey when he reached him.

Childers enjoyed a cordial relationship with the British embassy, not merely by virtue of his birth, but because of his second marriage to Rita Dudley.[2] She met him in 1952 while he was Minister for Posts and Telegraphs. They married in Paris later that year. Taoiseach de Valera was uneasy about the fact that she worked at the British embassy. She was obliged to step down from her post. She had worked in a number of secretarial positions for British government offices. Her abilities had drawn her to the attention of Sir John Maffey who ran the legation. She became the assistant press attaché in 1942. Impressed, Maffey had recommended her for a position at the Irish Desk in the Ministry of Information in London in 1943, an appointment she accepted. From there, she moved to the Foreign Office for a spell. During her interlude in London, she was permitted sight of classified intelligence files about the Holocaust that troubled her greatly. She returned to Dublin in 1946 to resume her role as assistant press attaché. John Betjeman held the role of senior press attaché, but this was cover for his assignment as a propagandist on behalf of the Ministry of Information. His work was performed in co-ordination with SOE, MI6 and MI5. It is not known what Rita Dudley knew of her superior's clandestine activities.

Some of the information Erskine Childers relayed to

the embassy was of a dubious quality. He appears to have been motivated, in part at least, by personal enmity. After Haughey and the other defendants were acquitted, Childers fed Peck a story which the ambassador relayed to London. The memorandum stated that:

> There is a Dublin businessman called Gerry Jones who is a close friend of [former government minister] Mr [Neil] Blaney and an associate of Mr Haughey in the various property deals and other transactions in which he specialises. The Deputy Prime Minister [Erskine Childers] told me that to his certain knowledge Mr Jones had tracked down and 'got in touch with' all 12 jurors in the [arms] trial.[3]

Since Childers was asserting that each member of the jury – without exception – had been approached 'to his certain knowledge', we can conclude that he was, at best, fantasising; at worst, lying. The charge that the entire jury was coerced by anyone on behalf of the defendants, let alone Jones, is manifestly untrue. Some of the jury had sided with the accused before the trial had ended. After John Kelly wound up his speech from the dock, he received the applause of at least one member of the jury. In his 2020 book, *The Arms Crisis, The Plot That Never Was*, the former RTÉ broadcaster and producer, Michael Heney, quoted two former jurors he had interviewed in 2001. They were responding to a claim by Garret FitzGerald that they had been intimidated. They wanted to tell a completely different story. One of them described how, after Gibbons had admitted some knowledge of the arms importation:

> You could actually sense the reaction in the jury box, because that was a turning point for the whole thing. A complete denial on

the one hand, and then an admission [by Gibbons] that he was aware of it … There was another lad on the jury and when we both – when we went in – we were saying, 'that's a revelation', and another few of the jury were in the vicinity and also of the same opinion … I suggested myself that the four lads shouldn't be up on trial, that it was Jim Gibbons [who] should have been up for perjury.[4]

Furthermore, the acquittal was reached quickly and unanimously. After the verdict, a number of the jurors rushed to shake hands with the defendants, again, hardly the act of people who had been intimidated.

Gerry Jones, the man maligned by Childers, was a charmer, not a thug. He was involved in shipping and engineering enterprises and a member of Fianna Fáil's National Executive.

Serious consequences flowed from Childers' deception: in the 1970s, the IRD would provide a series of briefings to media figures, during which Gerry Jones was named as a member of a group which was assisting 'US suppliers of firearms to the PIRA'.[5] This was a lie and placed his life in danger.

The Childers memorandum also reveals that the tánaiste was furnishing the embassy with information about Haughey's 'various property deals and other transactions'. A more cautious person might have paused to consider that such information, if it could have been substantiated, had the potential to be exploited by British intelligence as blackmail material.

Peck described Childers in his memoirs as 'a very remarkable man … when I knew him he was Minister of Health and a very steadfast supporter of Jack Lynch'; moreover, 'a very wise and experienced man, who had always been friendly and helpful' to the embassy and a welcome dinner party guest at the ambassador's residence.[6] Peck recalls that at one of the last parties he hosted:

> without warning Erskine Childers rose made a speech, very warm and simple and obviously straight from the heart, ... about Mariska [Peck's wife] and me and our time in Dublin. There is, of course, no text or record of it, but one of the points that he stressed went something like this: 'We in the Irish government soon discovered that the British ambassador interpreted our position and our problems faithfully and fairly to his government. But we also learned that he was a lucid and outspoken ambassador, and I would like people on both sides of the water to know that when, as often happens, there were differences between us, we were never left in any doubt what the British felt and why'.[7]

As an experienced diplomat, Peck would have been in dereliction of his duties had he not tried to absorb as much confidential information as he could from the gushing tánaiste. Gilchrist had probably milked Childers' political udders as hard as he could for years before Peck's arrival.

Yet, behind Childers' back, the embassy was scathing of the faction of which Childers, Lynch and Gibbons were members. On 24 August 1972, David Blatherwick sent a confidential report to FCO in London, Frank Steele, the senior MI6 officer in Belfast, and others, stating that Capt. Kelly was 'the fall guy, and Gibbons, by means of lying and eventually perjury preserved his head ... Mr Lynch and Mr Gibbons, the villains of the piece, continue to enjoy the fruits of a very dirty victory'.

The Fireball of the North

Peter Berry, the man who had been the cause of so much turmoil for Charles Haughey and Neil Blaney, retired from the DoJ at the end of 1970. By the time he gave evidence at the Public Accounts Committee (PAC) inquiry into the financial aspects of the Arms Crisis in 1971, he was carrying a loaded revolver. At one PAC session, he startled those present by taking it out and placing it on the table in front of him: a gesture designed to bring home to the politicians the dangers he believed he faced. The members of the committee decided that 'he had lost his marbles'.[1]

Berry's deputy, Andrew Ward, succeeded him. He was forty-four years of age when he took over from Berry in 1971 and remained in place until he reached the age of sixty in 1986.[2] Born in 1926, Ward hailed from Tourard, Co. Cork. He was a highly secretive man.[3] He was married and lived in Terenure, Co. Dublin. Over time, he earned the reputation of someone who 'was cute but did not lead from the front'. Smallish in stature, he was seen as 'a bit of a loner'.[4] One of his first orders was designed to preserve his anonymity. He dispatched a garda motorcyclist to Milltown Golf Club in Dublin to remove a picture of him with a group of golfers that was hanging on a wall at the club. When he spoke on the phone, typically, the first thing he said to the person on the other end of the line was 'press the scrambler button'.

Ward's accession to the top position at the DoJ meant that it was going to be business as usual, for Berry and Ward had worked well together. In his private memoirs, Berry described Ward as part of his circle of confidants within the department.[5]

Meanwhile, Neil Blaney had formed the opinion that a deal had been hatched at a meeting between Peck and Lynch on 5 May 1970 to have him and Haughey sacked. 'I think the British government pressed [Lynch] to do it', Blaney asserted in public. This was tantamount to a declaration of political war against London.

In his book on the Arms Crisis, *Arms and the Men*, Seamus Brady, a close friend of Blaney, provided an insight into what Blaney's circle suspected had happened: 'Whether it was through their agents in Ireland, or through the close watch which their M.I.6. network keeps on arms deals throughout their world of operation, the British counter-espionage agency got wind of the [arms importation] deal [with Otto Schlueter]. *The London Times*, following investigations on the Continent, has since reported that Austrian police had conducted inquiries into the arms shipment at the request of the British Embassy in Vienna. The evidence seems clear that word of what was afoot was passed to the Special Branch in Dublin, probably through the special branch in London, which maintains unofficial contact with its counterparts in Ireland.'[6]

For his part, Charles Haughey suspected British intelligence was responsible for informing Liam Cosgrave about the arms importation attempt in early May.[7] Cosgrave's intervention had caused Lynch to perform a u-turn on his earlier decision to retain Haughey and Blaney in his cabinet.

Blaney was a considerable threat to Lynch's grip on power. He had thrown his hat into the leadership ring back in 1966, only to whip it back out when he realised he was not going to succeed Seán Lemass as taoiseach. His blend of forthright republicanism was not then in vogue. But he still harboured leadership ambitions. The upheaval in Northern Ireland was now providing him with an opportunity to return to cabinet and possibly even open the door for him to replace Lynch as taoiseach. In 1969, the *United Irishman* newspaper, published by Official Sinn Féin, dubbed him the 'Fireball of the North'.

While Blaney had been arrested in 1970 alongside Haughey, Capt. Kelly and the other defendants, the evidence against him was wafer thin and the charges against him were dropped at a very early stage.

By 1971, Blaney was every bit as much a threat to the leadership of Jack Lynch, as was Charles Haughey. The JIC in London was concerned that if Lynch was toppled, his successor would probably be 'either less effective or less accommodating'.[8]

Ambassador Peck had little time for Blaney. He had come across him during the 'yearly butter wrangle' when London set a limit to the amount of butter that was to be imported from Denmark, Ireland and New Zealand. In 1970, Blaney as Minister for Agriculture led the negotiations. 'Of course it all ended in agreement, and there was the usual government lunch at Lancaster House, to which I was invited as Ambassador-Designate. There I had my first and last conversation with Neil Blaney. He was pleasant but he struck me as a bit dour – in fact he conformed exactly to my mental picture of a typical Northern Irishman, which indeed he is, from Donegal.'[9]

In May 1971, Blaney became the target of a manoeuvre which bears the fingerprints of Peck and Evans. It was designed to blacken Blaney's name in Washington. The first stage of the ruse was calculated to deceive the senior staff at the American embassy in Dublin. There were two key figures at the embassy in 1971, the ambassador, John Moore, and his 'political officer', Virgil Randolph III. Richard Nixon had appointed Moore in 1969. Before his appointment, he had served as a key adviser to Nixon. Born in 1910, Moore had a legal background and was well versed in the rough-and-tumble of politics in Washington. His grandfather had emigrated from Ireland to America during the famine, while his father had been closely associated with John Devoy and Clan na Gael in New York. Moore represented Washington's interests in Ireland until 1975. Such was his affection for the country, he chose to be buried in Deans Grange Cemetery, Co. Dublin, after his death in Manhattan in 1988 from bone cancer. His wife, who predeceased him, was also buried in Deans Grange Cemetery.

If Virgil Randolph III wasn't a CIA officer, he was certainly fishing in the same waters as the spooks from Langley.[10] In May 1971, Randolph III was contacted by 'an authoritative source in the Irish government' who gave him a very peculiar view of what was allegedly afoot in Ireland. The Irish official contended – deceitfully – that there were three separate wings of the IRA on the island: the Officials who were 'under Communist influence'; the Provisionals; and a 100 strong underground army he called 'Blaney's Private IRA'. The notion that such an organisation existed is so farcical that it does not merit rebuttal, but the 'government' official was sufficiently convincing so as to persuade Randolph III of its existence.

On 18 May, Randolph III sent an eight-page confidential assessment of the IRA to Washington. It was drawn up in coordination with the US consul general in Belfast. Randolph III provided a description of the events that had led up to the fracture in the IRA. He stated that he understood 'from an authoritative source in the Irish government that in the autumn of 1969, the Irish Minister for Agriculture, the unreconstructed Donegal man and powerful Fianna Fáil politician Neil Blaney, began beefing up his own political machine in the Republic and in Northern Ireland, ostensibly to further the Fianna Fáil interest but actually to further his own … Prime Minister Lynch, unable to curb Blaney's free-wheeling activities, which involved the diversion of Irish government and Fianna Fáil party funds to his supporters, waited for an opportunity to quash Blaney and his "Private IRA".'

Under the sub-heading, 'the Gun-Running Plot', Randolph III had more bunkum to impart, namely that:

it now seems established that during the spring of 1970 Neil Blaney sought to give muscle to his political ambitions by arranging for the illegal importation into Ireland of a substantial quantity of arms and ammunition for delivery to his Republican friends on both sides of the border. Despite the failure of the attempt to smuggle arms to Blaney's 'Private IRA', a quantity of guns and ammunition as well as money (some apparently from Irish government appropriations for 'Northern relief'), seem to have trickled into Northern Ireland during 1970, mostly into the hands of the IRA 'Provisionals'.

For the avoidance of any confusion, Randolph III was claiming that Blaney's IRA was a wholly separate organisation to that of the Officials and Provisionals. He described how, in January 1971, 'a responsible Irish government official' had estimated the 'combined active membership of both IRA groups [i.e. Officials and Provisionals] in the Republic at about 1300, with an additional half that number operating in Northern Ireland. These figures exclude Neil Blaney's "Private IRA", which may number a hundred men or so.'

Randolph III referred to Ruairí Ó Brádaigh, a co-founder of the Provisional IRA, by his English name, Rory Brady. According to the American: 'Brady's Provisionals are ... having nothing to do with Neil Blaney's ... current efforts to found a new 32-County Republican Party (whose real aim is to oust Lynch from the leadership of Fianna Fáil) ... Since it is doubtful that the new Republican Party will get off the ground, Blaney's "Private IRA" may eventually drift back into Fianna Fáil.' Since Blaney's IRA did not exist, the prediction that it would 'drift back into Fianna Fáil' provided a convenient escape hatch through which this source could slip with his credibility intact when – as was inevitable – this fantasy wing of the IRA failed to engage in any sort of activity.

It must have disturbed the recipients of the report in Washington, who were relying upon Randolph III's analysis, to hear that a mainstream European political party was prepared to absorb gunmen into its ranks.

Randolph III had more gobbledygook for his readers:

> In this connection, it should be noted that Fianna Fáil has very carefully avoided any confrontation with the IRA 'Provisionals' and the 'Officials' as well. In fact, the Lynch government has

turned a blind eye at clandestine 'Provisional' IRA training activities in the Republic.

The 'government official' responsible for this hoax was most likely a DoJ official. Why would a 'government' official pedal these ludicrous yarns to the American embassy? What was his agenda? It is hardly fanciful to suggest that he was a British agent who was handed a script by Evans – probably one written by Evans and Peck – and instructed to relay its content to the American embassy, to blacken the name of Blaney in Washington.

No doubt Evans and his colleagues were also busy circulating 'sibs' about Blaney to all sorts of gossips in Dublin. They probably fed the story that Blaney's official driver had taken one of Garda Fallon's killers to the Greenore ferryboat in a state car to Gerry L'Estrange, TD, who subsequently brought it up in the Dáil under privilege.

Blaney's star shone brightly after the Arms Crisis and its sequel, the Arms Trials, but it fizzled out amid bouts of internal feuding that convulsed Fianna Fáil during 1971. Blaney lacked patience – some would say he had a temper – and did not suffer lightly those he considered fools. Compared to Haughey, he lacked people skills. The friction between Blaney and the party hierarchy, resulted in his expulsion from the party during the first half of 1972. He would never return to the fold. On 24 August 1972, David Blatherwick sent a confidential report to the FCO in London and Frank Steele, a senior MI6 officer in Belfast, among others. It stated that while the Arms Crisis was 'now part of the past and seems likely to be treated as such in the Republic ... Mr Blaney's political career in Fianna Fáil has collapsed. Mr Haughey is still doing good deeds in the political wilderness.'

Henceforth, and with Blaney essentially no longer in contention for a leadership role in Fianna Fáil, MI6 and the IRD's attention would focus sharply on Charles Haughey.

SEXPIONAGE

In the 1970s, British Intelligence enlisted the underworld expertise of the Silver-Mifsud Syndicate of London to supply prostitutes for intelligence purposes in Ireland. Two partners, Bernie Silver, born in 1922, a former paratrooper, and 'Big' Frank Mifsud, a former Maltese policeman, born in 1926, ruled the Syndicate.

Silver visited Belfast to set up brothels in the city. The Syndicate's prostitutes served as 'swallows', women who variously flattered susceptible targets to collect pillow talk, or acted as bait in 'honey traps' to create opportunities for blackmail.

Mifsud had purchased a home for his family in Dublin, well away from his enemies in London. His wife was Irish. His residence was a short walk from the Old Shieling hotel in Raheny, a hugely successful music venue at which the cream of traditional Irish and folk acts performed before large audiences. The venue also attracted a lot of garda attention as leading republicans frequented it. Another point of interest for the gardaí and MI6 was that politicians, such as Charles Haughey, the local TD for the area, sometimes attended there. The gardaí had sources inside the hotel who passed on general information to them, some of which was relayed to MI6.

The use of prostitutes as intelligence assets was a tactic Maurice Oldfield had employed right from the start of his intelligence career in the British army. During the Second World War, he was once assigned the task of babysitting two Greek double agents, George Liossis and a man called Demetrios. The Greeks were being held in isolation at a villa near Damascus. There were long periods of boring inactivity and it was felt wise to keep them entertained. Oldfield's solution was to employ two prostitutes to visit them. His initiative backfired when the women insisted that the Greeks wear condoms, 'a suggestion that was considered grossly offensive' by them.[1]

The employment of prostitutes by British government officials was a common practice. After the Second World War, British intelligence employed call girls to coax secrets from Soviet targets in Germany and Austria. John Cornwell, who worked for MI5, and wrote novels as 'John Le Carre', described to his biographer how he once took a foreign delegation to a house of ill repute during their visit to London in the late 1950s.[2] In the 1960s and 1970s, the Foreign Office employed sex workers to pose as receptionists and secretaries. They were then introduced to foreign dignitaries and trade delegations on visits to the UK. The women were expected to sleep with the foreigners and thereby render them favourably disposed towards Britain. This backfired spectacularly when one of them, an Irishwoman, called Norma Russell, sparked a scandal in May of 1973. Russell, born Honora Mary Russell, the daughter of a Cork cattle dealer, had been employed to 'entertain' foreign diplomats but also had a portfolio of her own VIP clients.[3] One of them was Lord Antony Lambton, a government minister with responsibility for the RAF. He was photographed naked in bed, while smoking cannabis, with Russell and another prostitute, aged twenty-six. The pictures were taken through a two-way mirror by Russell's boyfriend, who sold them to the newspapers.

Some garda officers – including one extremely senior intelligence officer – who went to London for meetings or on training courses over the next decade – were invited to go on 'tours' of the city. Soho, the notorious vice centre which teemed with Syndicate brothels, was sometimes suggested as a destination. The officer in question – known for his suspicion of British intelligence – was aghast at the suggestion, surmising he was 'being set up' and declined the invitation.

MI5 were past masters at the exploitation of sex for the purpose of blackmail. Christopher Herbert, an Irishman, was one of the exponents of this dark art. Educated at Trinity College Dublin, where he had obtained a first-class degree in experimental science, he was recruited by MI5 in 1950. In 1970, he oversaw the blackmail and recruitment of a Soviet diplomat in London, Oleg Lyalin. The Soviet was conducting an affair with his secretary, Irina Templyakova. When MI5 felt they had enough material to blackmail him, he was confronted with his compromising behaviour and coerced into working for Britain. Lyalin supplied a list of all the KGB officers he knew in the UK to MI5. Based on the information provided by him, Edward Heath expelled 105 Soviet agents from Britain in 1971.

In Ireland in the early 1970s, the prostitutes controlled by the Silver-Mifsud Syndicate were used to gather information and create opportunities to blackmail the men with whom they slept. Gerry Lawless, a former IRA internee turned journalist, conducted an inquiry into their deployment in

Ireland. He described in the *Sunday World* how:

> After the illegal Falls Road curfew [in July 1970], the British
> Command was shocked at the duration of the battle necessary
> to take control of the Falls area – the longest gun battle between
> the IRA and the British Army since 1916. The RUC Special
> Branch, the traditional 'eyes' of the British in the North, had
> predicted a British walk-over, was discredited and a new ad-hoc
> intelligence unit was established. Many members of this new unit,
> drawn from both Scotland Yard and Military Intelligence, had
> served in Aden, and the unit soon became known as the Aden
> Gang. The unit operated from the top-secret HQ on one of the
> floors of Churchill House, the GPO building in Belfast. From
> this base, spy-brothels were established, one above the Munster
> and Leinster Bank near the Capitol Cinema on the Antrim Road,
> and the other, the Gardenia Massage Parlour, opposite Choline
> Gardens on the Stranmillis Road.[4]

The Aden gang retained the services of the Syndicate as
consultants for the project. The gangsters' task was to ensure the spy-brothels were run professionally. Mifsud and
Silver had taken over control of the sex industry in the West
End of London in the 1950s. They were well established by
the late 1960s and enjoyed the co-operation of the Metro-
politan police, many of whom were on their payroll.[5] The
pair controlled hundreds of prostitutes who worked at
thirty or more properties that they owned in Soho. Silver
was chauffeur driven about London, always in a Rolls
Royce, a car he changed a few times a year. He lived in a
Georgian mansion, tipped waiters £25 and never carried
less than £1,000 on his person. He is believed to have made
£5,000,000 during his career.

Mifsud was equally rich, but nowhere near as ostentatious
as Silver. Having retired from the Maltese police in the 1950s,

Mifsud had relocated to London where he joined forces with Silver and together they established the 'Syndicate'. The pair enjoyed the protection of the London police for decades.

Silver was flown into Belfast in 1970 and taken in an army vehicle to HQNI at Lisburn where the general objective of the spy-brothel operation was relayed to him. Over the next ten days, he scouted Belfast with a group of bodyguards in a search for suitable premises to convert into brothels and massage parlours.

The Belfast brothels were fitted with hidden microphones and 35mm Olympus cameras. One, called the Gemini Health Studio, was located on the Antrim Road. It catered for heterosexuals, while the Gardenia on the Stranmillis Road, attracted a gay clientele.

Men who liked to have sex with boys and male teenagers were catered for by the vice ring which revolved around Kincora Boys' Home in Belfast. This was a standard practice employed by MI6. Oldfield's close friend, Anthony Cavendish, described how the service used children in entrapment operations:

> Then there is the [foreign] agent who is set up for blackmail from the beginning. The groundwork having been laid and the agent having been photographed in bed with a small boy or his boss's wife, is then forced to provide information.[6]

Kincora was taken over by MI5 and MI6 no later than 1971. As noted earlier, in 2016, MI6 disclosed to the Hart Inquiry into child sex abuse that it possessed a 'small collection of papers ... which relate to the relationship [Oldfield] had with the Head of the Kincora Boys' Home (KBH) in Belfast'. The

'Head' of Kincora was Joseph Mains, who was convicted in 1981 for a series of rapes he had committed at the residence.

The Gemini opened its doors in the summer of 1970 promising 'very attractive masseuses' in advertisements in Belfast newspapers. A more upmarket brothel was located on the Malone Road.

Silver recruited the staff for the Belfast establishments in London. He picked out females with conversational skills and intelligence as well as good looks. At least one of them was from Dublin. The women were warned they would be participating in a risky enterprise but one that would be lucrative for them. They were required to sign the Official Secrets Act.

Two Catholics, a husband and wife, ran the sparsely decorated Gemini. For the sake of appearance, it had a rudimentary gym, sauna and a solarium, which were rarely, if ever, used. Visitors to the Gemini were taken to a lounge, where they were served complimentary cocktails or coffee when the establishment was busy. Otherwise, most clients headed for the dimly lit corridor flanked by a string of curtained cubicles. Inside there were iron-framed beds, wooden chairs and wardrobes. Large two-way mirrors were hung on the walls to hide the Olympus cameras, with their battery-controlled motors, taking pictures of the customers in *flagrante delicto*. Once a shot was taken, a mechanism would wind the film forward to the next frame. Piped music drowned out the occasional humming sounds from the cameras. Microphones were installed to record what was said inside the cubicles and competed with the piped music. The tape machines were in the attic.

The establishment on the Malone Road was plusher with soft lighting and thick pile carpets, but equipped with the same type of surveillance equipment.

In *Spycatcher*, Peter Wright of MI5 described how, for five years, he and his team had 'bugged and burgled our way across London at the State's behest, while pompous bowler-hatted civil servants in Whitehall pretended to look the other way'. By his own admission, Wright spent a lot of time in Northern Ireland. The cameras and microphones in Belfast were almost certainly installed by a team assigned, if not led, by him.

One of the objects of the operations was to gather information from customers who knew either a little or a lot about what was going on inside nationalist communities. In March 1971, the effort produced the names of the IRA unit which had killed three Royal Highland Fusiliers in Belfast. A Belfast SDLP councillor was compromised and forced to reveal the names of the IRA men. When Silver was subsequently put on trial for the killing of a London gangster, Thomas 'Scarface' Smithson, Chief Superintendent Kenneth Etheridge, the deputy head of Scotland Yard's Fraud Squad, gave evidence on his behalf.[7] He explained how Silver had assisted in the enquiry into the death of the three Scottish soldiers in Belfast.

The Provisional IRA uncovered the existence of the spy-brothels and attacked the Gemini on Monday, 2 October 1972. They claimed they shot dead a man codenamed 'Bossman Jim' and his female assistant during the assault. Bossman Jim was a retired British army major. His assistant was the daughter of an army brigadier.

After the attack, witnesses saw the British army removing

a series of cameras and tape-recorders from a separate brothel on the Antrim Road.

'Mr Frances', the Welshman who ran the Gardenia, disappeared after the attack on the Gemini.

The *Daily Mirror* quoted a senior British army officer, in April 1974, who confirmed that the Belfast brothels had been run by the military and were closed because, 'We had no option … the cover had been blown and the lives of everybody involved were at stake … It was a good source of information and we managed to pick up all sorts of information without being discovered.'[8]

Sadly, the abuse of children at Kincora continued unhindered until early 1980.

While the various brothels were open for business in Belfast, Frank Mifsud was commuting between Dublin and London. His presence in Dublin did not raise eyebrows as he was married to an Irishwoman and was not a public figure. He had purchased a modest semi-detached residence on Foxfield Avenue, Raheny, north Dublin, in the 1960s. Unlike Silver, Mifsud did not open any brothels in Dublin. There were no such establishments in the capital at the time. 'The city was too small for anyone to get away with that type of behaviour back in those days', a former garda officer familiar with the vice scene in the city has explained. 'You had girls on the streets and some of them had flats but you did not have actual brothels like they had abroad. There was an old tradition in the force that prostitution should be broken up but without making the girls' lives miserable. The older officers would explain to the younger ones that many of the girls came from poor backgrounds and broken homes; some had been abused. A lot of them had children. The courts normally just fined them instead of sending them to prison. Some of the older officers were very religious and felt it was "unlucky" to make their lives difficult. I think they were superstitious because Mary Magdalene was meant to have been a prostitute. There was no way a brothel could have been set up in those days without coming to the attention of Dublin's crime gangs and they were terrified of the Provos. There was no chance that an Englishman could have set up a brothel without the Provos finding out from the criminal gangs.'

'In the early 1970s, there were more British prostitutes on the streets of Dublin than there were local girls,' the same garda has revealed. Since the Syndicate controlled the London vice market, some of the British prostitutes who came to Dublin must have worked for it in London. This raises the very real prospect that MI6 asked the Syndicate to provide them with 'swallows' prepared to work in Dublin in flats and hotels instead of brothels.

Intriguingly, Foxfield Avenue, where Mifsud lived, was a short walk from the Old Shieling hotel which used to nestle in the leafy suburb of Raheny Village, but was demolished over a decade ago. Bill Fuller, who originally hailed from Kerry, owned it. The hotel employed IRA men as bouncers. Anthony 'Dutch' Doherty, a member of the IRA who had escaped from Crumlin Road jail in December 1971, found employment there. Martin Meehan, a senior Belfast Provisional, once took refuge there. Dáithí Ó Conaill, a resident of Raheny, was a visitor as was John Kelly. The hotel was a popular location for live music. Fuller was one of the first businessmen to combine live performances at a venue with a licence to sell alcohol. At one time, the hotel hosted weekly performances by the Wolfe Tones and The Dubliners among others. The activities at the hotel attracted a large number of breathalyser-wielding gardaí who tested patrons as they drove out its gates.

The IRD would later allege that Fuller was not merely a member of the Provisional IRA, but a member of its Army Council. An individual, who actually sat on that body and has an extensive knowledge of its history, is clear that Fuller was never in the IRA. He asserts that Fuller was 'on the republican side of Fianna Fail'.[9]

If, as appears to be the case, Mifsud came to Ireland to find a safe haven for his family, it is unlikely he would have engaged in espionage in Dublin for MI6 willingly, an activity that could have brought the wrath of the Provisional IRA down upon him. Equally, it is unlikely that Oldfield did not ask for his assistance. If he was asked to help MI6, it might have been merely to offer his views on how Syndicate 'swallows' might best mingle with the republicans who frequented the Old Shieling and other republican drinking holes and wheedle information from them, while they were animated by alcohol.[10]

Two of the prostitutes employed in Belfast by the Syndicate were killed in London shortly after that operation ended. One of them hailed from Dublin. It was never established if her death was linked to the Belfast operation or not. What is known is that Silver had no compunction about killing women. He killed his girlfriend and at least six of his prostitutes. The Dublin woman might have been murdered to keep her from talking about the operation in Belfast or possibly to protect the far more precarious position of Syndicate-MI6 activities in Dublin.

The Old Shieling was in Charles Haughey's constituency. His brother Jock lived nearby on Foxfield Avenue. Charles Haughey would drop into the hotel from time to time to meet with Jock and his wife, among others. Haughey, the politician who had once helped destroy the IRA, and even drove one supporter to go on a hunger strike, was suddenly a hero to those who had previously despised him. A soldier who later became a successful solicitor, observed the phenomenon. He recalls: 'My late friend … lived behind the [Old Shieling] hotel so [my wife] and myself met [him] there on a number of occasions. I have no recollection of seeing the owner [Bill Fuller] there but have a distinct memory of C J [Haughey] getting a standing ovation on one occasion. The whole evening consisted of rebel songs, a silent collection, and the sale of *An Phoblacht*. Good pints though!'[11]

Since Jock Haughey lived on Foxfield Avenue, the same road as Mifsud, the latter could have kept on eye on visitors to his home had he wished. Jock resided at number 25; Mifsud a little more than a dozen doors up from him. As signalled in the introduction to this book, this work is an attempt to shed light on at least some of the conspiracies that took place on this island during the period from the late 1960s–1980. An even fuller picture may eventually emerge if MI6's files become available one day. Mifsud is a case in point. If he did engage in any sort of espionage, he kept a very successful low profile and never drew the wrath of the IRA down upon himself. After the collapse of the Syndicate, he continued to live in Ireland. Although there are reports that he died in Malta, he was living in Ireland when he passed away in December 2017. He is buried in Sutton.

'The Dublin Press ... is the Priority Target'

Eunan O'Halpin discovered that, in 1967, Ambassador Gilchrist had attended a JIC meeting in Downing Street at which it 'was also suggested that "journalistic sources" should be tapped for information, and, in an aside worthy of Myles na gCopaleen, that there was much information available in public houses where a great deal of unguarded conversation took place'.[1]

Ambassador Peck shared this outlook. He instructed all the members of his staff in Dublin to seize any opportunity to find out what was happening in the Republic from 'Government Ministers, politicians of all parties in and out of office'. He made specific reference to 'the Press' which, he explained, 'means not only what is printed but what editors and political correspondents know or think they know and can discuss but cannot print'.[2]

When it came to forging contacts with journalists, Peter Evans of MI6 had a head start on his colleagues at the embassy as his cover was that of 'information officer', a designation that gave him easy access to the press.

In 1971, the IRD sent Hugh Mooney, a black propaganda specialist to Ireland. Mooney was an ideal choice as he had relatives in Ireland, was a graduate of Trinity College Dublin and, best of all, had been employed as a sub-editor at *The Irish Times*. The plan was to base him in Belfast while he would work on both sides of the border. He paid a visit to

Dublin in June in preparation for his assignment. One of those he consulted was Evans. In a letter Mooney wrote to his superior, the IRD's Special Operations Adviser, Hans Welser, he explained that his 'talks with Mr Evans shows that IRD can start working at once through the Dublin Press, which is the priority target. Though unable to place draft articles, [Evans] said he was willing to pass on absolutely accurate information to [the] journalists he meets regularly.'[3] Evans' media contacts were not named in the document.

Kennedy Lindsay, author of *The British Intelligence Services in Action*, developed sources who disclosed to him that 'the news media in particular has been infiltrated at all levels, including ownership, by either British or American intelligence'.[4] In the decades since the publication of Lindsay's work, FCO correspondence concerning Major McDowell has emerged. It lends credence to Lindsay's sources as it confirmed London's infiltration of *The Irish Times* at an 'ownership' level. As described in an earlier chapter, on 2 October, 1969, Ambassador Gilchrist was told by McDowell, that he was 'one of the five (Protestant) owners of the *Irish Times*, and he and his associates are increasingly concerned about the line the paper is taking under its present (Protestant, Belfast-born) Editor, [Douglas] Gageby, whom he described as a very fine journalist, an excellent man, but on Northern questions a renegade or white n[***]er. And apart from Gageby's editorial influence, there is difficulty lower down, whereby sometimes unauthorised items appear and authorised items are left out.'[5]

Lindsay did not reveal the names of the media figures in

his book, but spoke openly about one high–profile British ally in a conversation with me in the late 1980s. The individual was a businessman who was in a position to influence the media. Two UK intelligence sources with knowledge of the businessman have also been prepared to talk about him. One dealt with him directly. The second source worked at HQNI where MI6 was based. The HQNI officer was aware of plans to circulate Psy Op propaganda themes and began to notice a pattern, whereby they appeared in places where the businessman could exercise his influence. He concluded – as did some of his colleagues – that the businessman was a resource of British intelligence.

There was a possible third source with knowledge about the businessman, an Irish engineer codenamed 'Dr Kildare'. The Irishman had been coerced by MI6 into spying on a group of Soviets involved in a building project in Africa. Once, on a trip to London in the 1970s, MI6 tried to get him to take up residence in Dublin and to spy for them there. His handler had placed a few files on the desk in front of him. When he left the room for a fleeting moment, 'Dr Kildare' glanced at one of them. It related to an individual he later described in an interview on RTÉ radio in guarded terms as a 'businessman'. This businessman would engage in a series of anti-Haughey manoeuvres in the 1970s and 1980s.

Mooney, Evans and their successors soon found they did not have to engage in much heavy lifting with the Dublin media to accomplish Oldfield's cherished goal of undermining Haughey. According to Geraldine Kennedy: 'All of the senior big beasts as you would call them in the political correspondents' room [in Leinster House] did not trust Haughey after the Arms Crisis. They were all against him.'

One of the 'big beasts' was Dick Walsh who worked at *The Irish Times* for thirty years rising to become its political editor. He wrote a book about the *Arms Crisis* – in the Irish language – and another one on Fianna Fáil in 1986. Throughout the 1970s and 1980s, Walsh operated in a clandestine manner as a supporter of Cathal Goulding. He wrote the eulogy Goulding delivered at the funeral of an Official IRA volunteer who had been killed in Belfast in April 1972. Clearly, the killing of a chaplain and five of the kitchen staff at the Parachute Regiment's HQ in Aldershot two months earlier by the Officials had done nothing to make him think ill of Goulding and his colleagues. The kidnap and torture of Ranger William Best, a teenager from the Creggan on leave to visit his mother in Derry, did not trouble his conscience either.

Walsh's influence registered at the highest level of the Official IRA. He served as part of the Official IRA team that entered into negotiations to end a feud with the Provisionals in the 1970s. He sat across the table from Dáithí Ó Conaill at a series of discussions, at least one of which took place in a funeral parlour.

When it came to Haughey, Walsh was prepared to twist facts. In his 1986 book on Fianna Fáil, he alleged that before the Arms Crisis, 'Haughey, however, was one of those who, in [Conor Cruise] O'Brien's words, had not hitherto been suspected of more than conventional republicanism ... he was noted by a close parliamentary colleague as "never having uttered a peep at all about the North – at any party meeting or anywhere else".[6]

On the other side of the fence, there were at least two people inside *The Irish Times* who were favourably disposed towards Haughey. One of these was no less a figure than the editor, Douglas Gageby, who felt that the politician had been badly treated during the Arms Crisis. The other was John Healy who wrote a column for the paper and strove to elevate Haughey to the status of political divinity.

It is clear that by 1971 the British embassy and the IRD had begun to gain a measure of influence over the Dublin media.[7] Declassified documents provide us with a glimpse at what was going on behind closed doors. The documents relate to operations against the Soviet Union and indicate how the embassy was making progress in forging links with journalists and editors. These particular operations were designed to thwart the actions of three Soviet 'journalists' who were sent to Dublin between September 1970 and September 1972: Yuri Ustimenko, Yuri Yasnev and Victor Louis – all were exposed as Soviet agents by Peck, Evans and the IRD. The British embassy enjoyed the co-operation of the Department of Foreign Affairs in these efforts.

Yuri Ustimenko became the target of 'sibs' which exposed his true role. Within weeks of his arrival, Peck reported to London that the Russian was 'widely referred to as the KGB man or "the Spy".'[8]

Victor Louis was next in the cross hairs. The IRD supplied a brief that ended up as a story in the *Irish Independent* entitled 'Soviet Mystery Man Slips into Dublin'.[9]

As a direct result of Peck's efforts, garda special branch officers followed Ustimenko and Yasnev for the duration of their visits. Their movements were relayed back to the British embassy.[10]

In the 1970s, communists were viewed in Ireland as subversive, anti-Christian and a threat to democracy. According to Colin Wallace, who worked with Mooney, the IRD 'linked Ustimenko, Victor Louis and others to Haughey, Tim Pat Coogan [the editor of the *Irish Press*] and others', thereby attempting to bring them into disrepute.[11] Wallace recalled that in this instance, the smears 'would have been disseminated verbally *via* Mooney's personal contacts, or IRD staff at the Dublin Embassy'.[12]

While the British embassy and the IRD sought to sway the opinion of the Irish media against Haughey, Blaney and others in Fianna Fáil, as well as against the Soviets, they were far from the only enemy, the British had in their sights. The IRA was also high on their target list. When it came to darkening the reputation of the IRA in the eyes of the Dublin media, the IRD hardly had to lift a finger. The gunmen managed to shoot themselves in the foot repeatedly by committing atrocities that alienated the majority of the Irish media. The list of self-inflicted propaganda wounds during the first half of the 1970s includes Bloody Friday (July 1972; 9 killed, 130 injured); the Guildford pub bombings (October 1973; 5 deaths, 65 injured); the Birmingham bombings (November 1974; 21 dead and 182 injured). Four innocent people – the 'Guildford Four' – went to prison for the London attacks, while six innocent men – the 'Birmingham Six' – spent sixteen years in prison for the Birmingham atrocity while the IRA culprits enjoyed freedom and anonymity for the rest of their lives. The killing of Garda Fallon also had a profound effect upon public opinion in the south. In later years, more gardaí and an Irish soldier were killed during the course of their duties. Additionally, there were incessant bank robberies, the killing of informers, punishment shootings, knee-cappings, tarring and feathering and stories of torture which sickened the national media. Across the border, British soldiers and members of the RUC were killed and severely wounded on a regular basis, something which also troubled the media in the Republic. The trauma suffered by their families was all too evident at the funerals that followed.

Bad publicity was a two-way street as Peck and the IRD discovered whenever the British army engaged in violent behaviour. Bloody Sunday is a case in point. On 30 January 1972, British paratroopers shot and killed thirteen people in Derry, with another dying later. There was global condemnation. The following day, Ambassador Peck was dining at the Stephens Green club in Dublin with 'a distinguished businessman from Cork' who 'had become a close friend'. While he encountered 'no trouble' at the club, Evans rang to warn him: 'you had better bring the car to the back entrance to Chancery after lunch. Students from Trinity are beginning to picket the front, and there might be problems.' As Peck drove unobserved along Merrion Square to the back lane, he spotted an 'orderly file of students walking round in a circle in the street, carrying placards with predictable slogans about the thirteen dead of the previous day, with the words "Bloody Sunday" prominent'. His office was on the first floor, looking out on the square. 'More students arrived and started throwing snowballs at the Embassy and shouting slogans and abuse. Then they started putting stones in the snowballs. Then they dispensed with the snow. I had intended to have an office meeting to make our dispositions for what was evidently going to be a substantial riot. We closed the shutters, but the din was by now so tremendous that serious discussion was impossible. We made the normal demand for protection to the Irish Department of Foreign Affairs.'[13]

Peck was called to London to advise the government about what was happening in Dublin. On Wednesday 2 February, he telephoned the Dublin embassy from the FCO. 'I talked to Peter Evans, as the Chancery telephone was still working. The front door of the Chancery had been blown up by a small gelignite bomb which had badly injured one of the policemen trying to protect the building, and petrol bombs had been hurled in. David Blatherwick, the first secretary, and the security guard on duty had been sweeping the burning petrol out with buckets of water and brooms. The building could no longer be defended. The mob was not satisfied and clearly intended to destroy the place. The national day of mourning meant that the factories would be shut and the pubs open. The police fought hard and many had been burnt by petrol, but they were outnumbered. The staff were destroying the files and essential equipment and would then have to evacuate the building ... I could only agree, and said I would be back as soon as the Prime Minister consented; I asked Peter [Evans] to tell [my wife] Mariska I hoped to be back by six.'[14] By the time he returned, the embassy had been set ablaze.

Another organisation to suffer from bad publicity in 1972 was the Official IRA. Its response to Bloody Sunday was the Aldershot bomb atrocity in February 1972, during which seven people perished and nineteen were injured. This and other outrages so shocked its members that it called an end to hostilities later in the year. After the gun smoke faded, it became apparent that the Official IRA and MI6 had a common enemy in the Provisional IRA. The Provisional IRA believe that once the Official IRA stopped attacking British target, the RUC's special branch was directed to turn a blind eye to Official IRA criminal activity, of which there was plenty. The Officials ran protection rackets and tax frauds on building sites and continued to rob banks. The Provisional IRA point to the fact that despite rampant gangsterism, their opponents were largely left unmolested. Some Provisionals and other observers go further and contend that the Officials furnished information about the Provisionals to British intelligence, in return for the continued benefit of the RUC turning a blind eye.

Spooky Associations

A suspicious Charles Haughey once told Austin Currie of the SDLP that he believed the British-Irish Association (BIA) was a front for British intelligence.

Politicians such as Conor Cruise O'Brien and Garret FitzGerald attended the BIA in the 1970s and beyond. John Fleming, the head of the garda special branch and Sir John Hermon, chief constable of the RUC, paid visits as well. Suffice it to say that few, if any, of those who participated in the BIA in the 1970s and 1980s had any inkling of the hidden hand of MI6 behind-the-scenes; which is exactly what Oldfield wanted.

The origins of the BIA can be traced back to a suggestion made by Major McDowell, the ex-MI5 officer in charge of *The Irish Times*, to Andrew Gilchrist in 1969. Although McDowell had not presented London with 'precise ideas' about how he could help Anglo-Irish relations, he made one suggestion that caught Gilchrist's attention. The latter had noted how McDowell 'like so many others, laments the lack of contact between prominent people in the North and in the South. If some form of gathering to bring the two sides together could be contrived, then "*The Irish Times* would be happy to help, if need be contributing its name, finance, and administrative assistance".' Gilchrist added some thoughts of his own, such as that it 'should be possible to get a better audience – e.g. some M.P.s and officials, and perhaps even some Ministers – if the seminar or seminars avoided that contentious subject, where differences were bound to be restated, and instead took themes where inevitably North and South would find it made sense to co-operate'. The BIA emerged from this type of thinking and approach. Its membership was – and is – drawn not only from the north and south, but also Britain.

David Astor, one of Oldfield's assets, was placed in charge of the BIA. Astor had served with the Special Operations Executive (SOE) during the Second World War, and was close to MI6. He chaired the BIA for the first nine years of its existence. Astor knew Oldfield well. Both men were members of the Athenæum club in Pall Mall, London. Astor was the owner of the *Sunday Observer,* yet another conduit Oldfield used to promote his interests.

Astor had applied to join MI6 before the Second World War, but had not been accepted. He did, however, gain entry to the SOE, the organisation that supported resistance movements in Axis occupied countries, especially Europe. During the so-called 'phoney war' in 1939, Astor and some of his associates got together to oppose the 'crushing' of Germany. They advocated eventual Anglo-German co-operation with anti-Nazi Germans, such as Adam von Trott zu Solz. MI6 was also involved in these machinations. According to Astor's biographer, Jeremy Lewis:

> 'David is said to be doing Secret Service work', his cousin Joyce Grenville reported in 1939. He had, in fact, been turned down by MI6, but his eagerness to keep in touch with Trott and the German opposition brought him, for the first time, into contact with the Secret Service. 'I am going to Holland ostensibly as a special correspondent of *The Times* to see various people', he told TJ [Thomas Jones] in October 1939, and 'Geoffrey Dawson

has given me the necessary credentials'. Although it had been infiltrated by an Abwehr agent, MI6 had a strong presence in The Hague, including Nicholas Elliot, later to play a crucial role in the Philby saga, and Lionel Loewe, a barrister who hoped to put David in touch with the German opposition. On his return to London, David sent Lord Halifax, the Foreign Secretary, reports from *The Times'* reporter in Rotterdam as well as a passionate plea on behalf of anti-Nazi Germans.[1]

The Rotterdam mission, of course, did not topple Hitler.

In the 1950s, Astor gave Kim Philby, who had been pushed out of MI6 as a suspected KGB mole, a job at the *Sunday Observer*. He did so at the request of Nicholas Elliot of MI6, who approached him directly. Astor later denied that he knew that either Philby or Elliot had been in MI6.

In December 1968, the Soviet newspaper *Izvestia* published a copy of a secret MI6 document which listed various MI6 assets in the British press and at the BBC, including David Astor. The document was almost certainly one of those photographed by George Blake. Blake had been employed by MI6, but had betrayed its secrets to the KGB. Oldfield's friend, Anthony Cavendish, confirmed to Stephen Dorril that the document was genuine.

While the BIA was to be run from Oxford, the cabinet office was pulling strings in the background. Astor's biographer provided a sliver of information about this when he described how: 'Years later, as a founding member of the British-Irish Association, a body set up to work for peace and reconciliation in Northern Ireland [Astor], emerged from a meeting with civil servants in the Cabinet Office, and amazed his colleagues – Marigold Johnson, Lord Longford and Anthony Kennedy – by putting four fingers in his mouth to summon a taxi in Whitehall. "I didn't learn much from Eton, but I did learn that," he told them. As always, he was being far too modest.'[2]

Conor Cruise O'Brien, the politician who had supplied details of G2 activities to Ambassador Gilchrist in 1969, was another member of the BIA. After he lost his Dáil seat in the 1977 general election, his friendship with Astor, whom he knew through the BIA, landed him the editorship-in-chief of the *Sunday Observer* newspaper, 1978–81. Astor participated in the BIA until 1990. After Haughey became taoiseach, Astor occasionally called on him in Dublin.

Garret FitzGerald of Fine Gael was a founding member of the BIA. As an established friend of the British embassy in Dublin, he was a natural recruit to its ranks. In 1970, he had been appointed as a member of a Public Accounts Committee inquiry. It was tasked with looking at how £100,000 which the Irish government had assigned for the relief of distress in Northern Ireland in 1969 had been spent. Part of this sum had been used to fund the G2 operation involving Capt. Kelly that had precipitated the Arms Crisis. FitzGerald kept the British embassy informed of at least some of their private deliberations, behind the backs of his committee colleagues. Having spoken to FitzGerald, on 18 December, 1970, Peck was able to advise London that:

> Deputy Garret FitzGerald, a member of the [Public Accounts] Committee, told us last night that the Committee intends to question all those involved in the arms trial and to publish the proceedings in full. Evidence will be taken from people in the North, whose identities will however be protected. He said that of the £100,000 or so expended, it appeared that perhaps half had been spent on genuine relief works.

> It looks increasingly as if the proceedings of the committee could
> be a re-run of the arms trial and be awkward for Messrs. Haughey
> and Blaney.[3]

FitzGerald's membership of the BIA enabled him to become
acquainted with people from the FCO. Christopher Ewart-
Biggs, who served as the FCO liaison officer with MI6 in the
1960s, was one such individual.[4] According to FitzGerald's
first autobiography, *All In A Life*:

> Early in July [1976] I had attended, as I had done most years
> since its establishment, the annual conference of the British-Irish
> Association in Britain. There I met the newly appointed British
> Ambassador to Ireland, Christopher Ewart-Biggs. I found him
> charming and unconventional, and we would, I felt, be able to
> establish a good personal relationship.[5]

Fortuitously, the BIA grew into more than a mere forum
at which British diplomats and spies could play their cloak
and dagger games. When Mo Mowlam became Secretary
of State for Northern Ireland decades later, she was able to
use it to forge links with Irish politicians, a factor that undoubtedly helped her along the path to the signing of the
Good Friday Agreement in 1998.

   Unlike the BIA, it is impossible to find anything positive
to say about another project which was manipulated by MI6,
the Institute for the Study of Conflict (ISC).

THE SMEARMEISTER FROM DOWN UNDER

Brian Crozier of the ISC was an Australian journalist. He became one of Maurice Oldfield's most energetic and successful mouthpieces in the international press. There was no slur too nasty nor so preposterous that he was not prepared to circulate it for his friend Oldfield.

Crozier was the most notable and prolific propagandist of the Cold War. In 1966, he published *The Struggle for the Third World* in which he described Ho Chi Minh as a communist 'trouble-maker' in Vietnam. Another supposed miscreant on his radar was President Sukarno of Indonesia, who had engaged in what Crozier described as a 'policy of "confrontation" with Malaysia' in conjunction with 'his Communist allies'.[1] This was the same Sukarno toppled by the machinations of Andrew Gilchrist, MI6 and the IRD in the mid-1960s. A later chapter in Crozier's 1966 book was entitled, *The Yellow Hand*, which described Chinese intrigues in Africa. At the end of the book, Crozier predicted that 'the Communist problem will last at least as long as Communist rule persists in China. The struggle for the Third World will be a protracted one.'[2]

In 1967, he published a biography of General Franco of Spain, having secured access to the government files with the permission of Franco's officials. 'It brought me at least temporary fame, and long-term hostility,' Crozier recalled in his memoirs, *Free Agent*: 'I knew there would be hostile reactions. Franco was, and remains, a hate-figure, not only on the Left but among well-thinking (*bien-pensants*) liberals, who need hate-figures to divert hostility from themselves.' Some of his colleagues 'decided to boycott me for the mere fact of having written a book on Franco that was not a denunciation'.[3]

He was also an opponent of détente.[4] He participated in the CIA coup against President Salvador Allende of Chile in 1973, as did MI6 and the IRD. Crozier boasted about his involvement in his memoirs.[5]

Crozier was born in 1918 in Queensland, Australia. His father was a mining engineer. He chose a career in journalism which took him to Jakarta, Singapore and Saigon. In Saigon, he made contact with a MI6 officer at the British embassy, whom he described in his book as 'Ronald Lincoln', a pseudonym. He also revealed that in Singapore the 'huge intelligence complex at Phoenix Park, staffed by career personnel from MI5 and MI6, became one of my prime sources of news. Acquaintances I made there blossomed into friendships in later years.' Oldfield served as deputy head of MI6's station Singapore, 1950–53, and as head, 1956–59, and surely made his acquaintance there.

Crozier maintained his contact with 'Lincoln' who provided him with confidential briefings, which gave him an edge over other journalists and helped him land the job as editor of *The Economist*'s 'Confidential' weekly bulletin *Foreign Report* in 1954. For *The Economist*, he wrote leaders, chiefly on the Far East. Simultaneously, he delivered international commentaries for the BBC's overseas broadcast service, mainly in French, and later in Spanish. He left *The Economist* at the end of February 1964, after which he 'was approached by two secret services, and within weeks by a third ... The first "secret" approach was from a long-time IRD friend, H.H. ('Tommy') Tucker. I had already turned down a full-time job proposal from him, but he now made me an offer which I accepted immediately: a part-time consultancy for the IRD.'[6] Another MI6 officer whom Crozier styled 'Ronald Franks', worked for MI6 in London. One day he invited Crozier to lunch at his club, the Athenæum, and then asked him to visit Century House. There, he was quizzed by another MI6 man he called 'Noel Cunningham':

> That day and in future days, I met a number of people whom I had talked to, in the Travellers [club] or elsewhere, in the belief that they were 'Foreign Office'. One of them I had known as a colleague when he had worked for The Economist Intelligence Unit.
>
> Later on, at Century House, I met a number of non-officials I had known for years, whose 'contact' with MI6 was similar to mine. They included academic friends of mine specialising in matters of interest to me, including Vietnam and the Soviet Union.[7]

Cunningham wanted to know if he would be prepared, 'on occasion, to write analytical reports on themes in which I specialised'. These were to include, 'international Communism and insurgencies'. This, he revealed, would grant him 'occasional access to material not publicly available'.[8] He jumped on board with alacrity.

Later again, Crozier was chosen by MI6 to head up the grandiosely titled Institute for the Study of Conflict (ISC) which pumped out black propaganda on behalf of the CIA and MI6.

In London, Crozier and Oldfield often dined together at the Athenæum.[9] They became so close that Oldfield asked Crozier to plant a bug in the office of a Spanish political figure while he was researching his book on Franco. The Australian declined, as he feared the device would be discovered.

Crozier also had links with MI5. In his memoirs, he describes how he was once asked to lunch by the director-general of MI5, Sir Michael Hanley and Dirk Hampden, MI5's head of counter-intelligence.[10]

In early 1972, Crozier and his ISC associates published the *Annual of Power and Conflict 1971, A Survey of Political Violence and International Influence*. It promoted the notion that the IRA enjoyed safe havens in the Republic and implied links between Fianna Fáil and the IRA. The paramilitaries, he pronounced, had 'sanctuaries and unofficial support from Eire which claims sovereignty over the whole island'.[11]

More pointedly, he alleged that the 'support given by the Irish Republic to the IRA was much more serious. Mr [Brian] Faulkner [prime minister of Northern Ireland] estimated that up to 85 per cent of weapons and explosives come from the Republic. The supervision by the Irish Army of their side of the border was perfunctory. The Prime Minister of the Republic, Mr Jack Lynch, whose own position is precarious and his party Fionna Fial [*sic*], has historic links with the IRA, made some moves to curb them by depriving them of TV propaganda opportunities, and by investigating the alleged corruption of custom officials after the Schiphol arms discovery in October.'[12]

There was a statement elsewhere in the annual that

Catholics at the Harland & Wolff shipyard, a notorious stronghold of loyalist militancy, had marched to demand internment, thereby implying that the shipyard was a bastion of inter-community harmony and that internment had been introduced, due in part at least, to a clamour for it by ordinary Catholics.[13] Nothing could have been further from the truth.

The plight of the 'Hooded Men', a group of detainees who had been snatched up during the internment swoops of August 1971 and subjected to an array of torture techniques, was dismissed as mere 'physical ill-treatment'.[14]

Insofar as the politics of the Republic were concerned, Crozier and the ISC were responsible for a remarkable coup: they inveigled Garret FitzGerald, a future minister for foreign affairs and taoiseach, to join one of his front organisations.

The FitzGerald-Crozier Collaboration

Garret FitzGerald wrote for *This Week*, a magazine based in Dublin which featured some of the best writers of the time.[1] Joseph O'Malley, brother of Des O'Malley, the Minister for Justice, edited it. One of Brian Crozier's achievements was to infiltrate *This Week* on at least one occasion and thereby circulate his propaganda to a wide audience in the Republic. He managed this with the assistance of FitzGerald.

On 31 August 1972, the magazine published a cover story and eleven pages which were extracted from a 160–page paperback called *The Ulster Debate*. The cover of *This Week* ran with the title: 'The Options for Peace'. The book, *The Ulster Debate*, from which the extract was taken for the magazine was a compendium of the propaganda materials which the IRD wished to circulate in Ireland and beyond. It was produced by Crozier. *The Ulster Debate* went on to sell extremely well in the Republic and can still be picked up half a century later in second-hand bookshops across the island.

Crozier secured FitzGerald's co-operation by appointing him to his ISC Study Group on Ireland (ISCSG). As a senior ISC member, FitzGerald must have been in receipt of the ISC's *Annual of Power & Conflict 1971* yet he did not recoil from its dubious content. The association was an unusual one bearing in mind Crozier's reputation, particularly his views on General Franco. Curiously, neither of FitzGerald's autobiographies addresses their relationship. The pair may have met, or learned of each other, through *The Economist* as both had contributed to it. Before his election to the Seanad in 1965, FitzGerald had worked for a string of British publications and media including the *BBC*, the *Financial Times* as well as *The Economist*.

MI6 ran the ISCSG operation. *The Ulster Debate* contained an essay by FitzGerald, whom Crozier described as a 'Barrister-at-Law, Lecturer in Economics and shadow Finance Minister in Dáil Éireann'.[2] Crozier had the pseudo-academic jargon down pat claiming loftily that the 'guiding principle of the [Irish] Study Group was realism. The outcome is a guide to the Irish problem and proposals that respect the facts and possibilities of a dangerous and delicate situation. Each paper [including that of FitzGerald] is a separate contribution. It does not necessarily reflect the view of the other members of the Study Group.'

All told, the book contained five essays, including the one by FitzGerald, along with a chronology which served as a platform from which to fire a salvo of miscellaneous smears. Charles Haughey featured in the chronology as an IRA financier, while Jack Lynch found some favour being portrayed as anti-IRA in his public pronouncements: 'The Head of the Irish Special Branch accused Mr Haughey of offering £50,000 to help the IRA. Mr Lynch told the Provisionals they had no backing for violence.'[3]

Unfortunately, attention to detail was not a hallmark of the publication. According to the chronology, on 13 October 1971, 'Cathal Goulding, Chief of Staff of the Provisionals, was sent to trial in Dublin on charges connected with the

Explosives Substances Act and the Firearms Act. He was released on bail.'[4] Goulding in fact commanded the Official IRA, the bitter rivals of the Provisionals.

On page 129 of the book, it was alleged that on 10 March 1971 a 'feud between the Officials and the Provisionals broke out into open violence. There were murderous street battles in which it was estimated that 40 to 50 members lost lives.'[5] In reality, no one died on 10 March. Six people in total perished due to the Troubles during March 1971, of whom four were British soldiers.

Canadian readers would have been perplexed to learn that on '13 December 1971, the IRA hi-jacked a Canadian aircraft but were apprehended'.[6] Nothing of the sort had happened.

International readers would have been fascinated to learn that 'an opinion poll in the Republic of Ireland showed that a majority condemned IRA bombing and would not insist on instant reunification of Ireland'.[7]

Senator Edward Kennedy received a swipe from Crozier too. At this time the Foreign Office felt Kennedy 'was trying to exploit the situation in Northern Ireland' to attract Irish votes by attacking British policy in Ireland.[8] On 20 October 1971, Kennedy famously stated in the US Senate that Northern Ireland was 'becoming Britain's Vietnam'. When Kennedy sent letters to the press in Britain which the FCO felt were hostile, 'counter material was put into the media *via* various IRD contacts, including Lord Wavell Wakefield'.[9] Crozier used *The Ulster Debate* to nip at Kennedy by implying he that was not held in high esteem at the State Department. Crozier alleged that on 20 November 1971 a 'Senatorial resolution co-sponsored by Senator Edward Kennedy called for the withdrawal of British troops. The State Department repudiated the statement.'[10]

The allegation that IRA activists could find a safe haven in the Republic – something mentioned in the ISC's 1971 Annual Report – was regurgitated in *The Ulster Debate*.[11] There was a retelling of the yarn that Catholics in Belfast had marched for internment on 13 March 1971. This time it was claimed that: 'Over 6,000 shipyard workers, Protestant and Catholic march through the streets of Belfast to demand the internment of the IRA.'[12]

There was no mention of the white noise, beatings and injections that had been administered to prisoners after internment. Instead, it was contended that all that had occurred was the 'physical ill-treatment of a small proportion of internees'.[13]

The Civil Rights movement and the CDCs were tarred with the communist brush.[14]

One group that came out of *The Ulster Debate* well was the Parachute Regiment which had received much criticism after Bloody Sunday. According to Crozier, on 2 October 1971 a 'paratrooper gave his life in an effort to save some children'.[15] In reality, no one died on 2 October 1971, let alone a paratrooper.

A 'clear' account of Bloody Sunday, one that could be relied upon 'beyond doubt', was put forward by Lord Chalfont, minister of state for foreign and commonwealth affairs, 1964–70, in his paper: the IRA had been responsible for starting the violence of that day.[16] He blamed their tactic of using 'mobs as shelter for ambushes and snipers' something that 'sooner or later' was inevitably going to lead to 'a tragedy'. When this happens 'another weapon in the armoury of terrorism comes into its own – the weapon of propaganda. The actions of the security forces in London was the subject of unceasing IRA propaganda both before and after the Widgery Report was published, and much of it was swallowed whole in sections of the British press.'[17]

Garret FitzGerald addressed Bloody Sunday too, stating that 'against this long-term background the present unhappy state of Anglo-Irish relations can be seen as an aberration. An almost total – and unprecedented – failure of communications between the two countries.' He felt that the shootings in Derry had 'created a momentary mutual hostility that is uncharacteristic of their normal complex but basically friendly relationship with each other. That this could have happened in the face of the means of mass communications now available is astonishing and indeed deeply worrying. Past experience suggests, however, that in time the misunderstandings caused by such communications blockages will be dissipated.'[18]

FitzGerald looked to the future, opining that membership of the EEC might help alleviate the friction between Britain and Ireland. He pointed to a statement made by Prof. Ralf Dahrendorf, the EEC's Commissioner for External Relations, and argued that while 'the example of Londonderry [i.e., Bloody Sunday] was an important one; the participation of Great Britain and Ireland in the Community would not solve the Irish problem, but it will diminish the intensity'.[19]

Crozier did not refer to either FitzGerald or *The Ulster Debate* in his 1993 memoirs.

MI6 maintained a strong grip over the ISC. In 1977, Edward Peck, formerly of MI6 and chairman of the JIC, 1968–70, became one of its council members.

SMEARING JOHN HUME

John Hume of the SDLP became another target of British intelligence smears. Hugh Mooney, of the IRD, and Brian Crozier, of the ISC, led the assault.

The FCO did not like the fact that Hume was making trips to Washington where he was forging relations with the likes of Tip O'Neill, Ted Kennedy and other senior US politicians. Seán Donlon, who was Irish Consul General in Boston from 1969–71, has explained how Hume realised that he was 'going to have to break into the Washington scene ... I think very quickly John began to focus on: Where is the power? Who has the power? How can I enter that zone of power?'[1]

Another former Irish diplomat, Michael Lillis, has pointed out that the US President, the Secretary of State and the State Department are the 'three offices of the United States, which actually make up the foreign policy of America'. Before Hume's intervention they were 'completely controlled by the British. The British had enormous influence in Washington, more than any other country in the world.'[2]

According to Hume's biographer, Barry White, the British 'watched from a distance, wary that he might try to prise the US State Department away from its pro-London, anti-interventionist line. Indeed, it was partly to break the State Department's hold on policy that Hume concentrated on the politicians, who in America wield real power.' In his book, *John Hume in America*, Maurice Fitzpatrick summed up Hume's attitude thus:

For John Hume, it was clear that the British retention of a monopoly on Washington meant that their interests and their perspective on Northern Ireland would continue to be furthered, to the detriment of a fair solution. Somehow, a channel needed to be created to access the White House (which had been markedly unused during the JFK presidency), to break the indifference in Washington towards Ireland, an intransigence which was replicated in British policy towards the Northern minority.[3]

Adding insult to these political injuries – as the British establishment would have perceived it – Hume had helped smuggle details about the maltreatment of internees to *The Sunday Times,* in 1971, causing an international uproar.

Bloody Sunday occurred on 30 January 1972. The funerals of eleven of the victims took place on 2 February. Charles Haughey travelled to Derry for the ceremony, as did many other Dáil politicians. Haughey paid a visit to Hume's home in Derry on the morning of the burials. The picture Oldfield wanted to paint of Hume's post-Bloody Sunday efforts, however, was that of a wanted man. The entry for 16 February 1972 in Crozier's *Ulster Debate* made just such an assertion. It was silent about the crime he had allegedly committed, merely stating that a 'summons was served on Mr John Hume in the Bogside, by police escorted by armoured cars'.[4]

Some of Hume's US visits were as chairman of the Northern Ireland Resurgence Fund (NIRF), a charity which raised funds to encourage employment and self-help projects in Belfast. One of its early initiatives was to raise money to re-build Bombay Street, which rampaging loyalist mobs had torched in 1969. In August 1972, Mooney claimed some of the money raised by the NIRF had been diverted to the IRA while Hume had carved off a slice for himself.

The IRD's forgers manufactured a bank account purporting to show how Hume had stolen money from various US charities. A briefing paper was concocted which linked the Derry man with IRA fundraisers and hinted that he had stolen money which had been donated by the Ancient Order of Hibernians in America. According to the paper, Hume 'received 10,000 dollars'. Scribbled alongside this in red ink was 'see bank a/c'. The briefing paper was shown to certain American reporters.[5]

The slur oozed its way into *The Christian Science Monitor*, an international publication which, while it was available on subscription, was also distributed to influential political figures throughout the world free of charge. It is not clear how the publication could have afforded such generosity. The Hume story festered and spread until Hume was obliged to denounce it.

Various publications exposed the activities of Crozier in the mid-1970s. Anthony Crosland, the Labour Party Foreign Secretary, 1976–77, became concerned and began to make inquiries about the FCO's links to Crozier. In his book, *Free Agent*, Crozier recounted how Crosland instructed Oldfield to furnish him with 'background material' on Crozier. According to the Australian, Oldfield responded with a memorandum about his 'past informal contacts' with MI6. Then, in a stroke of luck for the Australian, Crosland died suddenly in mid-February 1977. 'Maurice told me', he wrote, 'that after Crosland's death the memorandum on my activities had been retrieved, by means which he left unstated. I never set eyes on it.'[6]

In April 1987, Barry Penrose of *The Sunday Times* confronted Mooney with the Hume briefing paper. At first, he denied he had written it or had seen the forged bank account. Later, afraid to be caught out in a lie, he conceded the handwriting on it 'could be' his.

IPU's propagandists also had a low opinion of Hume's political party, the SDLP. Col Maurice Tugwell, the man in charge of the IPU in the early 1970s, did not, however, understand much about Ireland. He revealed his rather peculiar thoughts in a secret internal report. It stated that both wings of the IRA had 'numerous front organisations' which disseminated propaganda on their behalf. One of these, he believed, was Hume's SDLP. Other groups 'willing to spread' IRA propaganda ranged from the Central CDC which was 'now heavily involved in promoting IRA interests' to *The Irish News*, 'a newspaper that has long represented Republican opinion in Ulster and is now an organ for printing IRA propaganda'.[7] Tugwell believed that the IRA could rely upon 'RTE and newspapers in the Republic to varying degrees, with *The Irish Press* particularly active'. The colonel was of the unsettling view that the 'indigenous Irish, once convinced that their cause is just, possess a breath-taking ability to lie with absolute conviction, not just in support of something they believe to be true, but to put across a story they know very well is untrue'.[8] The undeniable fact that part of Tugwell's brief was to dissemble seems to have been completely lost on him.

Gerry L'Estrange was suspicious about RTÉ too. He gave an interview to *This Week* in July 1972. The magazine described him as 'a political muckraker in the American journalistic sense of that term. He revels in the unveiling of political scandal, often coming dangerously close to abusing Dáil privilege in so doing. Those on the Government side see him as a political court jester, with a talent for sensational statements and outlandish criticisms. This talent has led to his being ordered out of the House more frequently than most back benchers. His latest obsession has been with subversives in RTE, largely unsubstantiated claims on I.R.A. bias in the media.' During the interview, L'Estrange described how he 'likes [his] confidential leads to be signed and indeed they normally are. He could only recall, he said, one anonymous document on which he acted.' His sources included 'Civil servants' whom he explained 'are often annoyed about decisions which have been taken. I have even been sent files out of Departments'. He did not volunteer a description of the source who had fed him the mendacities about the alleged garda driver who had spirited the killer of Garda Fallon to safety.[9] Declassified records disclose that Ambassador Gilchrist was one of those who fed him ideas, e.g., about the anti-British propaganda run by George Colley in 1969.

'It Has to be Deniable in the Dáil'

By the start of 1972, the Joint Intelligence Committee (JIC), the body that collects and assesses the information gathered by the various wings of British intelligence, was dividing Fianna Fáil into two camps, the moderates led by Jack Lynch, and 'the extremists' which included Charles Haughey and others.[1] The term 'extremists' underlines the hostility that was mounting against Haughey in London.

The JIC was relying on Maurice Oldfield and the diplomats at the Dublin embassy to keep it apprised of what was afoot inside Fianna Fáil. One of the committee's reports, from early 1972, recorded that Lynch's long-term aim was, and would continue to be, reunification, perhaps 'under a new constitution'. Describing the campaign by the IRA, they asserted that Lynch was thought to have had a 'strong political interest' in seeing the present situation brought to an end because it weakened his own position 'as against the extremists in his own party and outside'. The JIC also felt that the IRA's campaign was 'already starting to bring about a deterioration in the internal situation in the Republic which must eventually endanger the democratic system'.[2]

In the shadows, Oldfield was busily exploiting the turmoil in the Republic to spur Lynch on to enact effective anti-IRA legislation. During most of 1972, Oldfield ran two *agents provocateurs*, Kenneth and Keith Littlejohn in the Republic. Kenneth was a former paratrooper with a criminal record. On the ground, they were handled by John Wyman and, later, someone the brothers knew only as 'Oliver'. Some of the Littlejohns' tasks were to carry out bank robberies and attack garda stations. They petrol bombed at least two garda stations as the year unfolded. During the course of their mission, they behaved as if they were an IRA active service unit. Some members of a gang they formed had once been involved with the Official IRA. The object of this endeavour was to turn public opinion against republicans and create an appetite for stronger anti-IRA legislation. The impression is that Oldfield felt that the revulsion and anger generated by the slaying of Garda Fallon could be recreated with the deployment of the Littlejohns.

Meanwhile, Ted Heath was applying pressure on Lynch at the inter-governmental level. On 25 April 1972, he wrote to the taoiseach urging the immediate creation of security co-operation along the border. When questions were raised in the Dáil about his communications with Heath, Lynch denied that co-operation was broached.[3] Admirers of Jack Lynch's standing as a man of impeccable integrity will be disappointed to learn that behind closed doors Lynch was telling Peck that he agreed that 'discreet collaboration was clearly called for'.[4]

In what must have been music to Oldfield's ears, that same month Lynch gave Peck what he interpreted as *carte blanche* to pursue the establishment of security co-operation directly with the Departments of Defence and Justice in Dublin. Peck sent a telegram to London stating that the co-operation would be 'mutual and discreet, bearing in mind that it has to be deniable in the Dáil'. Afterwards, there was a meeting to kick-start the co-operation between the chief-of-staff of the Irish Army and the military attaché at the British embassy.[5] The point of contact for Peck at the Department of Justice was Andy Ward.

The following month, Lynch reinstated the Special Criminal Court by reactivating part V of the Offences Against the State Act, 1939. The court consisted of three judges who sat without a jury to determine charges brought against paramilitaries.

In October, section 31 of the same piece of legislation was used to prevent RTÉ from broadcasting any material that might promote or encourage violence. Sinn Féin's HQ was raided and shut down.

That same month the largest bank raid in the history of the state took place, perpetrated by the Littlejohn brothers. £67,000 was swiped from the AIB bank on Grafton Street at gunpoint during the second week of October. After the raid, the Littlejohns returned to England.[6]

It would take a while for the truth about the AIB heist to emerge. In the meantime, behind closed doors, Lynch strove to assure London that he was serious about curbing the paramilitaries. On 23 October, he spoke to Peck, who sent a revealing 'secret' report back to Kelvin White in London, the following day, about an obstacle to the security of the nation – at least in Lynch's eyes – but it was one he had resolved:

> … I said we had all been interested in rumours that the Minister for Justice [Des O'Malley] was going to introduce new legislation early in the current session of the Dáil. The Taoiseach replied, 'Well, I don't know about new legislation. Our quarrel is not

with the law but with the lawyers. We have a standing group of seven barristers working with us to see how the safeguards in our Constitution need not be used by [Chief Justice Cearbhall] Ó Dálaigh's boys [*a reference to the Supreme Court*] to block security measures – anyway you have seen that we have shunted Ó Dálaigh into Europe.

Peck added that this was the 'first indication I have had that the Chief Justice, who is a dedicated lawyer, historian and exponent of the Irish language, was regarded by the Fianna Fáil Government as an obstacle to internal security measures.'

Since Lynch's discussion with Peck was confidential, he was able to feign outrage, when, in 1976, Fine Gael's Minister for Defence, Paddy Donegan, called Ó Dálaigh, who was then president of Ireland, a 'thundering disgrace', in the wake of his referral of the Emergency Powers Bill to the Supreme Court to test its constitutionality.

Lynch also told Peck that he had sent Des O'Malley, Minister for Justice, to America to dissuade Irish-Americans from donating money to Noraid, the organisation that raised money for republicans. According to Lynch, O'Malley's mission was to steer their funds 'into genuinely charitable channels, and not into the purchase of arms'.

A momentous event took place at the end of 1972, the infamous bombing of Dublin on 1 December. Many senior gardaí and an array of Irish politicians concluded that British intelligence was behind the attack. Two people died and 127 were injured. Jack Lynch was one of those suspicious of British involvement in the attack. One consequence of the attack was that it cost Fianna Fáil victory in the general election that followed in February 1973.

The bombing took place on the night the Offences Against the State bill came before the Dáil facing almost certain defeat. The newspapers predicted a snap election for later in the month. Fine Gael was in disarray with Garret FitzGerald plotting the downfall of Liam Cosgrave. Then, two bombs exploded in Dublin and the bill mustered enough votes and abstentions to succeed. Had a general election taken place, the consensus was that Lynch would have won it. Although his party increased its share of the vote in the election that followed in February, it still lost power because Fine Gael and Labour used the intervening months to hammer out a vote transfer pact which gave them the advantage, even with Labour's vote decreasing. There would have been no such pact if an election had taken place in December 1972.

At least one of the loyalist paramilitaries involved in the preparations for the attack on Dublin was a British agent – Albert Baker.[7] In 1976, his brother told Frank Doherty of *The Sunday World* that a member of the UDA in Derry had supplied the explosives used in the bombing and that Baker had brought them from Derry to Belfast. According to the *Sunday World* report, the Derry UDA man 'had a close association with British Intelligence'. There is also evidence that implicates the UVF in the attack.[8]

While Lynch's defeat in the 1973 general election weakened his position within Fianna Fáil, it did not cost him the leadership of the party. Haughey meanwhile had topped the poll in his constituency with a massive majority and the prospect of a return to the front bench improved with each passing day.

The activities of British agents remained very much to the fore of Lynch's mind. In August 1973, the Littlejohns were convicted of the armed robbery on Grafton Street. Lynch now made an astounding statement to Ulster Television about the Dublin bombing of December 1972:

> Well my suspicions naturally are more aroused now, we have no, as I said, indication who was responsible [for the bombings] and it is now well known a lot of people in Ireland believe that many of these unexplained activities and actions could well be related to British Intelligence or other activities of that nature.

It is not possible to imagine a more serious accusation being levelled by a significant political figure against a department of the government of his nation's nearest neighbour. If there was substance in his misgivings, it must have alarmed Oldfield and his accomplices as their role in the affair was beginning to unravel. If Lynch was wrong, their blood should have boiled at the egregious insult. At the time Lynch made the remarks, Oldfield was experiencing difficulties with some of his staff, especially MI6's pool of secretaries, who were deeply upset at reports in the media of Kenneth Littlejohn's revelation that he had been asked to engage in assassination operations in Ireland on behalf of MI6. In response, Oldfield had gathered his staff together in the top floor canteen at his HQ, Century House, to assure them they were not part of a murderous criminal enterprise.[9]

The Dublin Molehill

Ambassador Peck had urged his staff at the Dublin embassy to seek out information from a 'multitude of informants' including 'civil servants'.[1] Maurice Oldfield was fishing in the same waters, but at a deeper level. His biographer, Richard Deacon[2] wrote that in the 1970s the spymaster had enjoyed 'some quiet successes' on both sides of the Irish border and attributed 'the comprehensiveness of certain of the Service's intelligence reports' to a network of 'agents and informants inside the Garda (Irish Republican police), the Irish Army and some Republic government departments'.[3]

Deacon, a former intelligence officer, was an informed and credible source of information about Oldfield. Their relationship had begun in 1974 after Deacon published a book on the Chinese Secret Service, which so impressed the MI6 chief that he approached the author and they became friends. Much of Deacon's biography of the spymaster was based on information provided by Oldfield and Anthony Cavendish. The book emerged three years after Oldfield's death. One of the motivating factors in the provision of information to Deacon was to counteract a campaign to discredit Oldfield run by a right-wing faction inside MI5 known as the 'Ultras'. While Oldfield's friends had a motive to inflate his accomplishments, there is corroboration for the claim made by Deacon that gardaí supplied MI6 with classified information. Furthermore, a number of cables sent by the US embassy to Washington raise the possibility that some at the DoJ had an unhealthy relationship with MI6.

Peter Evans was a key part of Oldfield's information-gathering apparatus. According to a source who worked with MI6 in the 1970s, Evans forged links with garda special branch and military officers during his assignment to Dublin. He also developed relationships with journalists in Dublin who had insights into what was going on behind closed doors. Evans was not the only MI6 officer at the embassy. Andrew Johnstone, who arrived in 1971, was another.[4] In addition, John Wyman was running the Littlejohns 'in the field' and liaising with Patrick Crinnion of C3.

Additionally, a number of people with information about the IRA – some possibly even members of the organisation – were furnishing reports to MI6. A military officer on attachment to MI6 in Northern Ireland travelled around the Republic to collect reports from them. 'They were often left in milk churns. In Russia you had dead letter boxes, in Ireland it was milk churns.'[5]

All of this information was pooled to compile a dossier that described the structure and activities of the IRA in the border region. The plan was to slam the dossier damningly on Lynch's desk and embarrass him into taking action against the men of violence. The end product became known as the Border Dossier. Kelvin White gave Anthony Craig an outline of what the British were trying to achieve with the document when he stated that the 'Irish government would have had to explain why it had acted as an accessory before the fact to [IRA] murder'.[6]

The dossier reflected one of the propaganda themes

Crozier had highlighted in *The Ulster Debate*, namely that 85 per cent of the IRA's arsenal had come from the Republic and that the 'supervision [of arms smuggling] by the Irish Army of their side of the border was perfunctory'.[7]

William Whitelaw, Secretary of State for Northern Ireland, and his spy chief at Stormont Castle, Allan Rowley of MI6, were centrally involved in the scheme. In a secret communication dated 21 November 1972, Whitelaw told Heath that the document showed 'exactly who, where and in what strength the IRA border units are, and what they are doing'. The Border Dossier relied heavily on material drawn from C3's Monthly Confidential Reports. They were written at Garda HQ and delivered by hand to Andy Ward at the DoJ. Once they reached him, they could flow onwards to government ministers in certain circumstances. All told, dozens of people had access to them as they meandered along the distribution pipeline.

MI6's milk churn network was far too small to account for the comprehensive nature of the dossier. The majority of detail must have emanated from the C3 reports.

The Border Dossier was passed to Peck who furnished a copy to the Irish government on 22 November 1972. Lynch's reaction to it was not quite what Heath, Whitelaw, Oldfield, Rowley and Evans had expected: Lynch realised there was a 'spy in the camp'. He must have feared that evidence that a government source was co-operating with London would be uncovered. He did not want to be implicated in the affair. He had warned Peck with impressive foresight the previous April that the security and intelligence co-operation to which he was giving a green light was to be 'deniable in the Dáil'. Lynch picked up the phone and spoke to John Fleming, head of the special branch, in his office at Dublin Castle and ordered him to run the source to ground. There are disturbing behavioural parallels between what Lynch was now doing and what he had done after the Arms Crisis erupted: he was feigning ignorance about what had been going on whilst pushing forward others into the firing line.

The perceived wisdom for decades has been that the source of the information in the dossier was Patrick Crinnion of C3 at Garda HQ in the Phoenix Park. Crinnion was arrested at Jurys hotel in December 1972 during an attempt to rendezvous with John Wyman. Both men were convicted of minor charges in February 1973 and released for time served. The more serious charges against Crinnion were dropped. There are substantial reasons to believe he was no more than a convenient scapegoat for the leaks. For a start, information continued to flow from Dublin to London long after his arrest.

The Crinnion affair is a hugely complex one, far beyond the scope of this book. For present purposes, it suffices to note that the Border Dossier affair is the tenth indication of the presence of a network of moles at the heart of the Irish state security apparatus.

The initial two pointers are faint. First, that the names of the new leadership of the Provisional Republican Movement were furnished to Ambassador Gilchrist within hours of the Sinn Féin split in January 1970. These names were relayed to garda special branch and the DoJ within the same timeframe.

Second, the possibility that MI6 was alerted to the existence of the Irish Army training programme at Fort Dunree by a government source in Dublin.

The third trace is a more substantial one: the accuracy of the information at the disposal of Capt. Markham-Randall in November 1969, relating to the CDC–G2 arms procurement operation including the name of the fictitious 'Dixon' bank account.

Fourth, the reference to a 'source' in the Ronnie Burroughs memorandum of 17 June 1970.

Fifth, the dubious nature of Peck's memoirs in which he denied any knowledge of G2 arms procurement operation before media reports emerged in May 1970. This has the appearance of a ruse designed to cover-up any hint of the embassy's access to sensitive information from the gardaí and DoJ.

Sixth, the existence of someone who was able to alert London to the trip that Jock and Kitty Haughey were about to take to Portugal in October 1970.

Seventh, the person, or people, who were able to convince Gerry L'Estrange, TD, that a garda driver helped the alleged killer of Garda Fallon escape in a ministerial car.

Eighth, the existence of 'an authoritative source in the Irish government' who fed Virgil Randolph III disinformation about a non-existent IRA splinter group run by Neil Blaney, as part of a sophisticated black propaganda operation against the politician.

Ninth, the reference to Oldfield's access to a network of sources consisting of 'some Republic government departments' in Deacon's biography of the spymaster.

The foregoing list is not exhaustive; there are more indicators that a British spy ring penetrated official Irish circles. The issue will be examined in later chapters. An array of yet further pointers involving the gardaí exists, details of which are beyond the scope of the present book.

While London was praying for Lynch's political survival, Haughey was not finding any favour among the ranks of Oldfield and his associates. During the next decade, British diplomats, spies and propagandists would target him relentlessly in an effort to derail his quest for rehabilitation and his ambition to become taoiseach. A mole, or moles, inside the Irish government would assist them.

THE SPOOKS IN THE CASTLE

The Information Research Department (IRD) of the FCO ran psychological operations ('Psy Ops') for the Foreign Office, most of which revolved around the dissemination of propaganda. It was deployed to Northern Ireland in the early 1970s. Another group, with a similar name and function, the Information Policy Unit (IPU), was responsible for running British Army's Psy Ops in Northern Ireland.

The essential difference between the IRD and the IPU was that the army's operatives devoted their time and energy to the fight against paramilitaries, whereas the IRD had politicians, such as Haughey, John Hume and Ian Paisley, in their sights as well as the gunmen. The IRD also viewed the world in Cold War terms whereas the army did not.

The army viewed the IRD as something akin to a cuckoo in its nest. 'No one wanted the IRD on their patch. They were political animals, but they needed a cover for what they were doing', recalls Colin Wallace, who worked with the British army's IPU.

Hugh Mooney of the IRD was never attached to the IPU, despite reports to the contrary.[1] The confusion is not the fault of reporters as he was 'accommodated' by it as part of his cover. According to Wallace, Mooney 'was just accommodated in the IPU because it was the logical place for him to be in that there was some spin-off for the British army in terms of political guidance. The IRD was created to counter Soviet expansion globally. Its role was political warfare.'[2]

At this time, the IRD was under threat from within Whitehall where its budget and staff were being cut by more than a half. As a result, the IRD welcomed a role in Northern Ireland. Mooney told the Saville Inquiry that the Northern Ireland crisis 'promised salvation', but he admitted that the role 'would probably end in disaster' for the IRD. According to Wallace, 'to justify its existence [to Whitehall], [the IRD] repeatedly overstated the significance of Soviet interference in the war in Ireland'.

In a letter dated 15 July 1972 to Philip Woodfield, a senior official at the Northern Ireland Office, Stewart Crawford, deputy under-secretary of state at the FCO, overseeing intelligence and security work, argued in favour of applying 'the IRD techniques of indirect, and where necessary covert, propaganda designed to counter hostile threats' in Northern Ireland.

Edward Heath was one of the driving forces behind the deployment of the IRD to Ireland. He told Lord Widgery who ran the first Bloody Sunday tribunal that 'we were in Northern Ireland fighting not only a military war, but a propaganda war'. The IRD derived its authority for its dirty tricks campaign in Ireland from a letter written by Robert Armstrong on 7 August 1972. Armstrong, who was Heath's personal private secretary, made it clear that 'the Prime Minister wanted to get hold of those who are ex-perienced in psychological warfare' and that 'he would like to see the place flooded with them'. Armstrong went on to say, the prime minister 'wanted an immediate, sustained, and continuing effort every day'. This would involve 'using money freely' to gain information, win friends and influence people.

The IRD had answered to the UK REP before direct rule was introduced in April 1972, thereafter to the secretary of state. The first holder of that office was William Whitelaw who was was based at Stormont Castle. The director and controller of intelligence (DCI), who oversaw all espionage activities, worked in the same building as Whitelaw. The first DCI was Allan Rowley of MI6. His team occupied the top floor of the castle. Born in 1922, Rowley had joined MI6 in November 1948 having won the military Cross in Burma at the end of the war, and had served in Egypt, Addis Ababa, Turkey and Rangoon. He served in Singapore, 1955–57 while Oldfield was MI6 Head of Station. His official designation was that of an under-secretary at the NIO. According to his successor, Denis Payne of MI5, Rowley carried out his duties 'in tremendous style … He lived like a king, he entertained like a king, he used to drink with Willie [Whitelaw] all night.'[3] He spent a year in Belfast.[4] Rowley most likely discussed the plots against Haughey with Whitelaw.

The work of the IPU and IRD overlapped to some degree. Hence, joint meetings took place on a regular basis at Stormont Castle out of sight and earshot of the Northern Ireland civil servants who were based elsewhere. Colin Wallace attended many of these. 'There were conference rooms on the ground floor for our meetings,' Wallace recalls. 'Security was tight. The rooms were "sanitised" in the sense that documents were not left lying around the building, unlike normal departments. The higher up you went inside the castle, the more important the office and the official occupying it became. Since visitors were not allowed upstairs, the officials on the higher levels could feel secure in the knowledge that no unauthorised people were in the vicinity. The conference rooms were pleasant places, well appointed. They had large tables and pictures on the walls. The meetings were often little more than "superficial" rubber stamping operations. Many of the decisions were already taken. The meetings lasted 90 to 120 minutes unless there was something pressing.' The language used at the meetings was often euphemistic. 'Wouldn't it be useful if X might do Y, that sort of thing. There was a lot of plausibly deniable behaviour.'

Cliff Hill and Hugh Mooney represented the IRD at the Stormont Castle conferences. Charles Haughey often featured on the agenda. Wallace and his army colleagues felt the IRD was unduly focused on smoke and mirror ploys to undermine Haughey. 'We wanted to take on the paramilitaries. We couldn't have cared less about Charlie Haughey. We couldn't understand [the IRD's] obsession with him,' Wallace has revealed.[5]

Ian Paisley was another target. In 1990, Michael Taylor, who also worked for the IPU stated: 'I saw forged documents, for instance that the Reverend Ian Paisley had a bank account in Canada.'

It emerged from these meetings – and discussions on the margins – that the IRD deemed Haughey a 'potential problem' for at least three reasons. Firstly, there were his suspected links to the Provisional IRA. Secondly, his threat to Jack Lynch's leadership of Fianna Fáil. At the time, Lynch was in London's good books as he was co-operating with the joint application by the UK and Ireland to join the EEC. Thirdly, there was a fear that if Harold Wilson returned to power and Haughey was taoiseach, they would hammer out a deal to reunify the country. That did not appeal to the right-wing hardline unionists at the castle.

Wilson, as leader of the British opposition, had met Jack Lynch in Dublin in November 1971. According to Wilson's press secretary, Joe Haines:

> At lunch with Mr Lynch, Harold Wilson aired some of the propositions he was later in the month to include in a fifteen-point plan for solving the problem of Northern Ireland: Ireland to rejoin the Commonwealth (a nonsense from which I was unable to budge him in an argument which the night before had gone on until nearly 3 a.m. in the hotel) and Irish unity, fifteen years after agreement upon it … The fascinating moment at the Taoiseach's lunch came when Harold Wilson put forward the plan for turning the dream of unity into reality. I had thought they would jump for joy. But their reaction was more akin to falling through the floor.[6]

Haughey, however, was deemed far more likely to embrace Wilson's vision. On 4 October 1969, Haughey had informed Ambassador Gilchrist that there was nothing he would not sacrifice to achieve a United Ireland, including Ireland rejoining the Commonwealth. Gilchrist had advised the FCO of this and stressed that, 'Mr Haughey's passion for Irish unity [was] greater than that of Jack Lynch and Patrick Hillery'.[7]

All of this put Haughey firmly in the IRD's crosshairs. 'When it came to Mr. Haughey, the tactic was a constant drip of negative information. They spoke to journalists and other opinion-makers at places such as the Europa Hotel. The idea was that people would eventually conclude that some of the dirt had to be true. This type of low-level offensive was seen as more likely to be effective than a focus on one major revelation. The IRD collected all sorts of trivia about Mr. Haughey from everywhere. They tried to stick it to him. The Dublin embassy was feeding the IRD with material on him too which wound its way to the North.'

During the Arms Crisis, Haughey had been hospitalised after a horse-riding accident. Wallace recalls that in 1972 the IRD studied rumours that Haughey had been hit over the head with a hurling stick 'by the husband of a woman' with whom he was allegedly having an affair.[8] Wallace says the hurling stick rumour was 'deployed later as part of a plan to draw public attention to Haughey's alleged "lack of morality"'.

Lurid rumours about the horse-riding accident persist to this day despite the fact that Haughey's daughter has long since gone on record stating that she was present on the morning of his fall and witnessed with her own eyes the condition of her father directly after it.

Another story doing the rounds was that Haughey had been involved in a 'punch-up with Eamon Andrews over an insult given to the latter's wife', something that 'made good beer talk in the bars and lounges of Dublin'.[9] Andrews was the host of the immensely popular *This Is Your Life*, show. Andrews was so annoyed about the slur, he eventually sued a newspaper that published the story. In later years the yarn mutated into a brawl between Haughey and Freddie Forsyth, the famous thriller writer. Forsyth in fact was a friend of Haughey's and wrote fondly of him after the politician's death.

A LICENCE TO DECEIVE

In Ireland, gossip-mongering, embellishment and conspiracy theorising are national pastimes. For officers of an organisation such as the IRD, the best smears to exploit are those that have already taken root in the soil of their target audience. In Ireland the smearmeisters did not have to dig to unearth dirt for their surreptitious intrigues, there was plenty of it being flung around by the locals already. The most effective smear the IRD directed against Haughey was one that had been in circulation for a number of years, namely that Fianna Fáil was linked to the IRA.

The first version of the Fianna Fáil-IRA conspiracy theory was concocted by William McGrath, one of Ian Paisley's more menacing lieutenants. Paisley and McGrath were incorrigible conspirators and exponents of sinister dirty tricks. They were key players in a series of loyalist 'false flag' bombings in Belfast in April 1969, i.e., they carried them out but blamed others. The pro-Paisley newspaper, *The Protestant Telegraph*, declared that a source 'close to [Stormont] Government circles' had informed the paper that a purported 'secret dossier' on the Castlereagh electricity sub-station explosion allegedly contained 'startling documentation and facts. Original reports suggested that the IRA could have been responsible, but in Parliament no such definite statement would be made ... We are told that the Ministry of Home Affairs is examining reports which implicate the Eire Government in the £2 million act of sabotage – By actively precipitating a crisis in

Ulster [*sic*], the Eire Government can make capital, win or lose. The facts, we hope, will be made public, thereby exposing the chicanery of the Dublin regime.' There was not one word of truth anywhere in this report.

McGrath used David Browne, the deputy editor of *The Protestant Telegraph*, to get his fabrication published in the paper. Browne had been present at a meeting in McGrath's house on the Upper Newtownards Road a few hours after one of the April 1969 bombs had exploded. At that gathering, McGrath had asserted that the attack had been carried out by a special unit attached to the Irish Army, nominating a figment of his imagination called Major Farrell as its leader. Farrell's mission, he alleged, was to destabilise Northern Ireland as a precursor to an invasion by the Republic. Browne later became editor of the newspaper.[1]

McGrath's conspiracy theory of a Fianna Fáil–IRA partnership has mutated over the years to become an accepted fact in the minds of many unionists, a string of respected historians and countless political commentators on both sides of the border. As late as 2021, *The Irish Times* was still reporting that Haughey had tried to import weapons for the Provisional IRA. Few of those who cling to the belief Haughey was an IRA godfather appreciate they are regurgitating the paranoid ravings of one of Northern Ireland's most notorious liars and hate-mongers, not to mention a brutal rapist of boys as young as ten years of age.

Suffice it to say, additional fuel was added to the Fianna Fáil–IRA theme by the webs of deceit which were spun during and after the Arms Crisis. When Chief Inspector

John Fleming testified at the Public Accounts Committee in 1971, he regurgitated some of the lies that Seán MacStíofáin had fed to the Special Branch about Haughey's links to the IRA. According to this version, Haughey was in league with Goulding to whom he allegedly gave £50,000. Somehow, this added ballast to the Haughey–Provisional IRA fable, at least among people who did not understand there was a difference between the Provisionals and the Officials.

Official Sinn Féin came up with another variation of the Fianna Fáil–IRA myth. It was circulated in a 1971 pamphlet, *Fianna Fáil and the IRA* and later again in a 68–page booklet, *Fianna Fáil, the IRA Connection*, printed in 1973. Official Sinn Féin alleged Haughey was guilty of attempting to import arms illegally and that Fianna Fáil set up the Provisional IRA. Stories circulated later in British intelligence circles that Dick Walsh had contributed some of the information included in the 1971 pamphlet. The fact that Walsh was an agent of Goulding, had made his name writing about the Arms Crisis for *The Irish Times*, and wrote a book about the affair, lends credence to this conclusion. Walsh, however, was not a reliable reporter of these events. The pamphlet promoted Goulding's conspiracy theory that Fianna Fáil created the Provisional IRA.

Neil Blaney became the subject of another reworking of the tale, the one fed to Virgil Randolph III at the US embassy in May 1971. It maintained the Donegal man had set up his own 'private' IRA.

In 1972, the IRD officers at Stormont Castle decided to jump on the Fianna Fáil–IRA bandwagon by reprinting

Official Sinn Féin's *Fianna Fáil and the I.R.A.* pamphlet. Hugh Mooney had a tattered copy of the pamphlet and decided to have it retyped before it fell apart. He gave it to Christopher Whitehead, an official from the MoD who was on a temporary assignment before a deployment to Germany.[2] A copy Whitehead produced was taken to the IRD's HQ at Riverbank House, in London, where the counterfeiters replicated it, but with subtle alterations designed to reinforce the image of Charles Haughey as a Provisional IRA godfather.

The IRD version included the entire content of the original document but was laid out in such a way as to make space for a few additions of their own. The compression technique can be viewed *via* the internet link contained in the footnote at the end of this sentence.[3] The extra space permitted Mooney to insert a new paragraph, on page 19 of the forgery, that contained a variety of allegations designed to call Haughey's integrity into question.

The replicated copy claimed that Haughey was in control of the Provisional IRA 'which he will almost certainly use to undermine Lynch and thus open the door to him becoming Taoiseach'.

In addition, the IRD version maintained that, 'Haughey is also said to be siphoning off huge sums of money donated by emotionally involved Americans and others who generously support the victims of the current pogroms in the North. It is estimated that for every dollar donated by well-meaning Americans, at least 50 cent goes into Haughey's coffers.' None of this was true. The charge that Haughey was collecting money in the US and pocketing half of it was concocted with an eye to Irish-American politicians in Washington. British diplomats and agents in the US capital disseminated copies of the pamphlet.

Mooney added that Haughey's 'skills as an accountant have enabled him to amass unexplained wealth by a network of corruption and by the misuse of government funds. Republicans must bear in mind that he will use the current crisis in the North to his own advantage, but abandon the Movement if and when he gains power.'

The IRD then employed a line of assault with which the Officials had not bothered. Mooney castigated Haughey as a 'an unashamed womaniser'.

One of those who circulated the forged copy of the pamphlet was William McGrath, the paedophile and insti-gator of the original Fianna Fáil–IRA conspiracy theory.[4] McGrath was also a MI6 agent. He had been given a job at Kincora Boys' Home in June 1971, where he set up 'honey trap' operations for MI6 and later MI5.

Not everyone was convinced by the authenticity of the IRD forgery. Gerry Lawless, a former Border Campaign internee who was now working as a journalist for *The Sunday World* in London, was a sceptic. He became convinced there was a 'MI6 connection' to the pamphlet and talked about his suspicions during conversations with other Irish journalists in London.

Mooney's efforts to undermine Haughey through the production of the forged pamphlet made little or no im-pact on the Irish public. Robin Haydon, a later British am-bassador to Dublin,[5] described this period in Haughey's career in a profile of the politician entitled: 'The Greatest Come-back Since Lazarus'.[6] According to him, Haughey had been 'relegated to the back benches [in 1970] in disgrace and all seemed lost yet slowly he managed to rehabilitate himself. He started by travelling round the Fianna Fáil constituencies all over the Republic, doing favours and winning friends. This was possibly because he was never really condemned by the rank-and-file of the Party, of whom an important element cherish extreme Republican views.' Haydon described how, in 1972, Haughey was 'elected Vice-Chairman of the Fianna Fáil Party ... During this period [i.e. early and mid-1970s] Haughey carefully avoided making any remarks about the North.' Haughey was in fact elected as vice-president, not vice-chair, of Fianna Fáil.

Haughey and the UVF Make a Killing

On 15 January 1973, Sir John Ogilvy Rennie's son Charles and his daughter-in-law were arrested for attempting to import heroin from Hong Kong. Rennie resigned as MI6 chief shortly afterwards and Ted Heath appointed Oldfield as his successor. Some accused Oldfield of having leaked details about the scandal to his contacts in the media. While no proof of this has ever emerged, it nonetheless provides an insight into how Oldfield was perceived by some of his contemporaries.

Once in the driving seat at MI6, Oldfield steered the service until his retirement under an appropriately misleading title, 'Head of the Foreign and Commonwealth Office, Research Department'. The next edition of *Who's Who* listed one of his hobbies as 'farming', a claim that was greeted with a measure of derision back in Over Haddon where he had grown up. He responded to his family's chiding by joking that 'farming' was a misprint and should have read 'farting'.[1]

He now occupied the top floor office of Century House, the HQ of MI6. The building was located conveniently across the Thames from Westminster. Oldfield retained a retinue of journalists in *The Telegraph* and other newspapers to keep him informed of what was going on behind closed doors at Westminster. This despite the fact that MI6's remit was to deal only with overseas activities.

Insofar as Ireland was concerned, it was business as

usual, especially in the area of black propaganda, with Haughey as its main focus. In 1973, the IRD created a press briefing document which predominately featured Haughey. According to Colin Wallace, 'there was a whole string of people who had tenuous connections allegedly with Mr Haughey. The idea was that this document put together a package really saying he was heavily involved in shady financial dealings both in the construction industry and also in the cattle business, and a lot of the money from these transactions was being diverted to get arms and explosives for the Provisional IRA.'

The document listed a number of people, some of whom – but not all – were involved with the IRA. They were fallaciously linked to Haughey.[2] One was Bill Fuller of the Old Shieling hotel. He was described as 'suspected of being a member of the Provisional Army Council and probably one of the IRA's bankers'. As noted earlier, Fuller was never in the IRA, although he was a supporter of the organisation.

The next sentence was placed between brackets. It read: 'See also Charles Haughey'. This was a tease designed to whet the appetite of anyone who was shown the IRD document and get them to ask more about Haughey and his links to the IRA. In reality, Haughey was doing little more than visiting the hotel while it was packed with his constituents to enjoy his new-found status as a republican hero – a significant electoral asset at the time. Nonetheless, his imaginary circle of paramilitary friends were next linked to the notorious Irish drug smuggler James McCann, the self-styled 'Shamrock Pimpernel' by the IRD press briefing document.[3] While McCann might once have smuggled guns for the IRA, he was never a key figure. In reality, he was an international drug smuggler who peddled his wares until 1979, when he was arrested in Europe. He then tried to use his past links to the IRA to halt his extradition from Europe. The IRA beat him up when he finally washed up in Portlaoise Prison for having tarnished them with drug smuggling. The idea that McCann and Haughey were part of an international Provisional IRA drug smuggling conspiracy is an entertaining notion but absurd.

A member of the UVF was also linked to the fantasy circle surrounding Haughey. His alleged role was to bomb parts of Belfast on behalf of Haughey so they could be rebuilt for profit, a ridiculous charge that no one in Ireland was ever going to believe. However, people living outside Ireland might not know any better and accept it at face value. The Provisionals were portrayed as part of the alleged scheme to bomb properties in Belfast and then purchase the derelict remains on the cheap.

A 'UVF' controlled company was listed along with the name of yet another individual, 'EC' who allegedly ran it. The UVF man was next linked to a nationalist from the Ardoyne who was supposed to have been 'retained by American business interests to advise on locating industrial projects in Northern Ireland'. The reference to 'American business interests' was certain to catch the eye of any American journalist afforded a glance at the briefing paper. The document proceeded to state that:

Although contributions to a variety of US organisations claiming to provide money for 'Relief' purposes in Northern Ireland probably reached their height in the period immediately following Internment in August 1971, the PIRA still relies heavily on American funds to finance its campaign of violence and to purchase weapons. Unfortunately, all too many well-meaning Americans have a very sentimental, but totally false Hollywood view, of what the conflict is really about. They do not appear to understand that the PIRA kills and cripples large numbers of totally innocent people throughout Ireland using weapons and explosives largely funded by generous US citizens.

The IRD document purported to identify 'the key people who provide support for the PIRA and its fundraising activities'. One of these was Gerry Jones, a Corkman who was a friend of Neil Blaney and had been close to Jack Lynch until 1970. Yet, Jones had no connection to the IRA. He became one of the more memorable figures of the Arms Crisis due to his elegant dress style and a rather dramatic eye patch.

One of the smears directed at him by the IRD was that he had been in the IRA during the border campaign. In reality, he was a former civil servant who had become a successful businessman. He started out as a civil servant in the Department of Local Government, 1937–40. During the Second World War, he was transferred to the Department of Defence, 1940–44, the department responsible for interning suspected IRA members. He then moved to the DoJ, 1944–50, where he worked with Peter Berry.

After the DoJ, he set up his own shipping and engineering business, the Jones Group plc, with his brothers, Christopher and John. At its peak the brothers employed more than 8,000 people. Jones had other business interests including Securicor, a UK company which had an Irish subsidiary. Its vehicles transported money about the country.[4] During the postal strike, which took place during the attempts to import arms for the defence committees, Jones had provided cash for some of their cheques as he had access to currency on account of his involvement in the security company.[5]

What led the IRD to target Jones for vilification? In 1970, Erskine Childers had falsely alleged in a conversation with Ambassador Peck that Jones had intimidated the Arms Trial jury. Childers had also alleged that Jones was involved with 'various property deals and other transactions in which [Haughey] specialises'.[6] This information was sent to London by Ambassador Peck, the former head of the IRD, and may very well have provided the inspiration for the IRD smears linking Jones and Haughey to the Belfast bomb and purchase smear.

The malicious IRD briefing paper contained the following personal information about Jones:

> Gerard (Gerry) Jones
> Dob: 15.06.1919
> Occupation: Building contractor
> In 1971, he was involved with Haughey in the arms scandal
> On the Board of Irish Shipping
> Former IRA member 1958–62
> Chairman of the Irish Arab Society
> Associated with [name withheld] (Estate Agent)
> Involved in the 'Committee for Relief in the North' in 1971
> Owns Celtic Coasters Ltd. Beach Hill, Dublin 4 with workshops at Anderson's Quay, Cork.

The company allegedly responsible for carrying out the

bombings from which Haughey and his associates profited was described as a 'scrap metal and demolition company that has arranged for the Provisionals to blow up buildings which the firm then contracts to demolish. The sites are then bought up by [Bill] Fuller and [Gerry] Jones.'

The Jones Group had a subsidiary in Northern Ireland. Unaware of the IRD smears linking him to the IRA, and the dangers this posed to his life, Jones continued to visit Northern Ireland on business trips. In November of either 1973 or 1974, he received a death threat communicated to him over the phone. It was one he took seriously and discussed with people he felt might be able to offer him helpful advice.

The Jones Group had business interests in Iraq and Saudi Arabia, which might account for the assertion that he was chairman of the Irish–Arab Society. The link to the society chimes with other IRD smears which attempted to connect Haughey and the IRA to Arab organisations such as the PLO and other groups perceived as anti-American.

In the mid-1980s, Jones moved to live in London. A more accurate appreciation of his character can be gleaned from the fact that he was involved in charitable work. He was a patron and life governor of the Royal Hospital, Donnybrook, Dublin and had an interest in cultural pursuits. While in England, he enrolled as a student at the Academy of Fine Arts.

'To my knowledge, my father was not aware of the IRD document', his son Gerard has explained.[7] 'He was a sensitive person who suffered greatly from the arms trial and his health was greatly impacted by these events.' He died in 1999.

All of these smears were useless without the means to

channel them to a selected audience. Forum World Features (FWF) was one of the vehicles Oldfield used to distribute the allegations about Haughey and other MI6 and IRD targets in the European press. In addition, the IRD used the North Atlantic News Agency, Trans World News and *Preuves Internationales* to disseminate its propaganda. FWF was a joint MI6-CIA venture based in London that fed weekly articles to newspapers, most of which were about 1,000 words long. At one stage, it was supplying 250 newspapers and magazines in fifty-three countries, with up to ten articles per week. Brian Crozier ran it until 1974. Crozier's successor at FWF was Iain Hamilton, a former editor of *The Spectator*.

In the summer of 1975, *Time Out* magazine, then going through a radical phase, linked FWF and Crozier to the CIA. Two months later, Philip Kelly and Stephen Weissmann of the magazine, exposed Crozier's links to the ISC. They reported that, 'the leak of literally hundreds of secret [ISC] documents to *Time Out* revealed a CIA hand behind the London Think Tank, the Institute of the Study of Conflict'.[8] Various exposés revealed the links between an array of other publications and the CIA and MI6.[9]

FWF closed down in June. Crozier admitted that FWF was a CIA-MI6 front in his memoirs.

The Mole who Conned the US Ambassador

US Ambassador John D. Moore became the target of an elaborate confidence trick designed to denigrate Charles Haughey in April 1973. It exploited the same fictitious information that Hugh Mooney and the IRD were circulating about the politician, namely that he was a sponsor of the Provisional IRA bombing campaign, and was deriving a profit from the endeavour.

Trying to unravel the inner workings of this operation decades later is not a straightforward task. The purpose of a secret service dirty trick is to deceive. It is something that is perpetrated by devious and manipulative people. Nonetheless, it is still possible to discern the role played by a senior Irish government official in the ruse. Yet again, my suspicion is that the key player was a mole at the DoJ. The official was either introduced to Ambassador Moore, or information from him was relayed to the ambassador.

The details the DoJ mole relayed – or were relayed on his behalf – were deceitful in the extreme. After Ambassador Moore digested the information, he sent a cable to Washington. Moore's cable – transmitted in April 1973 – alleged that the new government had learned that senior Fianna Fáil figures had been involved in a conspiracy, along with the IRA, to bomb Belfast and then purchase the damaged properties at a discount. Patrick Cooney, the Fine Gael Minister for Justice, 1973–77, was mentioned in the cable as having been aware of the scheme. Yet, he has stated that he was ignorant of such a project.

Crucially, the cable identified the 'source' as someone close to the Cosgrave government:

> Source close to new Govt, however, tells us that Cosgrave expects to make some major announcements and disclosures in near future ... Some of info is sensitive. Please hold carefully ... senior figures in previous [Fianna Fáil government] had formed a ring to buy bombed-out property in NI at low prices, using an American businessman as front for purchases ... Disclosures will inevitably raise suspicions that Dublin-based profiteers were in collaboration with IRA bombers...Source says that he has seen some of files on the case and found them 'extremely 'unsavoury'.[1]

Moore could only have swallowed these lies if he believed the source was an official with access to highly classified files. The special branch and DoJ had access to this type of information. It is also likely that Moore was given a copy of the IRD's reprint of the Official Sinn Féin pamphlet, *Fianna Fáil and the IRA*.

The cable stated that: 'Govt is likely to follow with full disclosure of scandal, though some in Govt believe that news should be withheld because it reflects badly upon entire Irish Nation'. The foregoing sentence displays a high level of cunning since the fictitious events predicted by the 'Govt' source were never going to materialise, and this caveat created an escape hatch out of which the source could slip with his credibility intact when nothing happened. Put simply, if challenged by the Americans later, he could defend his position by pretending that Cosgrave and Cooney had engaged in a cover-up in the national interest.

The cable also alleged that Cooney had 'found much evidence, hitherto undisclosed, implicating members of [the] previous [Fianna Fáil] Govt in arms-smuggling scandal of 1970'. The choice of words here elevates the probability that an official at the DoJ deceived Moore. Who else but a DoJ official could have pretended to have had access to what was going on inside Cooney's private office? If this analysis is correct, a senior official at the DoJ was involved, not a garda.

The cable proceeded to claim that: 'Outgoing Govt had made off with files on this and similar embarrassing topics, but a few career men kept personal photocopies which have now been turned over to new Govt. According to source, Justice Minister [Cooney] believes that evidence is sufficiently incriminating to allow new arms trial, with formal charges against three previous ministers: Haughey, Lenihan, and one other whom source did not recall.' The cable added that, 'This is first time we have heard that Lenihan may have been deeply involved in arms-smuggling episode.' Of course, no further trial took place. Again, the reference to 'career men' indicates that the man who misled Moore was a senior DoJ official.

Assuming the cable was the result of a MI6-IRD machination, it is interesting to note that the smear revolved around allegations that Haughey was involved in bombing for personal gain. This was far more likely to diminish Haughey in the eyes of Americans than his alleged backing of the IRA, something that would not have disturbed many Irish-Americans, including some of their political leaders. Furthermore, the reference in the cable to the use of 'an American businessman as a front for' the purchase of the properties that were allegedly being bombed and purchased by Haughey, was also more likely to attract interest in Washington than had the 'front' man been described as Irish, British or European. In addition, the IRD was running a parallel campaign which attempted to link the Provisional IRA to the Soviet Union, another association that would have reduced Haughey in the estimation of most American politicians and senior civil servants if it were believed to be true.

The denigration of Haughey as someone who 'had formed a ring to buy bombed-out property in NI at low prices' was perfectly in line with the approach the IRD had been taking in the US since 1972. The IRD had discovered that American targets were more interested in 'dirt' than in stories about links between their targets and the Soviet Union. The British Information Services (BIS) in New York, an organisation once led by John Peck, was an outlet for IRD propaganda.[2] It had prompted a number of journalists to publish articles on the IRA's Marxist leanings. However, by the end of 1971, the IRD was asked for more 'dirt'. The BIS asked Thomas Barker, the Head of the IRD, for 'a bit more digging' which would 'uncover other discreditable or disruptive material which could be produced'. Likely dirt included material on 'the IRA's treatment of their own members or of informers, or about the internecine struggle between the Officials and the Provisionals.' That sort of material was 'more likely to put people off [in America] than more serious studies of the Marxist background.'[3] In fact, 'Communist baiting is not as popular in the USA as once it was.'[4]

HAUGHEY'S 'SHADY' LAND DEALINGS

In 1973, an undercover IRD officer was assigned to the British embassy. He remained in place until 1976.[1] A declassified IRD document, created at the end of 1973, stated that 'it has never been considered appropriate to use the Dublin Embassy as an outlet for IRD material on any great scale'.[2] This makes perfect sense as IRD operations involving the IRA, Sinn Féin, Charles Haughey and John Hume were run from Stormont Castle. It appears that the new IRD officer at the embassy was given a bespoke role that involved a lot more than the mere distribution of propaganda to journalists. IRD operations in Dublin at this time involved the deception of the US embassy with the assistance of at least one mole working inside the bureaucracy of the Irish government.

Ambassador Moore transmitted a second US embassy cable on 11 November 1974. Again it reveals the likely hand of a DoJ mole working with MI6 and the IRD. It concerned Haughey's alleged 'shady' land dealings. On this occasion, the mole was probably briefed with a script by his MI6 handler and had a meeting in person with the ambassador to whom he relayed the smears directly.

Moore's resulting cable was entitled 'Haughey Tries For A Comeback' and detailed how Haughey:

> has been making a speaking tour that is clearly a bid for a front bench seat. Previously a minister, Haughey fell from power and grace during 1970 arms-trial crisis. (He was involved in misappropriation of public funds for Northern Catholic extremists.) Since then, he has kept quiet and worked hard on back benches. Newspapers have

always been fascinated by him, however, since he is one of party's few talented deputies. Current Fianna Fáil front bench is so weak that journalists love to speculate on 'when Charlie will return'. His reputation for shady real-estate deals does not seem to discourage his fans. Eventually, Haughey would certainly like to be party leader.[3]

In reality, Haughey was surviving on an astonishingly large overdraft from his bank but the disinformation in the US cable chimed with rumours that Haughey was involved in all sorts of lucrative business transactions. Erskine Childers had sprinkled a little fuel on those fires during his conversation with Ambassador Peck in 1970, as described in an earlier chapter, when he had referred to the 'various property deals and other transactions in which [Haughey] specialises'.

The cable's recommendation to Washington was that 'over the long-term, Haughey must be considered a serious challenger for Lynch's job, if only because the competition is so weak. We can entirely accept Lynch's judgment that Haughey would be dangerous: nothing is less needed now than Republican opportunism.'

The Dublin media remained cool towards Haughey. Tony O'Reilly, who had gained a controlling interest in a string of Irish newspapers including the *Irish Independent* between March and September 1973, togged out for the anti-Haughey squad. On 8 January 1975, the IRD officer at the embassy transmitted a cable to London revealing that O'Reilly had 'instructed his editors at lunch that no support whatsoever was to be given to Haughey's efforts to return to respectability'. O'Reilly had opined that Lynch was a 'decent man who was above [reproach] and should be protected from Haughey's machinations'.[4]

The IRD officer predicted that O'Reilly's ownership of regional newspapers might counter Haughey's attempts to secure support among the Fianna Fáil's grassroots throughout the country. Additionally, the IRD officer felt that O'Reilly's attitude might influence the political views of the country's businessmen 'who have taken the line that "Charlie may be a bit of a villain but he talks good sense on economics"'.[5] The IRD officer felt that they would not be 'so keen to push it if O'Reilly – who was a far more successful businessman than Haughey – takes a critical view of poor Charlie'.[6]

The IRD officer noted that this was the first occasion of which he was aware that O'Reilly had given his editors a directive 'on the handling of a political subject', adding that 'if he intends to make a habit of this, at least he has started sensibly'.

Haughey's possible return to Lynch's front bench was also being discussed in London at the time. An FCO official recorded that: 'I should have thought that the return to position and power of a man of Haughey's calibre was almost inevitable, especially in a country which has no excess of such talent.'[7]

In 1975, Lynch invited Haughey back onto the opposition front bench. If Lynch really believed that Haughey had attempted to import arms illegally for the Provisional IRA behind his back, in league with treacherous army officers, in a plot financed by stolen exchequer funds, he would hardly have brought him in from the political cold. It is worth recalling that back in May 1970, at the height of the Arms Crisis, Lynch had predicted a bright future for Haughey.

This had taken place during the marathon Dáil debate that month. Lynch's behaviour only makes sense in circumstances where Haughey had reluctantly played the role of scapegoat with the promise of rehabilitation down the line. Moreover, in a conversation with Ambassador Peck before the Arms Trial, Lynch said that he hoped 'Charlie' would be acquitted.[8]

Oldfield must have been dismayed at Haughey's comeback which represented a considerable professional failure on his part.

'SIR SPY'

In June 1976, Christopher Ewart-Biggs, yet another diplomat-spy, succeeded Ambassador Galsworthy at the Merrion Road embassy. Ewart-Biggs was undoubtedly briefed by the FCO about the on-going campaign against Haughey and expected to do his best to stymie Haughey's rehabilitation. Ewart-Biggs would not, however, live long enough to contribute to it. On 1 July 1976, the Provisional IRA assassinated him as he left his residence at Glencairn, Co. Dublin. He had only served as ambassador for twelve days.

After the assassination of Ewart-Biggs, the British embassy continued to monitor the progress Charles Haughey was making along the path to his political restoration. Some of the heavy lifting fell on the shoulders of the next ambassador to Dublin, Robin Haydon, 1976–80. Haydon was another example of a media savvy diplomat with a media and intelligence background. He had served as an officer with Britain's special forces during the Second World War. He later joined the Foreign Office where he served as the head of its News Department, 1967–1971, and as Downing Street's chief press officer, 1973–1974. As a member of the Special Forces Club in London, he had mingled with members of the intelligence community for decades.

Pádraig Ó hAnnracháin, who later served as Haughey's chief adviser in the civil service, referred to Haydon as 'Sir Spy'.

MI6 was taking every opportunity to place spies around

Charles Haughey and his family. They tried to recruit one of his secretaries, Sally Ann Egan, who worked in the private office he ran at his home, Abbeville, as an informant. She reported the unsolicited approach to him, received his thanks, and kept her job.

There are even indications that Haughey's family was targeted. In Dingle, 'CO', a bearded Scottish boatman and marine engineer, was employed by Haughey to render habitable Inisvickillane, the island he had purchased off the Dingle coast. The Scot may have spied on him too. The work CO conducted was physical and demanded his continued presence on the island transporting building materials, setting up hoists and pulleys and installing generators. He soon became a regular guest around the family campfire. One day he disappeared, never to return, or make contact again; leaving the family to wonder if he had been spying on them all along.

A female stable hand employed at Abbeville in the 1970s provided yet another pair of eyes to watch Haughey.[1] She gave Oldfield an insight into Haughey's social life and ability to network.

In addition, the gardaí were bugging Haughey's home and transcribing his conversations at garda HQ in the Phoenix Park. Some of the transcripts probably reached Oldfield's mole at the DoJ who passed them on to his MI6 contacts.

Oldfield suffered a setback in his ability to undermine Haughey and his other targets when the IRD, an organisation that had proved so useful to him came under attack during the mid to late 1970s.[2] It was gravely weakened in 1973 by cutbacks orchestrated by Oliver Wright, the chief clerk at the FCO. David Owen succeeded Crosland as British Foreign Secretary in 1977. He had little time for the propaganda mongers. Owen discovered that Brian Crozier of *Forum World Features* and the ISC, both of which had been exposed by *Time Out* magazine and other publications, had links to the IRD, and began inquiries that ultimately resulted in what Crozier described as the 'momentous decision' to abolish it.[3] The range of artillery available to Oldfield, from which to launch his bombardments, was dwindling in number with each passing year. This might account for the entry into the fray of *Private Eye*, a satirical magazine.

PRIVATE SPY MAGAZINE

By the mid-1970s, MI5 had become the dominant intelligence service in Northern Ireland but Oldfield and MI6 remained in charge of activities in the Republic. Both organisations were probably involved in the next phase of the campaign against Haughey which almost certainly involved the planting of acerbic and inaccurate stories about him in *Private Eye*, a London-based fortnightly magazine. It was the publication of choice for the circulation of MI5 and MI6 smears, some real, others imagined, especially after Forum World Features, the IRD, and other conduits for dragging people's names through the mud were shut down between 1975 and 1977.

In the 1980s, Pádraig Ó hAnnracháin revealed that he believed the British establishment had engaged in plots against Haughey. Ó hAnnracháin confirmed that Haughey believed this too.[1] Another of Haughey's key advisers, Martin Mansergh, became suspicious about the role played by *Private Eye* as a conduit for a campaign to tarnish Haughey.

The link between MI5 and the magazine is beyond question. In a book *Private Eye* published to celebrate its twenty-fifth anniversary, the magazine revealed that it hosted weekly alcohol-fuelled lunches to which many of its best establishment sources were invited. They made no bones about the fact that one of the guests, a man who presented himself as 'Mr Richmond', was a source of stories from inside MI5. After a while, he was replaced by another font of political gossip. As the book reveals, certain events appeared to them to have:

> prompted MI5 to replace 'Mr. Richmond' with someone even more reliable. One of those receiving adverse mention in the Eye's [Kim] Philby stories had been Capt. Henry Kirby, MP, who was a fluent Russian speaker working for MI5. After a suitable interval the captain wrote an adulatory letter to [the editor of *Private Eye*], praising a recent story ... It was not long before Kirby was also a regular attender at the Eye lunches ...

According to the anniversary publication, the editor of *Private Eye* was wary of intelligence sources, but continued to use them:

> The problem with spy stories is that it is more than usually difficult to work out who was leaking the information and to what purpose. But this detachment did not prevent *Private Eye* or the security services from keeping each other under somewhat bleary observation.

The fact that the editor's father had worked as a propagandist, economic warfare specialist and intelligence officer during the Second World War can only have informed his bleariness.

Private Eye magazine was a favourite conduit to which Oldfield turned when he wanted to start or quash a rumour. He even used it to suppress tittle-tattle about his private life. According to Oldfield's friend Anthony Cavendish, Oldfield 'worried constantly' that as a bachelor he was a 'natural target' for black propaganda and had once suggested to Cavendish 'half seriously' that his life would be 'so much easier and more pleasant' if Cavendish could 'find a wife for him'. His excuse for not looking for a bride himself was because he allegedly 'just did not have the time to devote to that sort of pursuit' because of work. His supposed psoriasis offered another more corporeal excuse. In September 1976, when rumours were circulating about his homosexuality, someone – almost certainly Oldfield – used *Private Eye* to report that the chief of MI6 was about to get married. Later, *Private Eye* reported that the relationship had gone sour and there would be no ceremony. The mini saga was fictitious but it was picked up by a number of newspapers and served to quell the gossip about Oldfield's homosexuality.

Charles Haughey featured in a *Private Eye* story ten days before the Irish general election of 16 June 1977. This was the first in a series of stories that would appear in the publication over the next three years. All of the themes developed by the IRD appeared therein, and more. At the time, the magazine had a respectable circulation in Dublin, especially in the more affluent areas of the capital. Politicians, journalists and people interested in public affairs read it. It was not, however, purchased by many outside of the capital. Hence, it would only make an impact if the national media repeated or 'ran with' what it was publishing.

The June 1977 article alleged that by 'his sneaky support of northern "Republicans", Haughey helped to ensure that the leadership of the Northern Catholics passed from the hands of decent Civil Rights people into the blood-stained hands of the IRA ... If it had not been for the way that the IRA at this time could terrorise justice, the ghastly Haughey might have been sent to prison. Now Haughey is once more one of the Fianna Fail leaders and if, as seems probable,

Fianna Fail loses the coming election, he may succeed Jack Lynch as leader.' The allegation about the terrorising of 'justice' was a reference to Haughey's alleged intimidation of the jury at his trial, something Erskine Childers had relayed to Ambassador Peck in 1970. Childers had not been telling the truth about the alleged intimidation.

The *Private Eye* campaign would also focus on Haughey's private life, another theme of the IRD's campaign against the Irishman. Colin Wallace had been present when the black propagandists from Stormont Castle decided to circulate stories about Haughey's personal behaviour. Hugh Mooney's reprint of the Official Sinn Féin pamphlet in 1972 had included a reference to Haughey as an 'unashamed womaniser'. The *Private Eye* story of June 1977 developed this theme with a far-fetched anecdote about 'a lady friend' who had objected on one occasion 'to something he said and threw into the nearest canal a £300 handbag he had presented to her' after which he 'plunged into the murky waters and reappeared, clutching the bag'.[2] Is it credible that Haughey would have 'plunged' into a rat-infested canal where he was likely to get Weil's disease, or hit a shopping trolley, or some such solid object that could have injured him badly?

A third IRD theme was Haughey's success as a 'shady' property dealer. Although this claim did not appear in the June 1977 article, it would feature in forthcoming pieces.

The style of the June 1977 story – and others soon to appear in *Private Eye* – was evocative of the snooty prose of Auberon Waugh, an acerbic *Private Eye* journalist with links to Oldfield and MI5. Readers of the magazine considered Waugh a great wit. Each edition carried a page devoted to his fantasy-comedy 'diaries' in which he poured scorn on a multitude of people and institutions. He was also responsible for the 'HP Sauce' column which attacked left wing British politicians.[3] In one of the articles about Haughey, an anonymous author referred to the Irish as follows: 'The leprechauns love democracy – for anyone else, that is'.[4] This type of language could have dripped straight out of Waugh's xenophobic pen.[5]

Oldfield had long since made it his business to get to know Waugh. Oldfield's nephew Martin Pearce revealed in his biography of his uncle that:

> There had been the hint of a dig at MI6 – and possibly, [Oldfield] thought, at himself – in a 1971 Auberon Waugh 'HP Sauce' column in *Private Eye* in which Waugh referred to 'Ogilvy's bum boys' – Ogilvy being John Rennie's middle name.[6] Only an insider would have worked out the intended target of the dig, but Maurice resolved to act. Henceforth he became friendly with Waugh, and the personal references became more favourable, if still irreverent, Waugh referring to 'my friend M' as his column prodded away at Harold Wilson – or 'Wislon', as the column preferred. Maurice even arranged for *Private Eye* to do a little cartoon and feature on his nephew John Pearce when John had to cry off a county rugby match after a cow he was milking sat on his knee and broke his leg.[7]

Waugh had other connections to the world of British espionage. He was the son-in-law of Lady Pamela Onslow, the woman who introduced the Littlejohns to British Intelligence.

In the mid-1970s, Waugh had been part of the campaign that called Harold Wilson's integrity into question. A cabal of disgruntled MI5 and some MI6 officers in London had run that project. They used *Private Eye* as a platform for a series of attacks denigrating Wilson. One of the principal anti-Wilson conspirators was Michael McCaul of MI5. By the late 1970s, McCaul was acting as MI5's liaison officer with C3, the garda intelligence directorate that oversaw the activities of the special branch in the Republic. When he visited Dublin, he invariably stopped off at the British embassy to discuss his operations with the intelligence officials stationed there. McCaul had multiple links to journalists in London such as Chapman Pincher who wrote for a number of newspapers.

Waugh was also the nephew of Auberon Herbert, a MI6 agent with connections to the Ultras. David Leigh, author of *The Wilson Plot*, has speculated that Herbert was one of those who fed Waugh smears about Wilson.[8]

Bearing all of this in mind, it is hardly fanciful to suspect the hidden hand of British Intelligence in the series of unrelentingly false and hostile articles published by *Private Eye* about Haughey in the late 1970s which relied on themes developed by the IRD earlier in the decade.

The Bid to Keep Haughey Out of Cabinet

In 1977, the consensus among political commentators was that Fine Gael and Labour would win the general election set for June of that year. However, Fianna Fáil swept back to power, securing a surprise overall majority with 84 of the 148 available seats. Yet again, Charles Haughey topped the poll in his constituency.

The Psy Ops officers at the Northern Ireland Office (NIO) reacted to the unexpected victory with a swipe at Haughey. At this time, officials from MI5 at the NIO directed Psy Ops in Northern Ireland. MI5 is a department that answers to the Home Office. Broadly speaking, it was staffed by former soldiers and police officers at this time. MI6, on the other hand, was part of the Foreign Office and recruited graduates from Cambridge and Oxford. Traditionally, MI6 has looked down its nose at MI5 whose officers it deemed intellectually inferior and lacking in sophistication.

The MI5 officials at the NIO launched a press campaign in an attempt to deter Jack Lynch from appointing Haughey to his forthcoming cabinet. The FCO was not happy about the way it was being run. The plot was soon exposed in an article published by *The Sunday World*.

Haughey rarely kept newspaper clippings about himself. Yet, he deemed the one from *The Sunday World* sufficiently important to preserve it in his private archive at Abbeville. Gerry Lawless wrote it in June 1977, after Lynch's landslide victory. Lawless was one of a handful of journalists who believed MI6 had been plotting against Haughey since the early 1970s. He had discerned 'the hand of MI6' in the circulation of the forged Official Sinn Féin pamphlet about the Arms Crisis. Lawless had become an admirer of Haughey and 'was forever defending him' to his journalistic colleagues in London despite the fact that Lawless had been interned by Fianna Fáil in the 1950s.[1]

An article by Lawless, 'Whitehall Row Over Bid To Block Charlie', read as follows:

> Last Monday's sudden dash to Belfast by Robin Haydon, the British Ambassador to Dublin, is believed in Westminster to be connected with an attempt by British government interests to influence Jack Lynch's selection of the new Dublin government, and to block Charlie Haughey from obtaining any senior governmental position … Haydon's trip was an attempt by the Foreign Office to get the Northern Ireland Office to tone down a bitter press campaign aimed at destabilising Fianna Fáil and influencing Mr. Lynch in his choice of Ministers. The Foreign Office feared that this campaign would backfire.

Lawless revealed that as soon as Fianna Fáil's election triumph had become apparent, 'British Army Psy Ops chiefs' had launched a campaign against Haughey. There had been briefings in London and Belfast for select British journalistic 'experts' on Irish affairs. There had been a 'press campaign which warned Mr. Lynch to watch out for the "Haughey clique" while at the same time revealing that Lynch would not give Haughey a top government post'.

According to Lawless, the operation had appalled the 'more sophisticated Foreign Office mandarins', who ordered Haydon to go to Belfast to warn '[Secretary of State for

Northern Ireland Roy] Mason's officials that this campaign could backfire' and that it should be suspended until after 5 July when Lynch would announce his new administration.

Where did Lawless get the information for his article? The most likely candidate was a man called Thomas E. Utley, who was an asset of Hugh Mooney of the IRD. Utley is a good example of an 'agent of influence'. Utley had been working with the IRD since at least early 1972. He was precisely the type of person who would have been invited to the 'briefings in London … for select British journalistic experts on Irish affairs' described in *The Sunday World*.

At the age of nine Utley had been struck with blindness, something that had caused him to cultivate an exact memory. He developed this skill at an early age by listening to people who read books to him aloud. He was privately educated and then went to study History at Corpus Christi College, Cambridge, achieving a first with distinction. He graduated during the Second World War and joined the staff of the Royal Institute of International Affairs at Chatham House, an institution with links to the Foreign Office. From there, he entered the world of journalism. By 1944, he had become a leader writer for *The Times*. As a journalist, he began his career by demonstrating that he was prepared to toe the Foreign Office party line in an obedient fashion.[2]

After the war, he also became leader-writer for *The Observer* and *The Sunday Times*. From this platform he grew into the 'in-house philosopher of the Conservative Party', producing pamphlets and delivering lectures on Toryism. In 1964, he became leader writer for *The Daily Telegraph*.

After the Troubles commenced, Utley began to visit Northern Ireland where he linked up with Hugh Mooney. At the time of the Bloody Sunday massacre, Utley was working for the *Daily Telegraph* and *Sunday Telegraph*, both pro-Tory papers popular with middle and upper class Britain. Mooney and Utley discussed the Bloody Sunday problem together. It was ultimately resolved that Utley would write a paperback about it. According to a confidential letter dated 24 March 1972, the FCO reported to the MoD that Utley hoped to 'complete the writing in about six weeks, though this may be a little over-ambitious'. According to the letter, he was 'obviously' going to 'need a certain amount of help from Army PR, particularly on the propaganda aspect'.[3]

While Utley failed to produce the book, in 1975 he published the rather grandiosely titled *Lessons of Ulster* which took a broader look at Northern Ireland and a litany of developments that had occurred in the meantime. An indication of his mind-set can be gauged from the fact that he objected to the use of the phrase 'Bloody Sunday', something he described as 'slavish obedience to IRA mythology'.[4] He argued that some of those killed were 'fresh-faced boys who might otherwise have lived to swell the ranks of patriotic militancy'. In other words, they probably would have joined the IRA if they had not been shot.

Utley's interpretation of the Arms Crisis was that:

> Among the factors which made the IRA campaign in the North possible – lavish financial support from deluded Americans, and guns and technical advice from Iron Curtain and Middle and Far Eastern Countries – the acquiescence of the Republic in IRA activity has almost certainly been the most powerful. To put it in

the mildest possible terms, the Republic has not prevented a war against a neighbouring friendly power from being waged from the Republic's territory. In 1970, Mr Lynch suddenly dismissed two senior ministers, Mr Haughey and Mr Blaney, for alleged conspiracy in gun-running in the North. Subsequently there were abortive prosecutions and investigations. All that emerged was that both armaments and public money had reached the IRA with more or less high-level connivance in the Republic. British opinion was momentarily scandalised, but the incident was rapidly dismissed as another example of the eccentricity of Irish politics.[5]

A friend of Lawless from the 1970s, another Irish journalist, has no doubt that the friendship between Lawless and Utley was genuine. 'They found each other fascinating and were completely open about their politics', he recalls. 'They often lunched together at the King & Keys pub on Fleet Street. The lunches sometimes stretched into the late afternoon.' Utley probably made a few remarks about the manoeuvrings against Haughey at one of these meetings. As a graduate of Cambridge, a doyen of Chatham House and an ally of the IRD, Utley might have enjoyed using Lawless to embarrass MI5 and thwart their attempts to muscle in on MI6's campaign to undermine Haughey, especially in circumstances where they had not agreed on a joint course of action with the FCO.

One senior advisor to Haughey has stated that 'I had lunch with [Utley] one day where he tried unsuccessfully to "pump" me. My view is that he had these connections with the [British] intelligence community.'

The NIO-MI5 anti-Haughey briefings about which Lawless wrote had no discernible impact on Jack Lynch's choice of his new cabinet. Lynch appointed Haughey as

Minister for Health and Social Welfare. The campaign Oldfield and the IRD were conducting against Haughey from the shadows was, however, far from at an end.

'You set People Discreetly Against one Another'

Daphne Park, one of Oldfield's most trusted officers, once provided a rather indiscreet insight into how MI6 dirty tricks worked:

> Once you get really good inside intelligence about any group, you are able to learn where the levers of power are, and what one man fears of another … You set people discreetly against one another … They destroy each other, we [in MI6] don't destroy them.[1]

Hugh Mooney used this tactic to bait the Official and Provisional IRA whom he wanted to feud with each other. His approach, as relayed to his superior, Hans Wesler, was to suggest that the Officials were 'seriously considering assassinating the dozen or so leading Provisionals in Belfast'. He also spread rumours that the Provisionals had betrayed the Officials in the aftermath of internment.[2] A soldier attached to the Special Military Intelligence Unit (SMIU) who was performing field work for MI6, recalls, 'I remember one night I sneaked into an arms dump in Belfast, I think it was a Provo one, and stole a few rifles and brought them to an Officials' dump. Then we told the Provos [through cut-outs] that the Officials had stolen them and where they could be found, and sat back and waited for the fireworks.'[3]

The same divide and conquer tactic, albeit without murderous intent, was applied to Fianna Fáil. Haughey already had an array of enemies inside Fianna Fáil who were determined to thwart his ambition to succeed Jack Lynch as taoiseach. They included George Colley, Des O'Malley and a new minister, Dr Martin O'Donoghue. They were unhappy about his return to cabinet. The festering resentments in Dublin provided fertile soil for the troublemakers in MI5 and MI6 to exploit.

In July 1977, *Private Eye* published an accusation that Haughey was an IRA supporter whose acolytes were drunken louts who were resentful of the Lynch faction in the party. The magazine alleged that the Clifden House Hotel 'was smashed and chairs came flying through the window' during a celebration of Fianna Fáil's general election victory.[4]

On 11 November 1977, *Private Eye* published a story that touched upon Haughey's alleged land dealings, the subject so favoured by the IRD. This article contended that: 'Mr Haughey's career is fairly well-known; a chequered one of political wheeling and dealing; of land-sales which helped make him the rich man he is today; of some flirtations with extreme Republicanism ...'

The article was meant to have been written in Ireland, hence it appeared under the title: 'Letter from Dublin'. Yet, it referred to a minister called 'Gary Collins'. While Gerry Collins served in the cabinet, there was no 'Gary Collins'. It is inconceivable anyone living in Ireland – especially a journalist – could have described Gerry Collins as 'Gary' Collins.

In addition to Haughey's alleged land dealings, the *Private Eye* article reported that his 'behaviour and demeanour have become more and more those of a man just waiting in the wings. His biggest rival when Lynch goes will be The Most Boring Man in Ireland, Finance Minister George Colley. Colley's latest fan is the new Minister for Economic Planning and Development, the Trinity College don, Professor Martin O'Donoghue. Haughey reckons that O'Donoghue is Colley's soft under-belly. He recently confided his opinion of O'Donoghue to a group of people in Dublin. "A total fool," said Haughey. And added, "A fuckin' eejit, too". Hmm!'

The following year, John Peck added his weight to the campaign against Haughey. Peck had chosen to stay in Dublin after he had retired as ambassador and produced a memoir in 1978. He used it to portray Haughey as a supporter of the Provisional IRA. He started by alleging haughtily that it was 'no business of an Ambassador, least of all a British Ambassador in the Republic, to interfere with domestic politics or the administration of justice', as if he, Evans, Oldfield and the IRD had nothing to do with the machinations that had surrounded the Arms Crisis. He described Lynch as someone who believed that 'reunification could never be brought by force, but only by consent'. That was a fair and accurate assessment of Lynch. He then had a swipe at Haughey albeit without identifying him by name:

> Whereas previous IRA campaigns had been utterly pointless, there was now a new IRA, under new management, with a programme designed to help Northern Catholics and perhaps, ultimately, to reunite Ireland. You did not need to condone violence or be a member of the IRA, still less a gunman, to feel some chord being struck in the national memory and to have a sneaking or indeed subconscious sympathy for the breakaway IRA [i.e. the Provisionals]. And since Fianna Fáil was the party which had always opposed the Treaty, it was in Fianna Fáil that sympathy with the notion of active

support for the Northern Catholics was mainly to be found. What was disclosed on 9 May 1970 [at the marathon Dáil debate about the Arms Crisis] was a *prima facie* case that this sympathy extended into the upper reaches of the government.[5]

Peck's book sold very well and can still be picked up in second hand bookshops in Ireland. None of these intrigues, however, had any real impact on Haughey's rehabilitation inside Fianna Fáil, or on his relationship with the Irish electorate. By now, people either loved or loathed him. Those who admired him were not going to be swayed by foreign reports, especially ones emanating from London, or by comments in a book by a retired British ambassador.

As 1979 ended, Jack Lynch, who had served thirteen years as leader of Fianna Fáil, was edging towards his retirement. On 14 September, *Private Eye* produced another trenchant attack on Haughey. Again, it was supposed to have been written by an Irish journalist living in the Republic and was published as a 'Letter From Dublin'. Curiously, the purported Irish correspondent did not know how to spell Haughey's name correctly:[6]

Why has Irish Premier Jack Lynch proved so hesitant in handling the IRA since the murder of Lord Mountbatten and others? The explanation lies in Jack's fear and jealousy of his Fianna Fail rival and colleague, Charles Haughy (*sic*), the Minister of Health ... Haughy (*sic*) remains popular with the IRA and their sympathisers in Fianna Fáil – the sentimental oafs who enjoy singing drunkenly about the martyred heroes of 1916, the rattle of the Thompson gun and other murderous nonsense.

Moreover, the immensely rich property speculator Haughy (*sic*) now has enough patronage (as well as a private island and helicopter) to win over the party big-wigs in Dublin.

> Charlie's popularity with the Irish public has increased with his recent publicity campaigns as Minister of Health. These include propaganda against smoking and alcohol and a 'go-for-a-walk' campaign based on the US mania for jogging.
>
> Less well known to the Irish public is Haughy's (*sic*) keenness for what might be termed 'horizontal jogging' – an exercise in which he loves to indulge with hackette Terry Keane.[7]

The piece also alleged that Haughey and Blaney had been dismissed after the arms trial, which was incorrect. They were sacked on 5 May 1970, long before the court case commenced the following September 1970. It is inconceivable that an Irish journalist writing in 1979 would have made such a fundamental error.

It was while Haughey was serving in cabinet in 1979 that he learned of another intrusion into his life, the bugging at his house in 1970 by the gardaí. Vincent Browne, the then editor of *Magill*, revealed it to him. According to Browne, one of those involved in the operation was still a serving member of An Garda Síochána.

THE FULL TIME WHISTLE

Maurice Oldfield stepped down as chief of MI6 in 1978. The retired spymaster can only have been dismayed at the momentum building up behind Haughey as he drew his pension and watched impotently from the side-lines at the Irishman's onward progress.

Then, suddenly, in late 1979 the new British prime minister, Margaret Thatcher, pulled Oldfield right back into the game. He was chosen for a new role, that of Northern Ireland Security Co-ordinator. The appointment took place in October 1979. By then, too many disparate intelligence cooks had congregated in Northern Ireland and were spoiling the spy broth. Oldfield was asked to knock heads and streamline their work.

No sooner had Oldfield placed his feet under his new desk at Stormont Castle, than Jack Lynch announced his retirement. If Haughey was ever going to become taoiseach, this was the moment. The leadership ballot took place on Friday 7 December 1979. Haughey beat George Colley by 44 votes to 38.

Robin Haydon, who was still ambassador to Ireland, drew up a profile of Haughey early the following year for Peter Carrington, Thatcher's Foreign Secretary. A section of it addressed the British take on Lynch's departure and Haughey's leadership victory. Haydon started by explaining that while he had not obtained the inside story, he believed that:

The mainspring of backbench discontent was the Government's poor record on economic and social problems. But there was also a distinctively 'Republican' strand of feeling based on dissatisfaction with Lynch's approach to Northern Ireland (the 'national question') ... [It] was alleged that Lynch had agreed to overflying of the Republic's territory by British helicopters within a so-called 'air-corridor' along the border and so had accepted a derogation of Irish sovereignty. In September, Sile de Valera, a young Fianna Fáil TD and grand-daughter of the late President, voiced strident criticism of Lynch's alleged softness on the North: she was called to order but remained unrepentant. Later, when Lynch was away in the States, another backbencher Bill Loughnane publicly criticised Lynch for allegedly revealing more in Washington about North–South security cooperation than he had in the Dáil.[1]

Haydon's view was that the 'writing was then already on the wall for Lynch, and probably also for Colley as his successor'. Haydon managed to speak to Jack Lynch who told him he could have 'soldiered on but that as he and his wife had decided to announce his departure on 7 January, advancing it did not make much difference. The Party wanted a new man to lead them into the next election and it was, therefore, time for him to go. He also admitted that he knew things as a whole had not been going well in the country. Moreover, he said his wife had "wanted me out for 25 years!"'

Haydon had a few unkind words to relay about Lynch's weakness for alcohol.[2] He described 'persistent stories that Lynch was fed up (his outspoken wife, Maureen, was to a large extent responsible for these stories), suffering from the Irish "thirst problem" or ill. I think he was fed up and he certainly showed signs of losing his grip on both the party and the running of the country.'[3]

The ambassador's profile continued to describe how

Haughey had 'distanced himself from the Government's increasingly unsuccessful attempts to improve the economy and used his position cleverly to publicise his own achievements. So, by the time the [1979] leadership election occurred, he had re-established the image of a highly efficient Minister who got things done.'

Others confirmed this analysis 'or at least echoed' it in conversations with Haydon. These included Mrs Lynch, George Colley, the cathaoirleach of the Dáil, Joe Brennan, Garret FitzGerald 'and many others'. Haydon felt the analysis was 'probably the truth or as near as we are likely to get to it'. There was 'another important factor' in the equation: when Lynch decided to retire 'and indeed right up to the election of Haughey, he believed Colley would succeed him'.

Interestingly, Haydon admitted that he had few, if any, reliable sources inside Fianna Fáil. Nonetheless there was:

> no doubt that [Lynch's] resignation was hastened by the revolt within the party. ... Haughey was the backbenchers' obvious candidate as Lynch's replacement. His involvement in the arms smuggling affair of 1969/70 gave him impeccable credentials as a Republican: his successful tenure of several major departments singled him out as a leader who should be able to get the economy right. Nevertheless, many thought that when it came to the crunch the events of 1970 would be his Chappaquiddick. They were wrong, but his success was deeply divisive. As the voting figures indicate – 44 to 38 – his victory over George Colley, the only other candidate, split the Party down the middle.[4]

Haydon also warned Carrington that Haughey was 'no friend' of the UK; moreover, that he was someone with the potential to become 'hostile' towards it.

Haydon's warnings about Haughey's latent 'hostility' were

risible. Haughey had crushed the IRA's border campaign in the early 1960s while minister for justice. He condemned the Provisional IRA at the press conference he held after his 1979 leadership victory, something that was welcomed by the British embassy. He repeated his denunciation of their campaign at his first Ard Fheis as taoiseach. He went on to increase the number of officers serving in the special branch significantly at the request of garda intelligence supremo Joe Ainsworth. This was to lead to unprecedented success against the IRA. Sir John Hermon, RUC chief constable, was particularly complimentary about Ainsworth's crackdown in his memoirs. But to the Dublin embassy and MI6, Haughey was never going to be more than a republican bogeyman and an on-going target of surveillance and intermittent vilification.

OVERDRIVE

Private Eye went into overdrive after the formal election of Haughey as taoiseach in the Dáil on 11 December 1979. On the 21st, the magazine produced an article entitled 'Haughey's Bricks'.[1] It was a masterpiece of mischief, albeit one strewn with errors. It made a blunder about where Haughey had gone to school; erroneously claimed he had been elected to the Dáil on his first attempt, not fourth; mistakenly maintained he had become junior Minister for Justice on his first day; inaccurately asserted he had advocated an invasion of Northern Ireland in 1969; speciously avowed he had been elected leader because he was 'popular with the IRA'; wrongly maintained he had made a 'huge personal fortune from property dealing'.

There was also a dollop of salacious and absurd nonsense about his relationship with Terry Keane.

Ted Kennedy, who had been attacked by Brian Crozier in *The Ulster Debate* paperback and monitored by the IRD as someone who was anti-British, featured in the article too: 'All in all, Haughey's lifestyle closely resembles that of US politician Teddy Kennedy. Both are ambitious, ruthless and ready to bend the law to cover up their misdoings. Both are Irish "Republicans" – i.e. hope to get into office by sucking up to IRA terrorists.'

Kennedy and Haughey were accused of neglecting 'their wives, who in turn suffer from "emotional" troubles and thirst', a clear euphemism for alcoholism. The mention of Maureen Haughey in the same breath as Joan Kennedy who, sadly, was an alcoholic at this time, was contemptible. Maureen Haughey was uniformly admired as a dignified and gracious lady.

While Haughey was no saint, the following passage from the article was patently untrue: 'When he stood for the Dáil for the first time in 1957, he was already assured of a seat, and the appointment of junior minister in charge of police. So much so that when, at 2 a.m., the police raided a pub near Hill Street, Dublin, and found the great man carousing with Fianna Fail canvassers, Charlie gave his name to the sergeant as "C.J. Haughey TD (MP), Parliamentary Secretary to the Minister of Justice as of tomorrow". As the embarrassed sergeant wrote down this information, Haughey asked him in menacing tones: "What do you do in a case like this?" "I refer it to higher authority, Sir". "How high, sergeant?" "The Department of Justice, Sir". To which correct answer Haughey wittily answered: "You will go places, Inspector".' Since Haughey did not become parliamentary secretary until March 1960, this story cannot be true.[2]

Overall, the cavalier disregard for facts was reminiscent of the mistakes that had littered *The Ulster Debate* book produced by Brian Crozier. Here, *Private Eye* asserted that Haughey 'used this time to increase his huge personal fortune from property dealing in and around Dublin. Much money went too on the purchase of racehorses, and a mansion on one of the Skerries Islands'.[3] Haughey was in fact surviving on bank loans. His island was off the coast of Kerry and did not feature a 'mansion'.

There were other mistakes: Neil Blaney was referred to as 'Nial'.

The next edition of the magazine banged much the same drum.[4] It contained yet another 'Letter from Dublin'. This one alleged that:

> Prime Minister Charles Haughey fears that the continued exposure of his extraordinary private life may hamper him in much the same way that a licentious background harms his hero, Senator Edward Kennedy. For this reason, Charlie's fancy, Terry Keane, may soon get the Big Dump. Charlie and Terry, are known as Cocky and Tease ... Charlie has now told Tease that he would be "banjaxed" if the faithful Party stalwarts became aware of their relationship. [Vincent] Brown (*sic*) has been spreading the word amongst Dublin journalists that Cheerful Charlie is looking for somebody a little less complicated than the attractive, but ageing Terry. That cold-blooded approach is very typical of Cheerful Charlie ...

Haughey had retained Frank Dunlop, who had served as the government's press secretary while Jack Lynch was taoiseach, after he assumed that office. The press office was sent a variety of newspapers and magazines. The spread included *Private Eye*. Someone close to Haughey tipped him off about the story in the 4 January edition of the magazine. Dunlop recalls that he received a call from Haughey as it was coming up to lunch. Haughey wanted to know if he had a copy of the magazine. 'I have it', Dunlop said calmly, to which Haughey replied, 'I'll come down'. Haughey walked into Dunlop's office a few minutes later. The press secretary handed it to him. 'What page?' Haughey asked dryly. Dunlop told him and Haughey left the room with the magazine reading it as he headed in the direction of the Dáil restaurant. When he got to the piece about the 'ageing Terry', Haughey remarked to Dunlop: 'She's going to bloody-well love this!' Keane was forty at the time.

Sometimes the press office was asked to respond to negative publicity which had appeared in the media. Dunlop never received any instruction to deny or counter anything that appeared in *Private Eye* about Haughey.[5]

A few months later, *Private Eye* produced another staggeringly improbable article concerning Terry Keane:[6]

Christopher 'Robin' Hitchens has been in Dublin recently and tells a number of amusing stories about Charles Haughey, the new Irish Premier.

Not long ago, according to Christopher Robin, the new Taoiseach – say – 'tea-sock' as if you are drunk – went to one of Dublin's most expensive restaurants for lunch with a cabinet colleague. Who should be sitting there lunching with another gentleman but 'Cocky' Haughey's inamorata Terry Keane.[7]

The Republican hero approached her and said, 'Hello Terry. That dress I bought you looks well on you.'

At this the plucky colleen stood up, grasped the dress at the neck and ripped it apart. She hurled the garment at him with the words, 'You can take that back and everything else you have ever given me, Charles Haughey', and stormed out of the restaurant in her undergarments.

The article did not elaborate on the other 'amusing stories' relayed to Hitchens.

Just who in Dublin fed this yarn to Hitchens? It has all the appearance of a 'sib' conjured up by black propagandists at the Riverbank House HQ of the IRD in London or the British embassy in Dublin. At the time, visitors to the embassy were sometimes entertained with stories of this nature. Hitchens, as a high-profile visiting English writer, may have been a guest of the embassy. Auberon Waugh, or some other MI5/6 asset, could have been primed to report it once Hitchens started regaling his colleagues with the story upon his return to England.

While it is easy to dismiss the inflated stories about Haughey and Keane as farcical, that is to miss the point. They were written to draw attention to their relationship in a way that excited comment. *Private Eye*, however, was mostly purchased by readers in the more affluent suburbs of south county Dublin and the gossip about Haughey and Keane did not gain traction much beyond those leafy greenbelts, certainly not in rural constituencies. Hence, there was great surprise when Keane went on the *Late Late Show* on RTÉ in 1999 and spoke about their relationship.

The 4 January 1980 edition of *Private Eye* had widened the scope of its attack on Haughey with a patently ridiculous, not to mention libellous, assault on Vincent Browne by someone who could not spell his name properly.[8] Browne was portrayed as both an IRA supporter and Haughey's 'unpaid spokesman'. Quite the contrary, Browne was about to publish a series of articles in *Magill* which would reopen all of the old Arms Crisis wounds, hardly the act of a lackey. The *Private Eye* article portrayed Browne as 'dangerous and devious' and alleged that his 'IRA involvement has recently attracted the attention of both the Irish Special Branch and Sir Maurice Oldfield'.

The piece, a hollow concoction of lies and insults, proceeded to claim that:

> Brown (*sic*) is a former foot-in-the-door hack from the *Sunday Independent*. He was removed by the Indo's owner, Heinz ketchup King Tony O'Reilly – one of the prime movers in a remove-Haughey campaign.
>
> Brown (*sic*) threw his cap into Cheerful Charlie's corner in the brawl to be Taoiseach. Now the balding, thin-lipped editor is telling his cronies that in return for his expert advice on managing the media, Charlie has promised him the coveted post of Director of the Government Information Service.
>
> But Cheerful Charlie seems to be having second thoughts about putting a dangerous hack like Brown (*sic*) in such a sensitive post. Instead he has told the venomous Vincent that when the next election comes in 1981, Brown (*sic*) can act as 'editorial consultant' to the Taoiseach. Then, if Cheerful Charlie gets back – highly doubtful – Brown will get that government information post.
>
> Already dubbed Dr. O'Gobbels, Brown (*sic*) is rapidly becoming insufferable. In his megalomania, he is saying that before the year is out he will be one of the most powerful men in Ireland.

The attack on Browne makes sense if, as this book contends, the *Private Eye* series on Haughey was being orchestrated by Oldfield. It has since emerged that the Dublin embassy perceived *Magill* as a publication which had IRA sympathies. In November 1981, Paul Whiteway, the then press attaché at the embassy, drew up a confidential four-page report on the disposition of the Irish media for London. The print media, Whiteway believed, was 'bitterly anti-IRA', although there was a 'scattering' of IRA sympathisers in 'newspapers and magazines'. These writers did not 'seem to have affected the editorial line of the main newspapers and magazines with the exception of *Magill*'. Whiteway complained that there was 'an almost blithe lack of responsibility in what they write and a failing, either to perceive that the Provisionals pose a serious threat to society in the South, or – if they are more perceptive – to feel that as journalists they have any responsibility for this situation or much loyalty to the society of which they form a part'. This analysis of *Magill* was grossly unfair. The magazine was a perfectly balanced publication which was respected and feared in equal measure by political parties across the board. It sometimes carried reports about, and interviews with, republicans. These gave the public an insight into what republicans were thinking, but did so in a balanced manner. To the embassy, however, anything except outright hostility and condemnation was tantamount to support for the IRA. Hence, I believe, Browne was lined up alongside Haughey and Ted Kennedy for vilification in the *Private Eye* series.

In yet another 'Letter from Dublin' at the end of May 1980, *Private Eye* carried a new slew of allegations – all untrue– that Haughey was gagging the Irish media:[9]

The doughty 4ft 5in millionaire horse owner has also been showing Ireland's broadcasting organisation, RTE, that he does not favour independence in the media. He refuses to give an interview to their This Week current affairs show until the interviewer is one Proinsias Mac Aonghusa, a long-time Brit-hater and Haughey fan. MacAnguish, as he is known, would no more think of asking Charlie awkward questions – like, say, about his trial for smuggling arms to the IRA, in which he was acquitted – than fly in the air.

... RTE's controller, Muris (*sic*) MacConghail (*sic*), refused to give into Haughey's demands.[10] And where do you suppose this has led? He has lost his job. Muiris has been the target for the Fianna Fail party since he interrupted the previous Taoiseach, Jack Lynch, who was droning into the Irish night long beyond the length of the programme. Haughey is clever at identifying hacks who will do his bidding. He often hires them for laughable jobs as a way of rewarding their 'loyalty'.

The comments in the May 1980 article have the appearance of remarks designed to deter journalists in Dublin from writing positive things about Haughey lest they be accused of being one of his lackies.

When the Dáil re-assembled, in the autumn of 1980, it held a debate on the revelations made by Vincent Browne in *Magill* about the Arms Crisis. Lloyd Barnaby Smith, a first secretary who acted as press attaché at the embassy, was sent to monitor the proceedings from the Distinguished Visitors' Gallery on its behalf. A lot of the information was new and political dynamite; some of it egregiously embarrassing to Jack Lynch and Des O'Malley as well as Haughey. In those days, Dáil debates were not broadcast on the television nor on radio. The political correspondents in Dublin had given the press attaché the nickname 'Spook'. When he left Dublin, *The Irish Times'* Saturday Column poked a little fun at him. 'Mr X Leaves' one of its short pieces announced. Having named him fully as 'Lloyd Barnaby Smith', the article then proceeded to report that:

> While here, he developed a paranoia against seeing his name in print. I shall therefore refer to him only as 'X'. 'X' had the task of advising the Ambassador, Sir Leonard Figg, on sensitive topics such as H-Blocks support and attitudes towards the North within the political parties.[11] His tall frame was a familiar sight at every Ard Fheis in the RDS and in the distinguished visitors' gallery in the Dáil, where his arm nearly fell off making mental notes during the debate last year on the *Magill* articles on the 1970 arms crisis.

Moles Inside 'Government Departments'

Maurice Oldfield had a tried and tested tactic for the recruitment of foreign police officers: he let his existing agents make the enrolment pitch on his behalf. MI6 expert Stephen Dorril has revealed that when Oldfield and Frank Steele were in Lebanon, they had deployed a similar method of agent enlistment. Oldfield had appointed Steele as the head of MI6's Belfast Station, 1971–73. Dorril has described how:

> Frank Steele worked mainly through the local security service. The head of the Lebanese security and intelligence service was Farid Hehab, who often met in the St George bar with Maurice Oldfield, who tasked him with recruiting agents. Hehab's officers were supplied with money for information which was used for recruitment. Once targeted, sources were recruited via intermediary 'cut-outs', usually agents, or via 'unofficial assistants, resident British middlemen'.[1]

If he remained true to form, Oldfield would have asked his garda contacts to find like-minded officials to help them. His biographer Richard Deacon wrote that in 1979–80:

> MI6's main success was in establishing agents inside the Garda, the Irish army and government departments. One of the most vital informants was a senior garda officer [who] provided information on the activities of the former Irish premier, Mr Haughey, and other prominent political figures.

Since Deacon penned the above, unassailable evidence of British espionage directed against Haughey has emerged from Britain's National Archives. It is to be found in a letter dated 24 April, 1980, from the then Northern Ireland Secretary, Humphrey Atkins, to Margaret Thatcher which makes reference to two intelligence reports on Haughey:

> For his part Mr Haughey, having made promises that he will pursue the question of Northern Ireland with other European political leaders, needs a meeting with you: he has been criticised at home for going to Paris before London. What use he will wish to make of a meeting, in terms of substance as distinct from presentation, is not clear (but you will, I expect, have noted two recent intelligence reports that throw some light on his approach).

Spying on Haughey was never going to be an easy task. He had become extraordinarily taciturn. His former attorney-general, Patrick Connolly, SC, once told me that the politician 'kept all of his cards very close to his chest. You never knew what he was thinking. He would ask questions without providing the context. You could guess, but you could never be sure you knew what was in his mind.'[2]

The attempts to gather information about Haughey were incessant and not limited to MI6. In 1979, Oldfield's colleagues at MI5 asked an Irish special branch officer on a training course in London about the new taoiseach. He refused to divulge any information.[3] 'Frankly, it was insulting but they had no qualm about it. They were asking everyone about Charlie. They never gave it a rest,' the officer has revealed.

Michael McCaul, of MI5, had forged excellent relations with a string of C3 officers at Garda HQ in the Phoenix Park where he was undoubtedly able to pick up plenty of gossip about Haughey. He got on so well with one senior C3 officer, that he invited him to spend his holiday leave with him.

While Haughey was perfectly content in the company of people from Britain, he could become wary of them if his suspicions were aroused. On one occasion he became apprehensive about a man from the UK whom, he believed, was edging into his social circle to spy on him and arranged for him to be shut out.

As Northern Ireland Security Co-ordinator, Oldfield called upon his former colleague, Daphne Park, to act as a sounding board while developing his plans for Northern Ireland. If a king is to be judged by his courtiers, Oldfield's association with Park does not reflect well on him.[4] John de St Jorre of MI6, who served with Park in Leopoldville in the Congo in the early 1960s, described her thus: 'I always thought of Daphne as a blend of Margaret Rutherford, the bosomy and beloved actress, and Rosa Klebb, the cold-eyed KGB dragon-lady with a poisoned blade in her shoe.' Park had retired in 1979 and had taken up a position in Sommerville College, Oxford. Her new appointment opened the door for her to become the organiser of the British-Irish Association. She asked Maggie Fletcher, who had been her secretary at MI6 to work for her at Oxford.[5] At the BIA, she befriended a string of Irish politicians including 'Dear Garret', as she referred to FitzGerald. Haughey still shunned the BIA. One of Park's duties would have been to supply Oldfield with the information she was picking up through the BIA. In addition, she served as a director of the Ditchley Foundation which often discussed Irish affairs and brought Irish and British politicians together for conferences.[6]

When Oldfield had been in charge of MI6 his tentacles

had reached out to an array of contacts and assets in the media. He tried to reactivate his control over access to key reporters upon his appointment as NI Security Co-ordinator. The espionage writer, Chapman Pincher, who knew Oldfield well, recalled that: 'Around the same time he learned that I was in regular touch with one of his former colleagues and sent a note, by courier, saying, "I would prefer that you do not go on seeing Harry Chapman Pincher." The retired officer happened to know that I was seeing Oldfield, so he simply returned the note with the inscription, "Maurice, fuck off!"'[7]

On the Anglo-Irish front, Oldfield must have been surprised when the new taoiseach managed to strike up a cordial relationship with Margaret Thatcher. Haughey even managed to garner some positive coverage in the British press. While the cordiality would not last, it would outlive Oldfield's brief return to the fray as intelligence supremo in Northern Ireland.

Endgame: Winner and Loser

In 1979, Haughey's political star had reached its apogee with his election as taoiseach. Meanwhile, dark clouds were gathering on the horizon for Oldfield. The spymaster had made dangerous enemies in MI5. A clique inside the organisation known as the 'Ultras' was now after his blood. They included Michael McCaul of MI5. They despised Oldfield for an incident that had taken place a few years earlier. In 1975, Harold Wilson had come to suspect that MI5 was plotting against him. In the summer of that year, Wilson summoned Oldfield to his office and asked him about the hostile rumours which were circulating about him. Oldfield replied that he knew about the rumours and pointed to a section of MI5 which he described as being unreliable. After the meeting Oldfield contacted one of the anti-Wilson conspirators, Peter Wright, whom he knew well, and advised him to go to Sir Michael Hanley, the D-G of MI5, and confess his involvement in the conspiracy. Wright did this the next morning and wrote in *Spycatcher* that Hanley:

> went as white as a sheet. He might have suspected that feelings against Wilson ran high in the office, but now he was learning that half of his staff were up to their necks in a plot to get rid of the Prime Minister ... Ironically, his first reaction was anger with Maurice [Oldfield]. 'Bloody Maurice', he raged. 'Poking his nose into our business'. When he calmed down he asked me for the names. I gave them. Having come so far I could not very well refuse.[1]

Wilson called in Hanley on the afternoon of 7 August 1975, and confronted him with what Oldfield had revealed to him. Hanley tried to convince Wilson the plotting had ended.

Some of the Ultras' anti-Wilson smears had been circulated *via Private Eye* with the connivance of their ally Auberon Waugh. Waugh was also reasonably friendly with Oldfield. There is no doubt, however, about which side Waugh took during the 1979 clash between Oldfield and the 'Ultras'. He deployed his caustic wit against the spymaster in his fantasy-comedy diary. In these chronicles he presented himself as the confidant of the high and mighty. This allowed him to make outrageous remarks about people without any real fear of libel. The entry for 16 November 1979, is a good example of how Waugh managed to weave a damaging element of the truth about Oldfield into his article while wrapping it up in enough claptrap and twaddle to disguise the true purpose of the piece. The 'diary' entry addressed Oldfield's homosexuality with the suggestion that he may have been blackmailed by the Soviet Union. He wrote:

> The atmosphere in Curzon Street [the HQ of MI5] is strangely formal. J [Sir John Jones, Director-General of MI5] tells me he is anxious to refute a Soviet-inspired campaign of denigration against Sir Maurice Oldfield, former head of the rival firm MI6. He asks me to make absolutely plain to all *Private Eye* readers that Sir Maurice is none of the following:
>
> 1. a homosexual;
>
> 2. a Jew;
>
> 3. a Soviet agent;
>
> 4. a friend of Sir Harold Wilson.
>
> I happily agree to this, most particularly since I know Sir Maurice well and can personally vouch for the fact that he is none of

these things. But I find the request puzzling in light of previous briefings, when J. and his colleagues used to make tasteless jokes about Sir Boris Oddfish; 'Sir' Morrie Sodfield etc.[2]

In late 1979, or early 1980, the police in London launched an investigation into Oldfield's private life. With too many enemies lined up against him, he was unable to block it. His former subordinates at MI6 failed to rally to his defence. He was forced to tell the truth when challenged about his sexual history by the police. A MI5 report submitted to cabinet secretary, Sir Robert Armstrong, on 31 March 1980, revealed that after 'some preliminaries' Oldfield acknowledged he 'had first been introduced to homosexuality at university and he admitted having engaged in homosexual practices, intermittently, up till the time of his acceptance of his Northern Ireland appointment. His relationships were, for the most part, with restaurant waiters and the like: he had none, he said, with (MI6) staff or agents.'[3]

When Margaret Thatcher was told Oldfield's secret, his security clearance was withdrawn while an inquiry was carried out to see if he had been compromised by a foreign intelligence service such as the KGB. It was determined that he had not.

While his career was falling apart, doctors diagnosed him with an inflammatory condition of the bowel. It later transpired he had cancer. The following May, he asked Margaret Thatcher to relieve him of his Northern Ireland post on the grounds of ill-health. On 12 June 1980, it was formally announced that he was to leave Northern Ireland within a few weeks.

Oldfield was admitted to King Edward VII Hospital in

Marylebone where he underwent two operations followed by chemotherapy. He died on 11 March 1981.

Oldfield and his colleagues in MI6 and the IRD spent over a decade trying to prevent Haughey's rehabilitation, his return to cabinet and, finally, his elevation to the office of taoiseach. It is doubtful if any western intelligence service engaged in an operation that endured for as long as the one to impugn Haughey. While the campaign failed to achieve its primary aims, it did contribute to a misconception of Haughey which he never fully shook off – that he was a covert supporter of the Provisional IRA. Yet, instead of destroying him, the allegations created a whiff of sulphur which would cling to him for the rest of his career. Paradoxically, it turned out to be something the media and public found intriguing, some even alluring.

Haughey was a renowned political fighter. Yet, he appears to have done little or nothing to counter the campaign against him in the 1970s. His policy was simply to ignore the harpoons Oldfield was firing at him. It is possible that he had no real appreciation of what he was up against. He could not have known about the US embassy cables or the fact the IRD had reprinted the Official Sinn Féin pamphlet and booklet. There was no one to show him a copy of the IRD press briefing linking him to Bill Fuller and the IRA. In the 1980s, I showed Pádraig Ó hAnnracháin a copy of the 1973 booklet which I conjectured had been printed by British intelligence. He responded: 'We suspected that there was a campaign but this is the first time anyone has produced something that might prove it.'

Haughey's policy of simply ignoring the campaign to discredit him worked: he became taoiseach.

When Charles Haughey read the newspaper reports about Oldfield's departure from Northern Ireland in 1980 and his death the following year, he may very well have suspected that the English spymaster had been involved in the intrigues directed against him, but, if so, he never made any public pronouncement about Oldfield.

The IRD and Oldfield's weakness all along was their inability to understand the nature of the Irish electorate. A few stories hinting that Haughey was a Provo supporter with a racy private life in a low circulation London magazine was never going to cut the mustard. The electorate was more interested in what they believed Haughey and Fianna Fáil could do for them when it came to bread and butter issues. Unlike the general British public, which saw the Troubles as a simple issue of 'good' (the British army) versus 'bad' (nationalists), the electorate in the Republic was angry about British transgressions which had taken place across the border such as the attacks on nationalist communities by the RUC and B Specials in 1969, the 1970 Falls Road curfew, internment in 1971, and Bloody Sunday in 1972. On top of this, many were concerned about the activities of the MRF, a string of suspicious bombings which had taken place in the Republic 1972–74, the torture of prisoners and shoot-to-kill programmes in Northern Ireland. Hence, the whiff of republican sulphur that clung to Haughey was unlikely to alienate him from Fianna Fáil's support base where many of these issues were of great concern.

Oldfield and his colleagues, however, might have

succeeded in derailing Haughey had they assailed him on another front, the one that ultimately proved his reputational undoing: his precarious personal finances.

Decades later the Irish public would learn that, before becoming taoiseach, Haughey had built up an overdraft on his AIB bank account. In December 1976, Haughey's debt exceeded £300,000. He wrote to his bank manager, Michael Phelan, saying that he would require an 'accommodation of up to £350,000 for another two years'. The bank acceded to his request.

By June 1978, his debt had risen to £580,000, something the bank deemed 'unacceptable' but it was still reluctant to pull the financial plug on him. One AIB official noted in 1979, 'that [Haughey] does not believe the bank will force a confrontation with him because of his position'. By June 1979, Haughey was offering £400,000 in full and final settlement although his total indebtedness was £913,000. The bank noted that 'Mr Haughey fails to see the precarious position he is in and obviously feels that his political influence will outweigh any other consideration by the bank'. By September 1979, Haughey appeared 'more anxious than previously to get to grips with his affairs'. On 9 September 1979, Haughey telephoned his branch manager and said he wanted to handle 'this dangerous situation' once and for all.

When he won the Fianna Fáil leadership contest in December 1979, his debt stood at £1.143 million. After his election as taoiseach, he settled his liability for the payment of £750,000. He financed the deal with donations from business interests.[4]

Had Oldfield unravelled the extent of Haughey's debt and let the Irish public know about it, the revelation might very well have punctured Haughey's image as an economic genius. Over and above this, if, after December 1979, Oldfield had let it be known that the debt had been cleared by donations made by business interests, the impact would have been devastating. The oft-heard sentiment amongst many of those who acknowledged Haughey's imperfections, yet voted for him nonetheless, was that 'he might be able to do for the country what he has done for himself' or that 'he has the magic touch'. To this day, and with the benefit of the wider picture, people in Ireland still comment with derision at the comments Haughey made during a televised address to the nation on 9 January 1980, during which he said: 'I wish to talk to you this evening about the state of the nation's affairs and the picture I have to paint is not, unfortunately, a very cheerful one. The figures which are now just becoming available to us show one thing very clearly. As a community we are living way beyond our means … to make up the difference, we have been borrowing enormous amounts of money, borrowing at a rate which just cannot continue.'[5]

While Irish journalists gossiped incessantly about Haughey's exploits – real and imagined – throughout the 1970s, they never intruded upon his private life in print or on the airways. The so-called 'red top' tabloids in Britain would never have shown such restraint. Oldfield and the IRD failed to appreciate that the Irish media deemed this as sleaze and beneath their dignity. 'There was a culture of not invading someone's privacy', one reporter recalls. 'We would not have wanted to hurt his wife and children either', he adds.[6] The language of *Private Eye* which portrayed the Irish as 'leprechauns', 'sentimental oafs', and drunks in the Haughey series was off-putting too. In addition, there was 'a level of respect for Haughey' in some quarters, as one reporter of the time put it, 'because he was seen as competent and effective'. A few more had republican sympathies themselves. Although Haughey had a policy of not suing for defamation, this was not quite apparent at the time and hence libel was also a concern. One reporter also believes, 'we didn't want to repeat history, you know, the fall of Parnell'. Many of the key male reporters of the Haughey era were womanisers – and well known for it. They were hardly in a position to point a finger at Haughey. Even if a reporter had been inclined to run with a salacious story, or even drop hints about it, he or she would still have had to get past an editor. Douglas Gageby and Tim Pat Coogan would have had no truck with such an initiative. All of these factors combined to safeguard Haughey from *Private Eye's* onslaught. The Irish media simply ignored the output of the magazine.

In early 1981, while Oldfield lay dying on his sick bed, Haughey was planning a general election campaign to secure a mandate of his own. Fianna Fáil's prospects of winning it were good. Haughey intended to announce the polling date at his party's Ard Fheis in February of 1981 but the Stardust discotheque fire tragedy of 14 February caused him to postpone it.[7] By the time the election eventually took place on 11 June, a republican H-Block hunger strike was underway in Northern Ireland. A number of H-Block candidates ran in the election in the Republic. Two of them took seats. Fianna Fáil's general secretary, Frank Wall, concluded that the H-Block candidates cost the party approximately eight seats due to the vagaries of the proportional representation system. When the counting was over, Haughey had seventy-eight seats to Fine Gael and Labour's eighty. Garret FitzGerald became taoiseach.

Maurice Oldfield was dead by the time the election results started coming in. Hence, he did not get the opportunity to contemplate the irony that, despite all the efforts of MI5, MI6 and the IRD to destroy Haughey by portraying him as a Provisional IRA godfather, he was ousted from power by the success of a democratic election campaign run by his supposed friends in the republican movement. In other words, the republicans succeeded in toppling Haughey where Oldfield had failed so consistently.[8]

The sustained plots against Haughey, a campaign to subvert the democracy of the Republic of Ireland, contravened all diplomatic norms. Maurice Oldfield, John Ogilvy Rennie, Allan Rowley, Thomas Barker, Hans Wesler, Peter Evans, Cliff Hill, Hugh Mooney and their co-conspirators rode roughshod over Irish and international law. A case could be made that ambassadors Peck, Galsworthy and Haydon acted with the protection of diplomatic immunity, but that does not exculpate them on an ethical basis. Putting all legal and ethical considerations aside, can a case be made that from a purely internal British perspective the campaign had the authority of their political masters? Ted Heath knowingly unleashed a pack of attack dogs on Ireland.[9] He gave them *carte blanche* to smear, sully, tarnish and denigrate anyone they pleased – the targets ranged from the IRA to Haughey and John Hume. The authority for their behaviour was – arguably – contained in Robert Armstrong's letter of 7 August 1972, and perhaps in other records which have yet to see the light of day. At best, someone briefed to defend the dirty tricksters could argue that the Armstrong letter was never rescinded, but that hardly impresses. The campaign was certainly consistent with the attitude of the JIC which had divided Fianna Fáil into two camps in 1972, the moderates led by Jack Lynch, and 'the extremists' which included Charles Haughey and others.[10]

Heath was defeated in two general elections by Harold Wilson in 1974. Wilson, who served his second and third terms as prime minster, 1974–76, was himself a victim of dirty tricks perpetrated by members of MI5 and MI6. So too was his deputy leader, Ted Short.[11] It was certainly not Labour's policy to besmirch Haughey. In fact, one of the reasons for the campaigns against Wilson and Haughey was a fear that they would conclude a deal to reunify Ireland if they ever managed to get their hands on the levers of power in Ireland and the UK at the same time.

In a similar vein, there is not a shred of evidence, let alone a whisper of suspicion, that James Callaghan, also of the Labour Party, who succeeded Wilson as prime minister, 1976–79, knew about, or sanctioned, the efforts to besmirch Haughey. In fact, the notion is absurd.

David Owen, who served as Foreign Secretary, 21 February 1977 to 4 May 1979, had many discussions with

Oldfield which dragged on into the evening. Owen got the impression that Oldfield lingered as he had nowhere to go and enjoyed the company while it lasted. Nonetheless, since Owen was known to be averse to dirty tricks, Oldfield would never have dared to reveal that he and the IRD were meddling in the political affairs of the Republic of Ireland. This was just as well since, in 1977, Owen began the process of finally shutting down the IRD.

Overall, the campaign was illegal on three fronts: Irish, British and in international terms. Whatever about the schemes which took place while Heath and Willie Whitelaw had their hands on the tiller, the continuation of the campaign against Haughey, during 1974–79, was unsanctioned and conducted by an out-of-control service behind the backs of the leaders of the Labour government.

The Foreign Office, which oversaw the activities of MI6 and the IRD during the Oldfield era, surely owes the Irish public an apology for the transgressions outlined in these pages. It is difficult to think of an organisation to which the description 'institutionally racist' is more apt. It is most unlikely that an acknowledgement of wrongdoing and apology will be forthcoming.

While the passing of Oldfield brought about an end to an era, Haughey's troubles with the British establishment as well as its secret intelligence and security services were far from over. If anything, those who replaced Oldfield had even less scruples than him in their dealings with Haughey. Their actions are, however, stories for another day.

Endnotes

Introduction

1 A short biography of Oldfield appears in chapter entitled, 'The Man from Gloom Hall'.

2 I have addressed some of the measures undertaken by British military intelligence in Northern Ireland in *Kitson's Irish War* (2021). They include shoot-to-kill operations and collusion with loyalist paramilitary gangs in Northern Ireland.

Haughey's Republican Pedigree

1 The Ulster Volunteer Force (UVF) began to regroup under Lieut-Col F.H. Crawford. Thirty-one people were killed in Belfast between 12–16 February 1922.

2 Hundreds of Catholics (and many Protestants) had been killed during sectarian riots that had erupted in July 1920. Between 1920 and 1922, 267 Catholics were killed, while 2,000 more were wounded; another 30,000 people were evicted from their homes and driven from their jobs, especially at Belfast's shipyards.

3 Kieran Glennon, *From Pogrom to Civil War* (Mercier Press, Cork, 2013), pp. 150–51.

4 Interview with family member 27 May 2022, Dublin. It was discovered that an arrest warrant was issued for Kathleen Diver for her post-Treaty activities, but it was never executed. Kathleen subsequently married Edward McBrearty, a Free State army commandant, who was based at Finner Camp. McBrearty had been a member of the IRA and participated in the first daylight arms raid at Drumquin, County Tyrone in August 1920. Before that, he had served in the British army during the First World War where he had been wounded. The couple had no children. Kathleen was born on 1898 and died on 30 March 1974. She is buried at Crossroads, Co. Donegal.

5 Tim Pat Coogan, *Michael Collins* (Arrow Books edition, London, 1991), p. 351.

6 See my article: https://villagemagazine.ie/unpublished-dick-walsh-wrong-about-haugheys-disinterest-in-northern-ireland/

7 Haughey family document in my possession.

8 Copy of Haughey family notes in my possession.

9 He received his education at Scoil Mhuire national school in Marino (with brief interludes at primary schools in Dunshaughlin and at Corlecky near Swatragh) and at St Joseph's Christian Brothers'

School, Fairview, where he invariably took first place in each subject. On the sporting field, he represented the Leinster colleges in hurling and Gaelic football. He maintained his relationships with his cousins in Northern Ireland. Having completed his leaving certificate in 1943, he holidayed with his classmate Harry Boland in Kilrea, Co. Derry with his – Haughey's – uncle, Owen McWilliams.

10 He remained a member of the Local Defence Force until he became a TD in 1957.

11 Private discussions with Seamus Sorohan, Senior Counsel, at the Law Library in the early 1990s.

12 *The Irish Times,* 8 May 2020, Ronan McGreevy.

13 Private discussions with Seamus Sorohan at the Law Library in the early 1990s.

14 The successor to the Local Defence Force.

15 Lemass, a former IRA man, had served in the GPO in 1916 with Patrick Pearse and had been a supplementary member of the 'Twelve Apostles'. In 1927 Lemass was elected to the Dáil as a Fianna Fáil candidate. He became a government minister in 1932. During the Second World War, Lemass served as a senior minister in a government which passed legislation to intern suspected IRA men. Hundreds were held in the Curragh; nine prisoners were executed.

16 Private discussions with Seamus Sorohan at the Law Library in the early 1990s. Sorohan went on to carry out intelligence work for the IRA including 'taking photographs of Special Branch officers. I have piles of pictures at home'. Decades later he pondered what he might do with them, once suggesting rather mischievously to me, that he might 'donate them to the Special Branch for their archives'. If Haughey had joined the IRA, this perhaps might have been the type of work he would have been asked to undertake.

17 *Ibid.* Sorohan developed a fascination with British intelligence and amassed an extensive library about their activities which he studied in detail. After his death, his colleague, Patrick Gageby SC, arranged for the sale of his library for the benefit of his widow. It featured an extensive number of rare books on a wide variety of topics. The ones on British intelligence were often marked with handwritten notes.

18 Haughey was articled to Michael J. Bourke of Boland, Bourke and Company, and in 1948 won the John Mackie memorial prize of the Institute of Chartered Accountants (ICA). Haughey became an associate member of the ICA in 1949 and a fellow in 1955.

Haughey, the RUC and MI5

1 Eunan O'Halpin, *MI5 and Ireland, 1939–45 The Official History* (Irish

Academic Press, Dublin, 2003), p. 22.

2 PRO DO 121/84; see also, Eunan, O'Halpin, *Spying on Ireland* (Oxford University Press, Oxford, 2008), p. 239.

3 PWE archive FO 898/70 'Procedure, General Correspondence And Reports'.

4 Clair Wills, *That Neutral Island* (Faber, London, 2007).

5 Private interview with a friend of Betjeman, 29 May 2022.

6 Betjeman later helped Patrick Kavanagh and other Irish poets find publishers in Britain.

7 Robert Briscoe served as a Fianna Fáil TD, 1948–65, and became lord mayor of Dublin in 1956.

8 Eunan O'Halpin, *Defending Ireland: the Irish State and its Enemies since 1922* (Oxford, 1999), p. 244.

9 Private interview with former Deputy Commissioner Joseph Ainsworth.

10 Seán MacStíofáin described himself as 'Seán MacStíofáin' as opposed to 'Seán Mac Stíofáin', on the cover of his memoirs.

11 Seán MacStíofáin, *Memoirs of a Revolutionary* (Gordon Cremonisi, London, 1975), p. 81.

12 Sir John Hermon, *Holding the Line* (Gill and Macmillan, Dublin, 1977), p. 37.

13 John Maguire, *IRA Internments & the Irish Government Subversives and the State 1939–1962* (Irish Academic Press, Dublin, 2008), p. 144.

14 From 1914–1924 the position was known as Minister for Home Affairs.

15 C3 was a department of An Garda Síochána, based at Garda HQ at the Phoenix Park. It co-ordinated and directed the activities of the special branch.

16 Private interview with Seán Garland.

17 John Maguire, *IRA Internments & the Irish Government Subversives and the State 1939–1962* (Irish Academic Press, Dublin, 2008), *passim*.

A Hate Figure among Republicans

1 Currie became a founding member of the SDLP, and later a Fine Gael TD in Dublin. He was Fine Gael's candidate in the 1990 presidential election (which was won by Mary Robinson).

2 Austin Currie, *All Hell Will Break Loose* (O'Brien Press, Dublin, 2004), p. 40.

3 *Magill*, June 1980. In 1963, the head of the Irish Special Branch at Dublin Castle was Superintendent Philip McMahon. His counterpart in Northern Ireland was Chief Inspector Smith. According to Berry, 'on 6th September Chief Inspector Smith of the [RUC]

Special Branch in Belfast had called to see Superintendent Mc-Mahon, the chief of our Special Branch in Dublin Castle, [and] had discussed IRA matters with him'.

4 *Magill* (June) 1980, p. 74.

5 *Ibid.*

6 *Ibid.*, p. 75.

7 *Ibid.*

8 Jonathan Bardon, *A History of Ireland in 250 Episodes* (Gill and Macmillan, Dublin, 2008), p. 518.

Taking the Gun Out of Republican Politics

1 Cathal Goulding held onto his position as IRA chief-of-staff until the IRA split in 1969, whereupon he became chief-of-staff of the Official IRA. He died in 1998.

2 MacStíofáin, p. 99.

3 Brendan Anderson, *Joe Cahill, A Life in the IRA* (O'Brien Press, Dublin, 2002), p. 155.

4 Stormont Premier Terence O'Neill had warned the Home Office in London of this in December 1965. O'Neill claimed that the IRA was training volunteers for hostile action in Northern Ireland in time for the 1966 Easter Rising celebrations. These views were shared by Stormont Minister for Home Affairs Brian McConnell, 1964–66.

5 Patrick Bishop and Eamon Mallie, *The Provisional IRA* (William Heinemann Limited, London, 1987), p. 28.

6 Eunan O'Halpin, *The British Joint Intelligence Committee and Ireland, 1965–1972* (Centre for Contemporary Irish History, Trinity College Dublin, March, 2007).

7 Kevin, Rafter, *Neil Blaney, A Soldier of Destiny* (Blackwater Press, Dublin, 1993), p. 36.

8 Bishop and Mallie, p. 59.

9 *Ibid.*, p. 90-1.

10 Private interview with an individual who was summoned to meet the Army Council in 1967.

The man from 'Gloom Hall'

1 Adam Sisman, *John le Carré: The Biography* (Bloomsbury Publishing, London, 2015), p. 404.

2 Anthony Cavendish, *Inside Intelligence* (HarperCollins Publishers Ltd, London, 1990), pp. 32–3.

3 *Ibid.*, p. 3.

4 *Ibid.*, p. 44.

5 *Ibid.*, p. 3.

6 John Leahy, *A Life of Spice* (BookPublishingWorld, England, 2006).

7 The Soviets also managed to penetrate the émigré groups which were being used to mount the operations.

8 Peter Wright, *Spycatcher* (Viking Penguin Inc., New York. 1987), p. 162.

9 Roger Faligot, *The Kitson Experiment* (Brandon Book Publishers Limited, Kerry, 1983), p. 87.

10 The Warsaw Pact was a defence treaty signed in Warsaw, Poland, between the Soviet Union and seven other Eastern Bloc socialist republics of Central and Eastern Europe in May 1955, during the Cold War.

An Ambassador 'Complicit in Mass Murder'

1 *Observer*, 5 September 1999. See also: https://www.theguardian.com/world/2021/oct/17/slaughter-in-indonesia-britains-secret-prop-aganda-war: https://www.theguardian.com/world/2022/may/14 secret-british-black-propaganda-campaign-targeted-cold-war-ene-mies-information-research-department

2 John Martin, *The Irish Times: Past and Present* (Belfast Historical & Educational Society, Belfast, 2008), p. 139.

3 *Observer*, 7 November 2021.

4 O'Halpin, 2008, pp. 26–7.

5 The MI5 SLO was probably Christopher Herbert, a graduate of Trinity College Dublin.

6 Tony Craig, *Crisis of Confidence* (Irish Academic Press, Dublin, 2010), p. 45. See also Peck to Gilchrist, 5 August 1969, FCO 33/764, National Archives.

7 Craig, p. 46

8 FCO 33/764/1. See also Angela Clifford, *The Arms Conspiracy Trial* (A Belfast Magazine, March, 2009), p. 657.

A Defenceless Community

1 The Shankill Butchers carried out a series of gruesome killings of nationalists, many of whom were tortured first. At least 23 people were killed. The gang was active between 1975 and 1982.

2 The Shankill Defence Association, a loyalist vigilante organisation, later amalgamated with other similar groups to form the UDA.

3 'Crisis in North', *Nusnight* magazine, October 1969; Mulroe, *Bombs, Bullets and the Border* (Irish Academic Press, Kildare, 2017), p. 26.

4 13 November 1969. Greenhill had served as chairman of the JIC, 1966–68.

5 Clifford, 'Ireland's Only Appeal to The United Nations' (*A Belfast Magazine*, Number 26), p. 82.

6 See chapter 5 of my book, *Deception and Lies* (Mercier Press, Cork, 2020) for further details.

7 This officer became one of a small number of gardaí who were friendly with Haughey during his years in the political wilderness in the 1970s. Haughey promoted him to high office after he became taoiseach. There is no evidence that he provided any assistance to the G2 operation.

Haughey and the Diplomat-Spy

1 Born in 1919, Fitzgibbon had served in the British and American armies during the Second World War. When the war ended, he had become a major in military intelligence and a specialist on the subject of the German general staff. He was the author of a number of books. In 1969, he published *Out of the Lion's Paw, Ireland Wins Her Freedom*, a book about the War of Independence. His work *High Heroics*, was a fictional account of the activities of Michael Collins.

2 Clifford (2009), p. 661.

3 British National Archives PROFCO 33 759; A guide to the Public Record Office of the Foreign and Commonwealth Office (PRO FCO) can be found at https://www. nationalarchives.gov.uk/ help-with-your-research/research-guides/foreign-commonwealth -correspondence-and-records-from-1782/; Clifford (2009) p. 663.

4 Clifford (2009), p. 664.

5 Rafter, Kevin, *Neil Blaney: A Soldier of Destiny* (Blackwater Press, Dublin, 1993), pp. 53–54.

6 Private interview with the civil servant, Dublin, 11 January 2019.

7 Clifford (2009), p. 662.

8 Burke (2020), p. 117.

The 'Concerned' Ex-MI5 Officer at *The Irish Times*

1 TNA FCO 95/588. C. MacLaren (IRD). IRD Work in Ireland, 19 November 1969.

2 O'Halpin, *The British Joint Intelligence Committee and Ireland, 1965–1972*, Centre for Contemporary Irish History, TCD, March 2007.

3 John Martin, *The Irish Times: Past and Present* (Belfast Historical & Educational Society Belfast 2008), p. 247.

4 Wright (1987), p. 369. King's role as a MI5 agent was disclosed by Peter Wright of MI5 in his book *Spycatcher*. In this context, an 'officer' serves an intelligence organisation as one of its employees whereas an 'agent' assists it from the outside. Wright revealed: 'Feelings had run high inside M15 during 1968. There had been an effort to try

to stir up trouble for [PM Harold] Wilson then, largely because the *Daily Mirror* tycoon, Cecil King, who was a longtime agent of ours, made it clear that he would publish anything MI5 might care to leak in his direction. It was all part of Cecil King's "coup", which he was convinced would bring down the Labour Government and replace it with a coalition led by Lord Mountbatten.'

5 Cecil King, *The Cecil King Diary 1970–1974* (Jonathan Cape London 1975), pp. 171–72.

6 Martin, p. 102.

7 MI6 and the CIA were recruiting war criminals, the most infamous of whom was Klaus Barbie, the Gestapo chief of Lyon.

8 Martin, p. 119.

9 *Ibid.*, p. 246.

10 *Ibid.*, p. 247.

11 Gageby ceased to be editor of *The Irish Times* in 1974. Thereafter sales went into decline and there was a clamour for his return which McDowell and his allies were incapable of resisting. He was re-installed in 1977 and remained at the helm until 1986.

12 Martin, p. 247

13 *Ibid.*, p. 248.

14 Peck made no mention of these events in his memoirs of his time as ambassador to Ireland.

15 Martin, p. 252

16 *Ibid.*

The TD who Divulged Military Secrets

1 In later years, the same car sustained a bullet hole to its rear while being driven away from a checkpoint by the captain. Interview family member, 26 February 2022.

2 The Department of External Affairs also sent officials across the border to get an idea of what was going on.

3 A meeting of CDC representatives from nearly all of the Six Counties also took place at a hotel in Baileboro in early October 1969. Capt. Kelly lived in Baileboro. There may have been other covert G2 bases located near the border.

4 James Kelly, *Orders for the Captain* (Kelly-Kane Limited, Cavan 1971), pp. 197 and 199; see also trial transcript Clifford (2009), p. 355. This discussion most likely took place on 17 March 1970.

5 O'Brien was the Labour Party's then spokesman on Northern Ireland, and later, a government minister in the FG-Labour coalition, 1973–77.

6 John Devine, report entitled: *Aspects of the Six County Situation*, undated.

I acknowledge receipt of this report from University College Dublin.

7 The reference to 'Duggan' in the Devine memorandum was to Capt. Jack Duggan. 'Doolan' may have been Capt. Finbar Drohan who was engaged in intelligence duties at this time. Both were officers of the Eastern Command

8 Boyne, Seán, *Gunrunners* (O'Brien Press, Dublin, 2006), p. 56.

Diplomatic Arm Wrestling

1 Clifford (2009), p. 664.

2 *Ibid.*, p. 660.

3 'Tell it not in Gath' is a way of saying, 'Don't spread scandal. Keep the story to yourself'. The source is II Samuel, i, 20. David said when he heard of the death of Jonathan in the war against the Philistines: 'Tell it not in Gath, publish it not in the streets of Askelon, lest the daughters of the Philistines rejoice.'

4 Clifford (2009), p. 665.

5 Conor Cruise O'Brien, *States of Ireland* (Panther Hutchinson & Co., London, 1972), pp. 228–29.

The Plot to Assassinate a British spy in Dublin

1 Liam Clark's interview with John Kelly, 17 August 2005. The section of the transcript referring to the Arms Crisis is reproduced in Clifford, *Arms Conspiracy Trial* (2009) starting at p. 615.

2 Godfrey's company was an entity he called, the 'Savoy Finance Company'.

3 James Kelly, *The Thimble Riggers* (Self-published, 1999), p. 21.

4 The Irish parliament, the Dáil, is located inside Leinster House.

5 Kelly (1999), p. 19.

6 Burke (2020), p. 128. John Kelly's true loyalty, which was to the emerging Provisional IRA, was concealed from Capt. Kelly. John Kelly planned to betray G2 by helping the Provisionals seize the consignment of arms when it reached the Republic, but it never made it to the seaport.

7 When Jock Haughey had signed in at the Irish Club on his first trip to London, he had used the alias 'George Dixon'. This clue might have brought the name of 'Dixon' to the attention of the security forces following him, but would not – on its own – have alerted them to the existance of the bank account.

The Cat Jumps Out of the Bag

1 Tom Conaty was chair of the Central CDC in Belfast. William White-law appointed Conaty as one of his political advisers in 1972. Gerry Fitt was less than candid about his association with John Kelly after

the Arms Crisis erupted. Fitt succeeded in distancing himself from any association with the gun procurement operation.

2 The Department of External Affairs became the Department of Foreign Affairs in March 1971.

3 On 8 October 2020, the Irish Minister for Justice, Helen McEntee, confirmed that the state still possessed files on the Arms Crisis which had not been released.

4 Kelly (1999), p. 23.

5 Angela Clifford, *Military Aspects*, p. 76.

The Hamburg Con Artist and MI6

1 Boyne, pp. 71–2.

2 This was not Aidan Mulloy's only encounter with someone who worked for British intelligence. When in Hamburg, Mulloy became friendly with David Cornwell who asked him to read a manuscript of a book he proposed to submit to his publisher and tell him what he thought of it. Mulloy thought the story was excellent and encouraged Cornwell to pursue his literary ambitions. Cornwell went on to publish many books under his pen name, 'John Le Carre'. At the time, he befriended Mulloy, he was serving with MI6 in Germany. Interview with Liam and Ciaran Mulloy, sons of the late Aidan Mulloy, Dublin 2020.

The Dirty Tricks Brigade descends upon Dublin

1 John Peck, *Dublin From Downing Street* (Gill and Macmillan, Dublin, 1978), p. 15.

2 Oldfield has served as deputy head of MI6's Singapore station, 1950–53 and as head 1956–59. Evans was stationed there 1957–59, and 1961–62.

3 Peck, p. 78.

4 Michael Cullis, *Independent*, 20 January 1995.

5 Sir John Ogilvy Rennie succeeded Peck as director of the IRD, 1954–58. He later served as chief of MI6, 1968–73.

6 Dr Stephen Dorril, *MI6: Fifty Years of Special Operations* (Fourth Estate 2001), p. 548.

7 Cavendish, p. 139.

8 *Ibid.*, p. 140.

9 Norman Darbyshire gave an interview on camera to Channel 4 which was suppressed. The entire interview later disappeared in mysterious circumstances but a transcript of it survived. In his documentary on the plot, *Coup 53*, director and presenter, Taghi Amirani, secured Ralph Fiennes to act the part of Darbyshire.

10 Another key MI6 figure in the Iran operation was Monty Woodhouse,

a future Tory MP and member of the House of Lords, who wrote a book about his role in the venture.

11 Peck, p. 89.

The Ambassador who Knew Nothing

1 Peck, p. 37.

2 The fact that Lenihan called Col Hefferon demonstrates that he was not only aware of the importation operation but that G2 was involved in it.

3 The DoJ was not privy to the operation as it was run by the Department of Defence. Moreover, there was bad blood between Berry and Col Hefferon after the former's attempts to seize control of G2 from the Department of Defence and hence Berry had been kept in the dark about the operation.

4 Peck, pp. 35–36.

5 *Ibid.*, pp. 40–41.

6 British Public Record Office CJ 4/23 122658, 6 May 1970, record of luncheon at the Irish embassy.

7 Public Records Office (PRO), Cabinet minutes 128/45, 7 May 1970.

8 PRO, CJ 4/23 122658, 8 May 1970.

9 *Ibid.*, 28 May 1970.

10 Oliver Wright later became ambassador to Washington.

11 Clifford (2009), p. 672.

12 Peck, p. 49. The 14th Earl of Home was Sir Alex Douglas-Home who became Foreign Secretary. Peter Carrington was the 6th Baron Carrington. He became Secretary of State for Defence.

13 PRO, Foreign and Commonwealth Office 33/1610 122676, 29 June 1970.

The Politics of the Bear Pit

1 Desmond O'Malley, *Conduct Unbecoming* (Gill and Macmillan, Dublin 2014), p. 63.

2 Albert Luykx served as a translator for Capt. Kelly during his trips to the Continent and a link to Schlueter.

3 Clifford, *Military Aspects,* p. 76.

4 Document in my possession.

5 The minister, Jerry Cronin, later apologised to Capt. Kelly for his part in the forgery. He explained that he had been manipulated by Lynch and had not fully understood what he was doing. He also said that he turned down a cabinet post in 1977 because he did not want to serve in a government led by Lynch.

6 The motives are explored by me in my book *Deception & Lies* (Mercier Press, Cork, 2020)

7 Interview with a member of Col Hefferon's family, March 2022.

8 Peck, p. 123.

9 Clifford (2009), p. 140.

10 Gerald Boland died on 5 January 1973.

11 Kevin Boland, *Up Dev* (Self-published, 1971), p. 19.

A Mouth-Watering Stockpile of Intelligence

1 Craig, p. 137.

2 Vincent Browne, *Sunday Tribune*, 26 February 1984.

3 Private discussion with a former garda special branch officer, 2022.

4 Vincent Browne, *Sunday Tribune*, 26 February 1984.

5 James Downey, *Lenihan, His Life and Loyalties* (New Island Books, Dublin, 1998), p. 82.

6 See my article: https://villagemagazine.ie/
the-phone-tap-on-the-family-home-of-captain-james-kelly/

7 Dáil Éireann, Thursday, 30 October 1969.

The Smear Campaign against Jock Haughey

1 Liz Walsh, *The Final Beat, Gardai Killed in the Line of Duty* (Gill and Macmillan Ltd, Dublin, 2001), p. 2.

2 Boyne (2006), pp. 46–7.

3 His experience inspired his celebrated play, 'The Borstal Boy'.

4 On Saturday 21 October 1967, a Dublin taxi driver had pulled up outside Pearse Street library to pick up a fare. He was confronted by a number of Saor Éire members armed with revolvers. The taxi was driven to the Furry Glen in the Phoenix Park where the driver was tied up and told to lie on the floor of his vehicle. The vehicle was then taken to Upper Mount Street where, at 9.30 p.m., members of the gang alighted and hurled two petrol bombs at No. 13 which was the HQ of Fianna Fáil. The bombs consisted of a pair of two-gallon tins containing a mixture of oil and petrol. A witness to the attack chased the taxi as it drove towards Government Buildings. A few shots were discharged in the direction of the witness but he was not hit. A statement delivered to *The Irish Press* that night demanded the release of three Saor Éire prisoners. They included Joe Dillon who had been sentenced to five years' imprisonment the previous May for attempted robbery. Later that night the special branch tracked the gang to a pub in the centre of the city and arrested them.

5 Private interview with the retired garda officer.

6 Seamus Brady, *Arms and the Men* (self-published, 1971), p. 89.

7 Kelly (1999), pp. vi–vii; see also Clifford (2009), p. 687.

8 *The Irish Times*, 10 February 1971, p. 4.

9 Kelly (1999), p. vi.

10 *Ibid.*, p. 23.

11 Clifford (2009), p. 665.

12 Boyne, p. 32.

13 Walsh, p. 11.

14 O'Malley was implying that a garda was killed with the complicity of Blaney and Haughey, and that this crime was covered up for decades. Yet, who but the Lynch, the Minister for Justice, senior officials at the DoJ, and garda top brass could have initiated such an audacious cover-up? This implies that the man he most admired, Jack Lynch, along with Peter Berry, the Secretary to the DoJ, and John Fleming, the officer in charge of the special branch, participated in the plot, or turned a blind eye to it. If he really believed this, why did he vote for Haughey to become taoiseach in 1989 and then serve as a minister in Haughey's 1989–92 government?

15 *Conduct Unbecoming* (Gill and Macmillan, Dublin, 2014). O'Malley portrayed himself in his memoirs as 'a fiercely principled' young minister who stepped forward to prevent the State from falling into the grip of the IRA. To sustain this narrative, it is necessary to believe that CDC figures such as Tom Conaty, Paddy Devlin and Paddy Doherty were IRA supporters when, of course, they were nothing of the sort. The impression of O'Malley as an uncommonly courageous politician was not universally shared within garda circles. Those who served in the special branch in the early 1970s recall a phone call he made to the gardaí during the protests that erupted in Dublin after Bloody Sunday. O'Malley wanted to know if they felt it would be safe for him to travel to his office at the DoJ on St Stephen's Green in the city centre. He was told there was no danger to him. Private interview with a retired garda special branch officer.

16 Private interview with the retired garda officer.

'Winning Acceptance and Confidence'

1 Peck, pp. 51–2.

2 Rita Dudley was born in Dublin in 1915.

3 PRO FCO 33 1207; Clifford (2009), p. 683.

4 Michael Heney, *The Arms Crisis, The Plot That Never Was* (Head of Zeus, London, 2020), p. 320.

5 This will be discussed in more detail in a later chapter.

6 Peck, pp. 120–1 and 151.

7 *Ibid.*, p. 152.

The Fireball of the North

1 Private interview with a former member of the committee.

2 Like Berry, Ward maintained good relations with his British counterparts. David Goodall, who served as deputy under-secretary responsible for intelligence and defence matters at the FCO (i.e., MI6 reported to him) in the 1980s got to know Ward during the negotiations that led to the signing of the 1985 Hillsborough Agreement. Goodall recorded in his memoirs that after the conclusion of the talks Ward 'thanked me in an aside for all that I had done, not least (he said) for having always made it unequivocally clear what were the points of real importance to the British side. See David Goodall, *The making of the Anglo-Irish Agreement of 1985, a Memoir by David Goodall*, National University of Ireland, Dublin, 2021, p. 125.

3 He died on 4 September 1998, aged 73.

4 Private interview with a former senior garda intelligence officer.

5 They were acquired and published by Vincent Browne of *Magill* magazine in 1980.

6 Brady, p. 113.

7 Cosgrave had two sources. One was Philip McMahon, the former head of the special branch. The second source was someone who sent him a note about the import anonymously.

8 Richard J. Aldridge, Rory Cormac and Michael S. Goodman. *Spying on the World, the Declassified Documents of the Joint Intelligence Committee, 1936–2013* (Edinburgh University Press Ltd, Edinburgh, 2014), p. 366.

9 Peck, p. 24–25.

10 Randolph III joined the US Foreign Service in 1955 and served in Haiti, Brazil, Peru, Venezuela, Ireland, Barbados, Colombia and Washington. He earned the State Department's 'Superior Honor Award' before retiring in 1985. He was killed on 11 September 1997, in an automobile accident in Brazil.

Sexpionage

1 Martin Pearce, *Spymaster* (Bantam Press London, 2016), p. 58.

2 Adam Sisman, *John le Carré: The Biography* (Bloomsbury Publishing, London, 2015).

3 Russell was educated by the Order of the Sisters of Mercy Order. Her parents had expected her to take vows as a nun.

4 Gerry Lawless, 'Jailed vice-czar organised Belfast spy-brothels for British Intelligence', *Sunday World,* 17 August 1975, pp. 12–13.

5 Some of these would eventually end up being prosecuted, convicted and imprisoned.

6 Cavendish, p. 4.

7 Smithson had been murdered in 1956 on the orders of Mifsud and Silver.

8 *Sunday World,* 17 August 1975, pp. 12–13.

9 Discussion with a senior republican, 8 June 2022.

10 Male prostitutes trained to extract information were known as 'ravens'.

11 Private interview with the former soldier, Dublin 2022.

'The Dublin Press … is the Priority Target'

1 Eunan O'Halpin, *The British Joint Intelligence committee and Ireland, 1965–1972,* Centre for Contemporary Irish History, Trinity College Dublin, March 2007. Annex to JIC minutes, 18 September 1967.

2 Peck, pp. 51–2.

3 Hugh Mooney document in my possession concerning Mooney's visit to Dublin on 21–23 June 1971 with the internal designation: 1971X OWRR/2/3/71.

4 Kennedy Lindsay, p. 242.

5 Martin, p. 247.

6 Dick Walsh, *The Party, Inside Fianna Fáil* (Gill and Macmillan, Dublin, 1986), p. 101.

7 Thomas Barker directed the IRD from November 1971 to October 1975.

8 Peck to Western Europe department FCO, 23 April 1971, FCO 33/1621, British National Archives.

9 *Irish Independent,* 24 October 1972; Craig, p. 138.

10 Craig, p. 138. See also Peck to RID and IRD, UK Rep and Moscow, 27 October 1972, FCO 87/24, NA

11 Interview with Colin Wallace, 9 March 2022.

12 *Ibid.,* 28 May 2022.

13 Peck, p. 2.

14 *Ibid.,* p. 6.

Spooky Associations

1 Jeremy Lewis, *David Astor* (Jonathan Cape, London, 2016), p. 91.

2 Lewis, p. 28.

3 Public record office FCO 33 1207.

4 Ewart-Biggs served as 'Foreign Office Advisor' to MI6, 1966–70. Some sources claim he was also he FCO liaison with GCHQ. It is quite possible that he liaised with both MI6 and GCHQ.

5 Garret FitzGerald, *All In A Life* (Gill and Macmillan, Dublin, 1991), p. 281.

The Smearmeister from Down Under

1 Brian Crozier, *Free Agent, The Unseen War 1941–91* (Harper Collins, London 1993), p. 97.

2 Brian Crozier *The Struggle for the Third World* (Bodley Head, London, 1966), p. 156.

3 Crozier (1993), pp. 74–5.

4 *Ibid.*, p. 99.

5 *Ibid.*, p. 109.

6 *Ibid.*, p. 51.

7 *Ibid.*, p. 55.

8 *Ibid.*, p. 56.

9 David Astor was also a member of the Athenæum. He published some of Crozier's propaganda on communist subversion in industry in the *Sunday Observer*. See Crozier (1991), p. 108.

10 Crozier (1993), p. 114.

11 *ISC Annual* (1971), p. 17.

12 *Ibid.*, p. 19.

13 *Ibid.*, p. 18.

14 *Ibid.*, p. 19.

The FitzGerald-Crozier Collaboration

1 Charles Haughey harboured a grudge against *This Week* magazine. Tony Gallagher had written a story for it which had appeared shortly after the Arms Crisis erupted which had played down the role of Gibbons in the importation operation. See Burke (2020), p. 229–30. Gallagher was related by marriage to the family of George Colley. Haughey agreed to speak to a reporter from the magazine a few years later. A meeting place was arranged at a pub in Donnybrook, just across the road from the RDS. When Haughey appeared he declared, '*This Week* is no friend of mine', and terminated the meeting. Private interview with the reporter, 31 May 2022.

2 Institute for the Study of Conflict, *The Ulster Debate: Report of a Study Group of the Institute for the Study of Conflict* (Bodley Head, 17 Aug. 1972).

3 *Ibid.*, p. 129.

4 *Ibid.*, p. 136.

5 *Ibid.*, p. 129.

6 *Ibid.*, p. 140.

7 *Ibid.*, p. 149.

8 William Beattie Smith, *The British State and the Northern Ireland Crisis, 1969–70. From Violence to Power Sharing* (United States Institute of peace press, Washington, 2011), p. 234.

9 Paul Lashmar and James Oliver, *Britain's Secret Propaganda War, 1940s–1977* (Sutton Publishing, Gloucestershire, 1998), p. 153.

10 *The Ulster Debate*, p. 138.

11 *Ibid.*, p. 60.

12 *Ibid.*, p. 129.

13 *Ibid.*, p. 138.

14 *Ibid.*, pp. 121–22.

15 *Ibid.*, p. 135.

16 *Ibid.*, p. 61.

17 *Ibid.*

18 *Ibid.*, p. 73.

19 *Ibid.*, p. 78.

Smearing John Hume

1 Maurice Fitzpatrick, *John Hume in America: From Derry to DC* (University of Notre Dame Press, Indiana, 2019).

2 *Ibid.*

3 *Ibid.*

4 *The Ulster Debate*, p. 145.

5 A copy of the reprint can be viewed in my article at: https://village magazine.ie/john-hume-never-received-an-apology-from-the-british-secret-service-for-the-character-assassination-campaign-they-conducted-against-him/

6 Crozier (1991), p. 120.

7 William Whitelaw did not share this view of the CDCs. He asked Tom Conaty of the Central CDC to become one of his advisers in 1972. See my article: https://villagemagazine.ie/questions-for-the-former-minister-for-justice/

8 Maurice Tugwell, *Public Opinion and the Northern Ireland Situation, A Note by the Colonel GS (Information Policy, HQ Northern Ireland)*, 9 November 1971. Tugwell's report is available *via*: https://wikispooks.com/wiki/Maurice_Tugwell#Information_Policy

9 *This Week*, 20 July 1972, pp. 22–27.

'It has to be Deniable in the Dáil'

1 Richard J. Aldridge, Rory Cormac and Michael S. Goodman, *Spying on the World, the Declassified Documents of the Joint Intelligence Committee, 1936–2013*, (Edinburgh University Press Ltd, Edinburgh, 2014), p. 365.

2 *Ibid.*

3 Patrick Mulroe, *Bombs, Bullets and the Border* (Irish Academic Press, Kildare, 2017), p. 85.

4 *Ibid.*, p. 85.

5 *Ibid.*

6 The Littlejohns were later extradited from Britain to Dublin. Their trial became an international sensation when they disclosed their connection to MI6.

7 Further details about Albert Baker can be found in Chapter 8 of my book, *Kitson's Irish War, Mastermind of the Dirty War in Ireland* (Mercier Press, Cork, 2021).

8 It is possible that both the UVF and the UDA were involved but the ultimate puppet masters were British intelligence.

9 An alternative account is that he merely circulated a memo to this effect. It is likely that he circulated the memo and then gathered his staff.

The Dublin Molehill

1 Peck, pp. 51–2.

2 Deacon's real name was Donald McCormick.

3 Richard, Deacon, '*C*' *A Biography of Sir Maurice Oldfield, Head of MI6* (MacDonald, London, 1984), p. 173.

4 Johnstone was implicated in the Littlejohn and Wyman affairs. He slipped out of Dublin after these scandals erupted.

5 Private interview.

6 Craig (2010), p. 150.

7 *The Ulster Debate*, p. 19.

The Spooks in the Castle

1 Before his deployment to Ireland, Mooney had been assigned to Indonesia and Bermuda. After Direct Rule in 1972, Mooney was assigned to the NIO. Then, from January 1973 he became part of the staff of the DCI. Mooney left Northern Ireland in December 1973.

2 Interview with Colin Wallace, 28 May 2022.

3 Christopher Andrew, *The Defence of the Realm: The Authorized History of MI5* (Allen Lane, London, 2009), p. 107.

4 Rowley left Stormont Castle in 1973 and became a divisional head of MI6. After Oldfield retired, Dick Franks became chief and Rowley deputy chief of MI6. He retired in 1979.

5 Interview with Colin Wallace, 13 March 2022.

6 Joe Haines, *The Politics of Power* (Jonathan Cape, London, 1977), pp. 123–4.

7 Clifford (2009), p. 664.

8 The propagandists rejected an alternative account of the cause of the injury which had appeared in *Private Eye* in 1970, namely that he had been beaten up by garda special branch officers in Dublin

Castle after he descended upon it with armed soldiers to secure the release of his brother Jock from custody. According to this yarn, Jock Haughey was being held and questioned at the castle by the police. In reality, Jock Haughey was never arrested nor taken to Dublin Castle for questioning.

9 *Fianna Fáil – the IRA Connection* (Dublin, 1973, no name given).

A Licence to Deceive

1 Chris Moore, *The Kincora Scandal* (Marino Books, Dublin, 1996), pp. 61–3.

2 Christopher Whitehead, then in his early thirties later became the Head of Information at the Home Office. When he was interviewed by the Calcutt inquiry, he could not remember this task but could recall typing something up about Ian Paisley.

3 The compression technique can be viewed at https://villagemagazine.ie/smear-sheet-the-document-that-proves-charles-haughey-was-the-target-of-british-secret-service-vilification-after-the-arms-trial/

4 At the same time, McGrath was distributing propaganda materials linking left-wing British politicians to communism and the IRA. This was in furtherance of a parallel campaign Mooney was running to undermine the British Labour Party. Documents which annotated by Mooney referring to communism in the British Labour Party were being circulated across the UK.

5 Haydon served as ambassador, 1976–80.

6 PRO PREM/19/283, Profile of Charles Haughey by Ambassador Robin Haydon, 9 April 1980.

Haughey and the UVF Make a Killing

1 Pearce (2016).

2 A revised 1974 copy of the document is in my possession.

3 McCann was played by David Thewilis in the 2010 film, 'Mr Nice'.

4 Jones was also a director of Dublin Shipping Ltd, Irish Hotels Ltd, H. A. O'Neill Ltd, Climate Engineering Ltd, John Jones Ltd, Concast Ltd, and Irish Shipping Ltd. He was honorary Belgian consul in Ireland as well.

5 The role Jones played in cashing cheques was examined at the PAC hearings in 1971 where he testified under his Irish name, Gearóid MacEoin. See Reference 16.2.1971 Book 14 Questions 7498-7578.

6 PRO FCO 33 1207. See also Clifford (2009), p. 683.

7 Interview with Gerard Jones, 28 and 29 June, 2022, Dun Laoghaire, Co. Dublin.

8 Paul Lashmar and James Oliver, *Britain's Secret Propaganda War*,

1940s–1977 (Sutton Publishing, Gloucestershire, 1998), p. 167.

9 A root and branch unmasking was published in *Rolling Stone* magazine in October 1977 by Watergate journalist Carl Bernstein. See: https://www.carlbernstein.com/the-cia-and-the-media-rolling-stone-10-20-1977

The Mole who Conned the US Ambassador

1 The cables can be found on Wikileaks: https://search.wikileaks.org/?q=Charles+Haughey

2 John Peck, who served as head of the IRD, 1951–53. He became director-general of the BIS in New York, 1956–59. He served as Britain's ambassador to Dublin 1970–73.

3 One writer who was interested in the Soviet Union's alleged control of the Provisional IRA was John Barron, an American author of a number of books about the KGB. He was one of a string of visiting journalists who received briefings about the alleged relationship from Denis Payne, DCI NI 1973–75.

4 TNA FCO 95/1400, F. MacGuinness to Thomas Barker, Head of the IRD, 23 Dec. 1971; Rory Cormac, 'The Information Research Department, Unattributable Propaganda, and Northern Ireland: Promising Salvation but Ending in Failure?' *English Historical Review*, 131(552), pp. 1074–1104. https://doi.org/10.1093/ehr/cew342.

Haughey's 'Shady' Land Dealings

1 The IRD officer later went on to serve in Nicaragua (during the Contra era), Chad, Costa Rica and Bolivia.

2 TNA FCO 95/1478, I. Knight Smith, 20 Dec. 1973.

3 https://search.wikileaks.org/?q=Charles+Haughey

4 *Sunday Business Post*, 1 January 2006.

5 *Ibid*.

6 *Ibid*. In 1984, O'Reilly acknowledged that, 'in many cases we [in Independent Newspapers] try to lead public opinion, not follow it.' See Matt Cooper, *The Maximalist: The Rise and Fall of Tony O'Reilly* (Gill & Macmillan, Dublin, 2015), p. 159.

7 *Sunday Business Post*, 1 January 2006.

8 Heney, p. 252

'Sir Spy'

1 Private interview with a source in Lisburn.

2 The head of the IRD, Thomas Barker, had retired in October 1975 and was succeeded by Ray Whitney, who led it until 1978 when he retired and became a Tory MP.

3 The IRD was replaced by the Overseas Information Department which was headed by James Allan of MI6 who had served as an assistant secretary at the NIO between 1973 and 1976. He was one of the MI6 officers who negotiated with the IRA in the mid-1970s under the direction of Sir Frank Cooper, the permanent under-secretary at the NIO. Allan acknowledged his intelligence background in the early 1980s in the wake of his appointment as high commissioner to Mauritius stating that he now occupied a 'respectable position'.

Private Spy Magazine

1 Private discussions with Pádraig Ó hAnnracháin in the 1980s.

2 *Private Eye*, Issue 404, 10 June 1977, p. 6.

3 'HP' stood for Houses of Parliament.

4 *Private Eye*, Issue 471, 4 January 1980, p. 10.

5 Richard Ingrams, the editor or *Private Eye,* 1963–86, was unable to assist in identifying the author or authors of the series of articles about Haughey 'as it was so long ago' he could not remember. Email exchange with me, 9 June 2022.

6 This is a reference to Sir John Rennie, the chief of MI6, 1968–73.

7 Pearce (2016), pp. 261–2.

8 David Leigh, *The Wilson Plot* (Heinemann, London 1988), p. 196.

The Bid to Keep Haughey out of Cabinet

1 Private discussion with a friend of the Gerry Lawless, September 2021. Lawless died in London in January 2012.

2 After the plot to bomb Hitler on 20 July 1944, Utley highlighted the fact there were anti-Nazi forces in Germany. The Foreign Office objected, fearing it might encourage talk of a negotiated peace with the anti-Nazi forces. Utley dutifully rewrote the piece omitting any mention of support for German resistance to Hitler.

3 Letter in my possession bearing designation: OWRR 18/8/72.

4 T.E. Utley, *Lessons of Ulster* (J. M. Dent, London, 1975), p. 55.

5 *Ibid.*, p. 63.

'You Set People Discreetly Against One Another'

1 Philip H. J. Davies, *MI6 and the Machinery of Spying* (Frank Cass publishers, Oxon, 2004), p. 298.

2 BSI, Mooney to Welser, undated. See also the article by Rory Cormac entitled, *The Information Research Department, Unattributable Propaganda, and Northern Ireland: Promising Salvation but Ending in Failure?*

3 Private interview with the former SMIU officer, England, 2013.

4 *Private Eye*, Issue 407, 22 July 1977, p. 3.

5 Peck, p. 43.

6 There have been rumours that the author of at least one of the *Private Eye* pieces was a named Irish journalist – now deceased. It is inconceivable, however, that he could have misspelt the names of Charles Haughey and Gerry Collins (and later Vincent Browne), or made the litany of other mistakes that would appear in the series. While the magazine may have drawn on the wit and knowledge of Irish reporters, the parallels with the IRD campaign are too strong to discount by contending that the series was the work of one or two Irish reporters acting entirely on their own accord.

7 *Private Eye,* Issue 463, 14 September 1979, p. 10.

The Full Time Whistle

1 PRO PREM/19/283, Profile of Charles Haughey by Ambassador Robin Haydon, 9 April 1980.

2 Rumours had been doing the rounds about Lynch's problems with alcohol for more than a decade. Ambassador Peck was aware of Lynch's fondness for Paddy whiskey and once brought a pair of bottles with him to England during a summit between Lynch and Ted Heath. Heath was prompted to tell Lynch that it was usual at such meetings to take a break for a drink in the mid-morning. He then offered Lynch a whiskey. This was a ruse to either save Lynch embarrassment or to take advantage of his weakness for alcohol. (Private discussion with a friend of John Peck.)

Frank Dunlop, who worked as press secretary to Lynch during the 1970s recounts in his memoirs, *Yes Taoiseach,* that the Corkman liked to drink whiskey while at work, and considered it a good day if he got as far as Mallow, i.e., if the spirit level in his bottle of Paddy sank as far as Mallow on the map on the label.

Haughey believed that the British would ply his officials with alcohol during summit meetings and forbade them – on the pain of dismissal – from drinking any alcohol when in the presence of British delegations. Private discussion with Pádraig Ó hAnnracháin.

3 PRO PREM/19/283, profile of Charles Haughey by Ambassador Robin Haydon, 9 April 1980.

4 *Ibid.*

Overdrive

1 *Private Eye,* Issue 470, 21 December 1979, p. 19.

2 Moreover, he ran for the Dáil for first time in the 1951 general election without success. He failed again in the 1954 general election, and also lost a by-election in 1956.

3 He owned Inisvickillane off the coast of Kerry on the western side of Ireland. It did not feature a 'mansion'. Skerries is on the opposite side of Ireland, off the Dublin coast.

4 *Private Eye*, Issue 471, 4 January 1980, p. 10.

5 Interview with Frank Dunlop, 8 June 2022.

6 *Private Eye*, Issue 478, 11 April 1980, p. 6.

7 Gossip in Dublin subsequently suggested the other man was a well-known 'urbane' Irish diplomat. The entire story was probably a tall tale from start to finish.

8 *Private Eye*, Issue 471, 4 January 1980, p. 10.

9 *Ibid.*, Issue 481, 23 May 1980, p. 11.

10 The man spelled his name Muiris Mac Conghail.

11 Sir Leonard Figg became British ambassador to Dublin in June 1980.

Moles inside 'Government Departments'

1 Dorril, p. 665.

2 Private discussion with Patrick Connolly, SC, in the Law Library Dublin in the 1990s.

3 Private interview with the officer.

4 In 1960, while she was Head of MI6's Congo Station, she was involved in the assassination of the country's prime minister, Patrice Lumumba. Margaret Thatcher appointed Park to the BBC's Board of Governors in 1982, a post she held until 1987.

5 Paddy Hayes, *Queen of Spies, Daphne Park, Britain's Cold War Spymaster* (Duckworth Overlook, London 2015), p. 270.

6 Brian Crozier organised at least one ISC conference at Ditchley Park, the home of the Ditchley Foundation; Crozier (1993), p. 124.

7 Pincher (1991), p. 40.

Endgame: Winner and Loser

1 Wright, p. 371.

2 Auberon Waugh, *The Diaries of Auberon Waugh. A Turbulent Decade 1975–1985* (Private Eye Productions Ltd, London, 1985), pp. 86–87. The use of the invented name 'Sodfield' was an unsubtle reference to Oldfield's practice of sodomy.

3 These quotes are taken from a four-page Special Branch Report on Oldfield by Detective Inspector G. Catherall.

4 Vincent Browne, the editor of *Magill*, was one of a small number of journalists who probed Haughey's finances. Ironically, he was cast as one of Haughey's menials in *Private Eye*. Garret FitzGerald received the benefit of a write-off of a sum in excess of €250,000 from the Allied Irish Bank in 1993.

5 The clip is shown on repeats of RTÉ's perennially popular *Reeling in the Years* television series.

6 Private interview with the journalist, 31 May 2022.

7 The tragedy cost the lives of forty-eight people; forty-six in the fire and two later on with the last recorded death occurring on 11 March 1981 – 214 people were injured.

8 Haughey regained power in the February 1982 election, but lost it again in November 1982.

9 Heath appointed Howard Smith as UK REP to Northern Ireland in 1971. He knew that Smith had urged the assassination of the prime minister of the Congo in the 1960 because he – Heath – had received a circular containing the recommendation. Daphne Park later had Patrice Lumumba murdered in conjunction with the CIA. See *Village* magazine: https://villagemagazine.ie/britainted/

For an account of Heath's sexual abuse of boys see https://village magazine.ie/not-just-ted-heath-british-establishment-paedophil-ia-and-its-links-to-ireland/

10 Richard, Cormac and Goodman (2014), p. 365.

11 The IRD forged a Geneva bank account implying Edward Short had access to dubious funds. See my article in *Village* magazine: https://villagemagazine.ie/john-hume-never-received-an-apology-from-the-british-secret-service-for-the-character-assassination-cam-paign-they-conducted-against-him/

BIBLIOGRAPHY

Aldridge, Richard J., Cormac, Rory and Goodman, Michael S., *Spying on the World, the Declassified Documents of the Joint Intelligence Committee, 1936–2013* (Edinburgh University Press Ltd, Edinburgh, 2014)

Aldridge, Richard J., Cormac, Rory, *The Black Door: Spies, Secret Intelligence and British Prime Ministers* (William Collins, London, 2016)

Anderson, Brendan, *Joe Cahill, A Life in the IRA* (O'Brien Press, Dublin, 2002)

Andrew, Christopher, *The Defence of the Realm: The Authorized History of MI5* (Allen Lane, London, 2009)

Bardon, Jonathan, *A History of Ireland in 250 Episodes* (Gill and Macmillan, Dublin, 2008)

Bishop, Patrick and Mallie, Eamon, *The Provisional IRA* (William Heinemann Limited, London, 1987)

Boland, Kevin, *Up Dev* (Self-published 1971)

Boyne, Seán, *Gunrunners* (O'Brien Press, Dublin, 2006)

Bower, Tom, *The Perfect English Spy* (Heinemann, London, 1990)

Brady, Seamus, *Arms and the Men* (self-published, 1971)

Burke, David, *Deception & Lies, the Hidden History of the Arms Crisis* (Mercier Press, Cork, 2020)

___ *Kitson's Irish War, Mastermind of the Dirty War in Ireland* (Mercier Press, Cork, 2021)

Cadwallader, Anne, *Lethal Allies* (Mercier Press, Cork, 2013)

Callaghan, James, *A House Divided* (Collins, London, 1973)

Clifford, Angela, 'The Arms Conspiracy Trial' (*A Belfast Magazine*, March, 2009)

—— 'Military Aspects of Ireland's Arm Crisis of 1969–70' (*A Belfast Magazine,* September, 2006)

—— 'Ireland's Only Appeal to The United Nation' (*A Belfast Magazine,* March 2006)

Coogan, Tim Pat, *A Memoir* (Phoenix, London, 2009)

—— Michael Collins (Arrow books edition, London, 1991)

Cooper, Matt, *The Maximalist: The Rise and Fall of Tony O'Reilly* (Gill & Macmillan, Dublin, 2015)

Craig, Tony, *Crisis of Confidence* (Irish Academic Press, Dublin, 2010)

Crozier, Brian, *The Struggle for the Third World* (Bodley Head, London, 1966)

—— *Free Agent, The Unseen War 1941–91* (Harper Collins, London 1993)

Currie, Austin, *All Hell Will Break Loose* (O'Brien Press, Dublin, 2004)

Curtis, Liz, *Ireland the Propaganda War* (Pluto Press, London, 1984)

Davies, Philip H. J., *MI6 and the Machinery of Spying* (Frank Cass publishers, Oxon, 2004), p. 298.

Deacon, Richard, *'C' A Biography of Sir Maurice Oldfield, Head of MI6* (MacDonald, London, 1984)

Dillon, Martin, *The Dirty War* (Arrow, New edition, London, 1991)

—— *The Shankill Butchers: A Case Study of Mass Murder* (Arrow, London, 1990)

Downey, James, *Lenihan, His Life and Loyalties* (New Island Books, Dublin, 1998)

Dorril, Dr Stephen, *MI6: Fifty Years of Special Operations* (Fourth Estate 2001)

Dunlop, Frank, *Yes Minister, Irish Politics from Behind Closed Doors* (Penguin Ireland, Dublin, 2005)

Ewart-Biggs, Jane, *Pay, Pack & Follow* (Weidenfeld and Nicolson, London, 1984),

Faligot, Roger, *The Kitson Experiment* (Brandon Book Publishers Limited, Kerry, 1983)

Faulkner, Brian, *Memoirs of a Statesman* (Weidenfeld and Nicolson, London, 1978)

FitzGerald, Garret, *All In A Life* (Gill and Macmillan, Dublin, 1991)

Fitzpatrick, Maurice, *John Hume in America: From Derry to DC* (University of Notre Dame Press, Indiana, 2019)

Glennon Kieran, *From Pogrom to Civil War* (Mercier Press, Cork 2013)

Goodall, David, *The making of the Anglo-Irish Agreement of 1985, a Memoir* (National University of Ireland, Dublin, 2021)

Haines, Joe, *The Politics of Power* (Jonathan Cape, London, 1977)

Hermon, Sir John, *Holding the Line* (Gill and Macmillan, Dublin, 1977)

Hayes, Paddy, *Queen of Spies, Daphne Park, Britain's Cold War Spymaster* (Duckworth Overlook, London, 2015)

Institute for the Study of Conflict, *The Ulster Debate: Report of a Study Group of the Institute for the Study of Conflict* (Bodley Head, London, 1972)

Johnston, Roy, *A Century of Endeavour* (Lilliput, Dublin, 2003)

Kelley, Kevin, *The Longest War, Northern Ireland & the IRA* (Brandon Press, Kerry, 1982)

Kelly, Capt. J., *Orders for the Captain* (Kelly-Kane Limited, Cavan, 1971)
—— *Thimble Riggers* (self-published, 1999)

Kennedy Lindsay, *The British Intelligence Services in Action* (Dunrod Press, Antrim, 1981)

Keogh, Dermot, *Jack Lynch: A Biography* (Gill and Macmillan, Dublin, 2008)

King, Cecil, *The Cecil King Diary 1970–1974* (Jonathan Cape London 1975)

Lashmar, Paul and Oliver, James, *Britain's Secret Propaganda War, 1940s–1977* (Sutton Publishing, Gloucestershire, 1998)

Leahy, John, *A Life of Spice* (BookPublishingWorld, England, 2006)

Leigh, David, *The Wilson Plot* (Heinemann, London, 1988)

Lewis, David, *Sexpionage, the Exploitation of Sex by Soviet Intelligence* (Heinrich Hanau Publications, London, 1976)

Maguire, John, *IRA Internments & the Irish Government Subversives and the State 1939–1962* (Irish Academic Press, Dublin 2008)

Martin, John, *The Irish Times: Past and Present* (Belfast Historical & Educational Society Belfast 2008)

McCann, Eamon, *War & An Irish Town* (Penguin Books, Middlesex, 1974)

McDonald Henry and Cusack, Jim UDA, *Inside the Heart of Loyalist Terror* (Penguin Ireland, Dublin, 2004)

McDonald, Henry and Cusack, Jim, *UVF The Endgame* (Poolbeg Press, Dublin, 2016).

MacStíofáin Seán, *Memoirs of a Revolutionary* (Gordon Cremonisi, London, 1975)

Moore, Chris, *The Kincora Scandal* (Marino Books, Dublin, 1996)

Mulroe, Patrick, *Bombs, Bullets and the Border* (Irish Academic Press, Kildare, 2017)

O'Brien, Conor Cruise, *States of Ireland* (Panther Hutchinson & Co., London, 1972)

Ó Dochartaigh, Niall, *From Civil Rights to Armalites; Derry and the Birth of the Irish Troubles* (Cork University Press, Cork, 1997)

O'Halpin, Eunan, *MI5 and Ireland, 1939–45 The Official History* (Irish Academic Press, Dublin, 2003)

—— *Intelligence, Statecraft and International Power* (Irish Academic Press, 2006)

——O'Halpin, Eunan, *Spying on Ireland* (Oxford University Press, Oxford, 2008)

O'Malley, Desmond, *Conduct Unbecoming* (Gill and Macmillan, Dublin,

2014)

Pearce Martin, *Spymaster* (Bantam Press, London, 2016)

Peck, John, *Dublin From Downing Street* (Gill and Macmillan, Dublin, 1978)

Pincher , Chapman, *The Truth about Dirty Tricks, from Harold Wilson to Margaret Thatcher* (Sidgwick and Jackson, London, 1991)

Rafter Kevin, *Neil Blaney, A Soldier of Destiny* (Blackwater Press, Dublin, 1993)

Sisman, Adam, *John le Carré: The Biography* (Bloomsbury Publishing, London, 2015)

Smith, William Beattie, *The British State and the Northern Ireland Crisis, 1969–70. From Violence to Power Sharing* (United States Institute of Peace Press, Washington, 2011)

Stone, Michael, *None Shall Divide Us* (Blake Publishing; New Edition, 2003)

Utley, T. E., *Lessons of Ulster* (J. M. Dent, London, 1975),

Urwin, Margaret, *A State in Denial* (Mercier Press, Cork, 2016)

—— *Counter-Gangs, A History of Undercover Military units in Northern Ireland 1971–1976 (*2012) available for download on Spinwatch: https://spinwatch.org/images/ Countergangs1971–76.pdf

Walsh, Dick, *The Party, Inside Fianna Fáil* (Gill and Macmillan, Dublin, 1986)

Walsh, Liz, *The Final Beat, Gardai Killed in the Line of Duty* (Gill and Macmillan Ltd, Dublin, 2001)

White, Barry, *John Hume, Statesman of The Troubles* (Blackstaff Press Ltd, Belfast, 1984)

White, Robert A., *Ruarí Ó Brádaigh The Life and Politics of an Irish Revolutionary* (Indiana University Press, Bloomington, 2006)

Waugh, Auberon, *The Diaries of Auberon Waugh. A Turbulent Decade 1975–1985* (Private Eye Productions Ltd, London, 1985)

Wills, Clair, *That Neutral Island* (Faber, London, 2007)

Wright, Peter, *Spycatcher* (Viking Penguin Inc., New York. 1987)

Index